D1376995

2-PK699 00/-
40⁰⁰/-
#26 W-6

BIRDS
of Fiji, Tonga and Samoa

BIRDS
of Fiji, Tonga and Samoa

BY DICK WATLING

ILLUSTRATED BY CHLOË TALBOT-KELLY

MILLWOOD PRESS

WELLINGTON • NEW ZEALAND

For Amerita

First published 1982

MILLWOOD PRESS LTD
291b Tinakori Road
Wellington
New Zealand

Copyright 1982 Dick Watling

ISBN 0-908582-36-6

All rights reserved. No part of this book may be used
or reproduced in any manner whatsoever without
written permission except in the case of brief
quotations embodied in critical articles and reviews.

Typography and design by Bob Henderson

Set by Fred Witham Ltd, Wellington, New Zealand
Printed in Hong Kong by Wing King Tong Co Ltd

Contents

Acknowledgements

As I am sure is always the case, a book of this type involves the help of a great many people. Certainly this one is no exception and I know it would never have seen the light of day without the enormous amount of help that I have received.

The genesis of this book lies with Shirley Charters and the publishers — Millwood Press, without their initial approach and subsequent encouragement, it would never have been written.

In the initial stages, Ian Galbraith of the British Museum of Natural History, Mary LeCroy of the American Museum of Natural History and Con Benson of the Cambridge University Zoology Museum provided much assistance whilst I was examining skins. All three were subjected to a variety of requests by correspondence whilst I was soaking up the sun in fairer climes, and all generously helped where they could. To Con Benson — an experienced hand at this game, I am particularly grateful for some sound advice in moments of my impatience. Fergus Clunie of the Fiji Museum has a store of local information on the birds of Fiji which far outweighs that which is found in this book. He answered many enquiries and read the first draft, providing much positive criticism. He very kindly allowed me to incorporate many of his own findings and greatly lengthened the list of Fijian bird names. The book is much enhanced by his help. John Hatch, smarting from many defeats on the squash court, obviously took delight in straightening out the sea bird and wader section. To him and his compatriots who helped, I am very grateful. I extend and amplify this to David Holyoak who very kindly combed the second draft of this section for errors and inaccuracies.

David Todd provided me with unpublished information on the Niuafo'ou Megapode and Tongan bird names, as well as some useful comments on the first draft. Kurt Stunzner and Ulf Beichle supplied me with the Samoan names for many birds and also information on habits, distribution and status.

Gil Dixon took on the formidable task of typing the manuscripts and to her I am especially grateful.

Dr Kathy MacKinnon kindly corrected the proofs, an onerous job which is much appreciated.

Murray and Shirley Charters carried much of the burden of organising material for the text photographs, as well as many other administrative details in times when I had carefully placed myself incommunicado. They made many constructive criticisms on each of the drafts and were responsible for translating them into English. It was a suggestion of Shirley's that was responsible for the genesis of the book, but I acknowledge Murray as being responsible for my development as a naturalist. If he had known that it would result in my errant ways, he might have thought twice in the early days.

Whilst pursuing my zoological interests and especially during the earnest years of thesis preparation, I have — I hope, been able to maintain a balanced perspective. If this is so, it is in a large part due to the light-hearted bantering of Charles and Vani Eaton, and Ian and Maria Partridge with whom I overstayed my welcome on many occasions; and to Andrew Laurie and Robert Olivier in Cambridge who never could comprehend anything smaller than a pachyderm.

The artwork of Chloë Talbot-Kelly requires no foreword from me, its excellence is evident in the ensuing pages. I can only express my gratitude to her for accepting to illustrate the book.

I could not conclude this piece without conveying my gratitude to the many Fijian families whose overwhelming hospitality I have enjoyed during my wanderings over the past fourteen years. Much of my knowledge of Fijian birds was gained in the company of Simione Kawabu and a mob of scruffy dogs. If the dogs had been more proficient in the pursuit of wild pig, perhaps I would not have had so much time to observe birds, and the book would not have been written.

I reserve for the last, some apt words from my erstwhile hero Huckleberry Finn:

> "...and so there ain't no more to write about, and I am rotten glad
> of it, because if I'd knowed what a trouble it was to make a book I
> wouldn't a tackled it and ain't agoing to no more."

Note: The manuscript for this book was completed in August, 1978; only minor alterations have been made to it since. I have no illusion as to its perfection although I have strived to make it complete and accurate. I would be grateful if all those who find errors, new distributional or species records, etc., or have any ideas for improvement would contact me in care of: The Fiji Museum, Suva, Fiji. I would appreciate it if all those who publish papers of relevance would forward reprints.

PART ONE
Introduction

THE BACKGROUND

Primarily, my deepest concern in writing this book has been the lack of realistic conservation in the South Pacific. While a book of this nature will do little directly to further the cause of conservation, it is my belief that it is only when the people of the region develop an awareness of, and an interest in, wildlife, (which is at present sorely lacking) that any conservation measures will become effective. If this book in any way helps to promote or develop that interest in their avian or other wildlife heritage, then I will be well satisfied.

The book is intended for the interested layman — both local and visitors — in a style which I hope is interesting and informative. Many ornithologists may find it lacking in biological detail. In some cases I have sacrificed these, in order to hold the interest of the more general reader, but in most cases they are simply not known. I hope that this book will give some idea of how little ornithological research has been done in the region, and so stimulate a great deal more fieldwork, especially in the spheres of ecology and distribution.

The book is divided into five parts: the first contains a general introduction to the geography and vegetation of the region with several sections on general ornithological subjects. The second part comprises coloured illustrations of each bird. The third part contains individual species' accounts of the region's land birds, which are the most interesting and probably least known members of the region's avifauna. To many this will be the most informative part of the book since much of the information will be new to the majority of readers. The fourth part deals with the sea and shore birds of the region. I make no apologies for the fact that I am not a good sailor and have never paid more than a passing interest to the sea birds of the region. In consequence, this section relies heavily on the observations of others, which I hope I have collated completely, and in particular to two fine books, to which I refer the reader — Warren B. King's *Seabirds of the Tropical Pacific Ocean* (Smithsonian Institute, Washington DC), and *The Handbook of Australian Sea-birds* by J. Serventy, V. Serventy and J. Warham (A. H. & A. W. Reed). Whilst our knowledge of the resident sea birds and common passage migrants in the region is reasonably complete, we have a great deal to learn about the rarer migrants and vagrants in the region. The final part of the book contains a Bibliography which I hope many will find useful if they wish to pursue their ornithological studies more deeply. In the text I normally avoid including references for the sake of clarity and continuity. However, in a few cases specific pieces are referred to by means of superior reference numbers. Readers should look up the number in the Bibliography to locate the reference.

The Species Accounts
Each resident species and all the migrants or vagrants which are liable to be seen in the region, are given separate treatment, whilst rare vagrants are mentioned under the Remarks and Allied Species section of a close relative.

Each bird has been given a species number and this number is used for indexing and reference to that bird.

The Species Accounts are divided into sections where the information is available.

Nomenclature

Several birds in the region are known by local English (or vernacular) names. I have standard-ised these so that the currently accepted vernacular in ornithological circles is used. For species that also occur in Australia, I have — with only one or two exceptions — followed the R.A.O.U. list of recommended English names (Emu, 1977). For other birds the use of some names are open to question, but I have attempted to be objective. Commonly used alternative names are also listed.

In each species account the local names for the bird are given. The source of these names is from:

1. A search of the material listed in the Bibliography.
2. My personal knowledge of Fijian bird names, in collaboration with Fergus Clunie, whose wide ornithological experience in Fiji enabled him to add considerably to the list.

Those local names in capitals are the most commonly used. For Fijian birds these are names which Fergus Clunie or I have found to be reasonably widespread. For Tonga they are the names given by B. Carlson in his work on the Tongan Avifauna,[31] and checked and sup-plemented by David Todd during his recent ornithological fieldwork in Tonga. For Niue they are those collected by Kazimierz Wodzicki[235] and for Samoa, they are the names recorded by Mr Kurt Stunzner, a lifetime resident of Samoa, who has a profound knowledge of the Samoan fauna.

There can be little doubt that several writers have collected local names indiscriminately, without checking the knowledge of the donor or the name itself. This has led to some incorrect identifications and probably some fabrications. However, the greatest problem in the use of local names lies in the real variation between different localities. In Samoa and Tonga, such variation is not as widespread as it is in Fiji, although there are differences between islands. In Fiji, the situation is complicated and dialectical differences, even over comparatively short distances, are normal. Consequently, the same bird is liable to have a different name in separate localities or else the same local name is used for different birds.

An added complication is the generally poor knowledge of birds by Fijians. Whilst this is to be expected in urban dwellers, it is more surprising to find that the majority of villagers are poorly versed in bird lore.

This situation is compounded by a characteristic and genuine willingness to help, usually resulting in an evasion of any answer involving "I don't know". If a question is asked, then an answer will be given even if it is incorrect or fabricated. It is also worth emphasising that unless the local names are correctly pronounced, they will not be recognised, and this applies even to the commonest names. To facilitate correct pronunciation, important stresses are marked with a macron and one must be aware of the different orthography used by each of the countries of the region. For these reasons, visiting ornithologists must be exceedingly careful in the reliance that they place on the use of local names both by themselves or by locals.

In the majority of cases, the scientific names follow Ernst Mayr's classic book *The Birds of the South-west Pacific*.[153] There are, however, a few changes based on more recent work. For widespread species with subspecies found outside the Fiji region and more than one within the region, the binomial is used and subspecies are listed. For similar species — but having only one geographical subspecies in the region — the trinomial is used. For species endemic in the Fiji region (and its immediate environs) the binomial is used and subspecies listed if they occur.

Identification

The identification of the region's land birds is a relatively simple affair, a few exceptions apart. This is because of the small number of species present, and on any one island only a proportion of these birds will be found. Thus distribution is an important consideration in their identification. For these reasons this section gives only a brief description of the most noticeable field characters of the plumage, and for standardisation I describe the subspecies found on the island of Viti Levu, Fiji if the species occurs there. For the Samoan endemics I describe the subspecies found on the island of Upolu. Subspecific variation in plumage is pronounced in some birds, e.g., Island Thrush, and brief descriptions of these are added in the subspecies section.

Only one measurement — the total length, bill tip to tail tip — is included. Many people may be unfamiliar with metric lengths, and in many cases total length is of little practical value unless direct comparison with another bird is possible. The following common birds may be useful for comparison:

Red-headed Parrotfinch	10 cm.
Polynesian Triller	15 cm.
Common Mynah	23 cm.
Feral Pigeon	30 cm.
Swamp Harrier	55 cm.
Reef Heron	60 cm.

Flight
Flight characteristics are described if they are sufficiently distinct to be useful aids in identification.

Voice
The commonest calls of most birds are given, but beware of geographical variation in calls, especially between islands.

Food
Basic information on the food and feeding behaviour is given in this section.

Breeding
If available, the nest, eggs and normal clutch are described.

Habitat and Range
In many cases habitat is very important in determining the distribution of birds, but whilst in many continental areas birds are often finely tuned to habitat types, island birds generally have broad niches with subsequent wide habitat tolerance. In consequence, only wide habitat definitions are used. For instance I do not generally make any distinction between forest type or altitude. Despite the fairly large areas of forest remaining on the larger islands of the region, it is doubtful if any of it is primary or virgin forest, but much of it is certainly mature. For this reason I make the distinction between mature forest, which contains old, large trees and has not been recently disturbed, and secondary or immature forest which has been relatively recently logged or affected in other ways. There is a continuum from this type of forest through secondary bush, open woodland, etc., to native gardens and heavily affected vegetation on the periphery of rural villages.

Other habitat types such as agricultural land, suburban, etc., are self-explanatory.

The range of each species with a restricted distribution within the region is given in precise terms; widespread species are given in more general terms. I avoid a long list of island names on which the bird has been recorded, for few people will ever visit the vast majority of these islands and in most cases such a list would be incomplete anyway. However, distribution is an important aid to identification and so I have added distribution maps to give more specific and easily assimilated information. The recorded presence of a bird on large islands is marked exactly, but if the bird has been recorded on one or more island of a natural group of small islands, then the whole group is included in the range.

Remarks and Allied Species
In this section of a species account, any birds with which it may be confused are indicated and the distinguishing features given.

Other information, of a general nature, is also given in this section.

Subspecies
I have included this section, which will really only be of interest to serious ornithologists, for the state of completeness and because there are very great differences in the plumage of some subspecies. These subspecies are not described in detail (a fuller description may be found in J. du Pont's *South Pacific Birds*),[66] but a knowledge of their distribution, which is included, will enable ornithologists to know where different plumage types are to be expected.

A NOTE ON ORTHOGRAPHY
Local orthography for place and bird names is used in this book. Whilst this will, no doubt, be slightly puzzling and awkward for visitors, I feel that the local people are entitled to spelling with which they are familiar.

In Fijian:
b is pronounced as *mb* in *number*
c is pronounced as *th* in *that*
d is pronounced as *nd* in *end*
g is pronounced as *ng* in *singer*
q is pronounced as *ng* in *finger*

In Samoan:
g is pronounced as *ng* in *singer* (Tonga and Niue formerly pronounced *g* as *ng,* but have now adopted the symbol *ng.*)

In Samoan, Tongan and Niuean:
An apostrophe marks the glottal stop. This represents a catch in the voice, similar to that found in the Cockney pronounciation of *letter* as *le'er.*

In all cases:
A macron marks long vowels, e.g., *kakā.*

Some islands are known on charts and maps under two or several names or under various forms of the same name. The accepted local names are used.

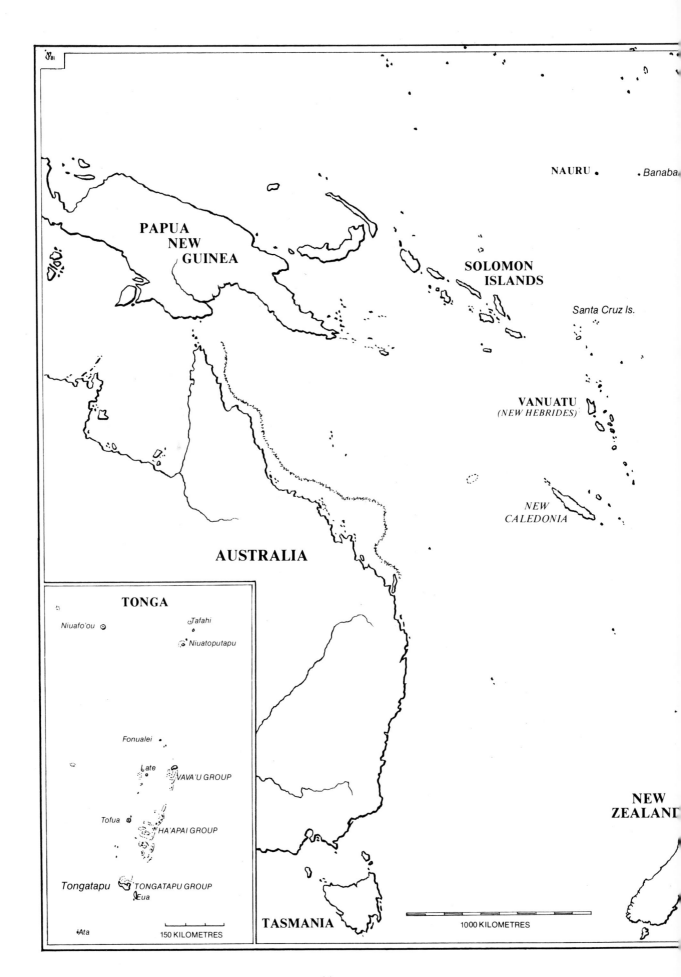

NAURU · · Banaba

PAPUA
NEW
GUINEA

SOLOMON
ISLANDS

Santa Cruz Is.

VANUATU
(NEW HEBRIDES)

NEW
CALEDONIA

AUSTRALIA

TONGA

Niuafo'ou ⊙

Tafahi

Niuatoputapu

Fonualei ·

Late

VAVA'U GROUP

Tofua

HA'APAI GROUP

Tongatapu

TONGATAPU GROUP
Eua

Ata

150 KILOMETRES

TASMANIA

NEW
ZEALAND

1000 KILOMETRES

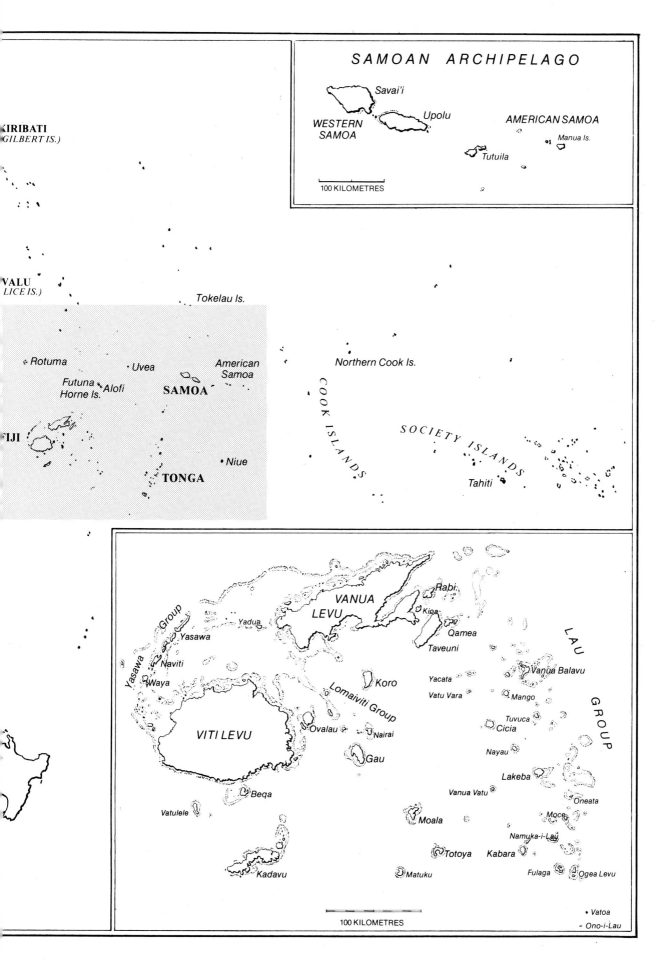

SAMOAN ARCHIPELAGO

Savai'i

WESTERN
SAMOA

Upolu

AMERICAN SAMOA

Manua Is.

Tutuila

100 KILOMETRES

KIRIBATI
(GILBERT IS.)

VALU
(LICE IS.)

Tokelau Is.

Rotuma

Uvea

American
Samoa

Futuna
Horne Is.   Alofi

SAMOA

Northern Cook Is.

FIJI

COOK ISLANDS

SOCIETY ISLANDS

Niue

TONGA

Tahiti

VANUA
LEVU

Rabi

Yasawa
Group

Yadua

Kioa

Yasawa

Qamea

Naviti

Taveuni

LAU

Waya

Koro

Yacata

Vanua Balavu

Lomaiviti Group

Vatu Vara

Mango

VITI LEVU

Ovalau

Nairai

Tuvuca
Cicia

GROUP

Gau

Nayau

Beqa

Lakeba

Vatulele

Vanua Vatu

Oneata

Moala

Moce

Namuka-i-Lau

Totoya

Kabara

Kadavu

Matuku

Fulaga

Ogea Levu

100 KILOMETRES

Vatoa

Ono-i-Lau

15

ORNITHOLOGICAL HISTORY

The first important contribution to the ornithological knowledge of the South-west Pacific was made on James Cook's second voyage, for whilst the expedition was visiting Tonga and Niue its naturalists — John Reinhold Forster and his son, George — were making observations and collecting specimens. This was followed, in 1827, by Dumont d'Urville's expedition which visited Tonga and Fiji and made a small collection. However, it was the United States Exploring Expedition of Wilkes, 1838 to 1842, that began what may be described as the first phase of ornithological exploration. The expedition's naturalist was Titian Ramsay Peale, and he made the first substantial collection of birds, and painted several species.

Subsequently, important material was gathered by collectors from the Museum Godeffroy of Hamburg in Germany. The museum had been founded by J. Caesar Godeffroy who had widespread mercantile interests in the South Pacific, based in Samoa. He sent out several professional collectors, most notably Dr E. Gräffe and Messrs T. Kleinschmidt, F. Hübner and J. Kubary. Between the years 1850 and 1880 they made valuable collections and their specimens were studied by two eminent German ornithologists, Professor Otto Finsch and Dr G. Hartlaub, who in 1867, published a forerunner of the present volume *Ornithologie der Viti, Samoa und Tonga Inseln.*

Titian Ramsay Peale.
Courtesy of the American Museum of Natural History.

Theodore Kleinschmidt.
Courtesy of the Fiji Museum.

In Fiji, the British Consul, Edgar Layard, who had been sent out to investigate a possible annexation of the Fiji Islands to Britain, also pursued his ornithological interests, and together with his son, Leopold, made a large collection of skins and contributed some notable papers on the ornithology of the South-west Pacific. The bulk of their collection is at present in the Liverpool Museum of Natural History in England—the Layard Collection.

Shortly before the Deed of Cession was signed in Levuka in 1874, the Royal Navy Challenger Expedition visited the Group, and although primarily concerned with oceanographical research, its naturalists made a small but useful collection of Kadavu birds. This was briefly examined by Layard who indicated the presence of two species new to science—the Kadavu Honeyeater and Layard's White-eye.

Meanwhile, in Samoa three missionaries had been devoting some of their characteristic zeal to ornithological matters. The skins that were acquired and the observations made by the Reverend J. B. Stair and the Reverend S. J. Whitmore, in Western Samoa, and by the Reverend T. Powell in American Samoa, were significant contributions.

Other important collections of skins were made during this period by Baron A. von Hügel, during his anthropological wanderings in the South Pacific; by J. Stanley Gardiner who visited Rotuma in 1896; by J. Lister in the 1880s, and by the ill-fated Lionel Wiglesworth in 1901, who died of dysentery not long after his arrival in Fiji. Their collections are presently housed in the Cambridge University Zoology Museum, UK. During the same period J. A. Boyd, H. and W. Abbott and C. Pearce, each made small collections which are at present in the Australian and Macleay Museums in Sydney. This material was initially examined by E. P. Ramsay, who infuriated Edgar Layard, not only be persuading Layard's former butler and collector, Charles Pearce, to work for him, but also by describing new species in the *Sydney Morning Herald*.

Although the collections made during this first phase laid the foundation of our present knowledge of the region's ornithology, there was, nonetheless, a great deal of taxonomic confusion. This was the result of generally small collections being gathered from a variety of location, and worked upon by several taxonomists, in different countries, all of whom wished to take part in the flush of new species' description which was prevalent at the time. It was not until the end of the second phase of ornithological research — in the 1940s — that these problems were resolved.

Apart from the visit of P. Bahr to Fiji in 1912 and Lieutenant R. C. Reed to Samoa in 1921, and the important work of Casey A. Wood and Alexander Wetmore in 1925-26, the second phase of ornithological endeavour really belonged to the Whitney South Sea Expedition. Mention must, however, be made of William Belcher, who during the eleven years from 1924 to 1935 produced over ninety paintings of Fijian wildlife. He illustrated some fifty birds species and made many orchid studies. Although his paintings cannot be considered classics, they are a magnificent contribution to Fijian ornithology. The result of great dedication, his subjects were usually depicted with great accuracy, not only in details of plumage, but in the surrounding vegetation and plant species. The existing collection of his paintings can be found in the Fiji Museum in Suva. He was not only an artist; but together with A. and G. Martin, he also collected and prepared a large number of skins which were presented to the American National Museum of Natural History, Washington, by Casey A. Wood.

Science, and in particular ornithology, owes much to Harry Payne Whitney and his family, who so generously sponsored the Whitney South Sea Expedition that visited nearly every significant island in the South Pacific, except New Zealand, to collect birds, over a period of twelve years from 1920. The expedition visited Fiji, Samoa and Tonga between October 1923 and August 1925 under the direction of its principal collectors Rollo H. Beck and José Correia. It worked under the auspices of the Museum of Natural History of New York, and its findings and the work done on its collections by Professor E. Mayr and his associates has given us a thorough knowledge of the taxonomy of the South Pacific avifauna.

Leo Layard.
Courtesy of the National Archives of Fiji.

HMS *Challenger* at anchor — from "Sketches of Many Shores
Visited by HMS *Challenger*".
Courtesy of the Royal Geographical Society.

HMS *Challenger* shortening sail — from the Report of HMS *Challenger*, 1873-76.
Courtesy of the Royal Geographical Society.

LINNEAN SOCIETY.

The ordinary monthly meeting of this society was held in the society's room, 64, Hunter-street, on Monday last. The Hon. Leopold Fane de Salis, Esq., M.L.C., in the chair.

Messrs. Thomas Francis, J. Belisario, and M. C. H. Hawkes, were proposed for election at the next monthly meeting.

The following paper was read by Mr. E. P. Ramsay, F.L.S.:

TRICHOGLOSSUS

(*Glossopsitta*) amabilis. Nov. sp. (Ramsay).

Adult Male.—Forehead (all above a straight line from the eye to the nostril) and the whole of the upper surface bright green, darker on the wings and tail, brightest on the rump and upper tail coverts, but having a slight olive-green tinge on the upper wing coverts, interscapular region and back; the first primary quill, the tips and all but a narrow green margin to the outer webs of the remaining quills, blackish brown; the inner webs of the secondaries and concealed portions of the wing coverts blackish brown; primaries and secondaries below, and the outer series of the under wing coverts, dark brown, the first two secondaries having a faint spot of yellow near the base of their inner webs, being visible only on the under surface; the remainder of the under wing coverts and margins of the shoulders bright green of the same tint as the under surface of the body; lores (all below a straight well-defined line from the eye to the nostril), cheeks, and throat bright vivid crimson, bounded below by a crescent-shaped band across the chest of bright yellow, which reaches to the sides of the lower neck; legs bright vivid crimson, with a few feathers of bright yellow, and of violet at the thighs; under tail coverts green, tinted with yellow, near the base; round the vent a small patch of crimson feathers, and a few tinged with violet; ear-coverts, sides of the neck, lower part of the chest, and the remainder of the under surface bright green; two or three yellow feathers on the sides of the chest under the wings in some specimens, and a few of crimson and of yellow scattered over the abdomen; the central portion of most of the feathers on the abdomen tinged with yellow; tail above dark green, below blackish brown; the terminal third portion of all the feathers yellow; on the inner webs, near the base of the three external quills, on either side is a large oblong blotch of bright crimson, margined below with pale yellow. Bill and cere, orange red; tip of upper and lower mandible, dark horn colour; orbits, orange yellow; tarsi and feet, flesh red. Total length, 6·7 inches; wing, 3·6; tarsus, 0·46; tail, 3·25; bill, 0·5; culmen, 0·35.

Adult Female.—Similar in size and markings to the male, but less highly coloured; the tail not so extensively tipped with yellow, and only an indication of the yellow band across the chest; the four exterior tail feathers on either side are blotched with crimson, as in the male, the crimson being more distinctly margined near the base and sides with yellow, but, as in the male, confined to the inner webs of the feathers. The abdomen and legs are less ornamented with crimson and yellow, no yellow spot at the base of the secondaries as described in the male. Total length, 6·5; tail, 3·05; wing, 3·6; *habitat*, Ovalau, Fiji Group, S. S. Islands.

Remarks.—This very beautiful species was found at Ovalau by Mr. Charles Pearce, who was fortunate enough to procure both sexes from a large tree bearing bunches of yellow blooms, from which they extracted a honey-like fluid; they had not previously made their appearance, and only remained while the tree was in flower. The flock consisted of about thirty individuals, the stomach contained nothing but the fluid extracted from the blossoms and a little pollen from the stamens of the flowers.

This species differs very little from those of the genus *Trichoglossus* and its sub-genus *Glossopsitta*, except perhaps in the proportionably greater length of the tail, and the relative length of the tibia and tarsus, as will be seen by the accompanying measurements:—

Average sized specimen of *G. Australis*: Total length, 0·8 inch; wing, 3·8 inch; tail, 2·3 inch; tibia, 1·05 inch; tarsus, 0·3–6. T. (G.): Total length, 6·7 inch; wing, 5·0 inch; tail, 3·25 inch; tibia, 1·15 inch; tarsus, 0·46–6.

A vote of thanks to the author for his valuable contribution, and another to the Chairman, was then passed, and the meeting separated.

E. P. Ramsay took the unprecedented step of publishing formal descriptions of new bird species in the *Sydney Morning Herald* — in this case for the Red-throated Lorikeet on 28 July, 1875.
Courtesy of the Mitchell Library, Sydney.

Red-throated Lorikeet *Charmosyna amabilis*, by William Belcher. *Courtesy of the Fiji Museum.*

Pacific Swallow *Hirundo tahitica*, by William Belcher. *Courtesy of the Fiji Museum.*

Harry Payne Whitney sponsored the Whitney South Sea
Expedition which collected birds for twelve years.
Courtesy of the American Museum of Natural History.

Rollo H. Beck, the Whitney South Sea Expedition's principal
collector during its two years in the Fiji region.
Courtesy of the American Museum of Natural History.

The third and present phase of ornithology (1950 onwards) began with an excellent taxonomic knowledge of the land birds present. Yet the ecology of the vast majority of species is still almost as little known as when the birds were first discovered. There is, however, an awakening interest in the study of the ecology of some of the native species which has been greatly stimulated by the activities of Fergus Clunie and Robin Mercer, two resident ornithologists. These two apart, there has been little enthusiasm demonstrated internally, despite the presence of a large regional university; it is from abroad that interest is being generated. Although this is to be encouraged, real progress — if it is to be made — must be based on the work of resident ornithologists or long-term visitors. One hopes that such activity will increase, as it must do if naturalists are to be able to put forward a sound case for the conservation of the region's avifauna, in the face of mounting pressure from habitat destruction that results from alternative land use.

COMPOSITION OF THE AVIFAUNA

A characteristic of oceanic islands is the paucity of bird species compared with a continental area of similar size. The more remote and the smaller the islands, the more this is accentuated. The islands of the Fiji region are no exception, and although there are sixty-nine indigenous breeding land birds in the region (two of which are considered extinct), far fewer than this are found on any one island.

Table 1: Breeding land birds of Viti Levu, Savai'i and Tongatapu.
Includes indigenous birds now possibly extinct. *Includes the Red-breasted Musk Parrot.

Island	Area (Sq. km)	Indigenous breeding land birds	Introduced birds
Viti Levu, FIJI	10,386	47	9*
Savai'i, SAMOA	1,820	32	2
Tongatapu, TONGA	260	13	3

This paucity of species, combined with the retiring habits of many of them, has led many ornithologists to become disillusioned and disinterested in the avifauna. Even Edgar Layard, referring to Fiji wrote, "The whole country is, however, singularly destitute of birds." Perhaps his previous ornithological work in Ceylon and South Africa had spoilt for him what can be a rewarding experience, for the meagre number belies a rich degree of endemism in a characteristic and interesting avifauna.

As with all oceanic islands, the fauna and flora of the Fiji region arrived by crossing sea barriers and then colonising the islands. The ancestral stock of virtually all the birds came from the west, despite this being contrary to the prevailing winds. With their power of flight birds are more successful colonisers than other faunal groups, so it is not surprising that they are far better represented in the region than other terrestrial vertebrates. Some birds are better invaders and colonisers than others, and this results in some groups being richly represented whilst others are totally absent. Thus the land bird fauna of the South-west Pacific is without such families as bee eaters, rollers, hornbills and drongos, all of which are widely distributed in the Indo-Australasian islands. On the other hand, the efficient colonisers like the pigeons, parrots, flycatchers (of the family Muscicapidae) and honeyeaters, are comparatively well represented.

During the Ice Ages great areas of land and ocean were frozen, locking away water and consequently lowering the level of the seas. Islands and island arcs then appeared which are at present submerged (see map on next page). These, together with the concommitant increase in area of many existing islands, made island hopping considerably easier than at the present time. The bulk of the region's endemic avifauna probably arrived during this period.

Fiji, Tonga, Samoa and their outlying islands form a relatively discrete, isolated group. It is, therefore, not surprising that they share a related and characteristic avifauna. In fact, it is so similar that the region is considered a distinct zoogeographical unit by some authorities,

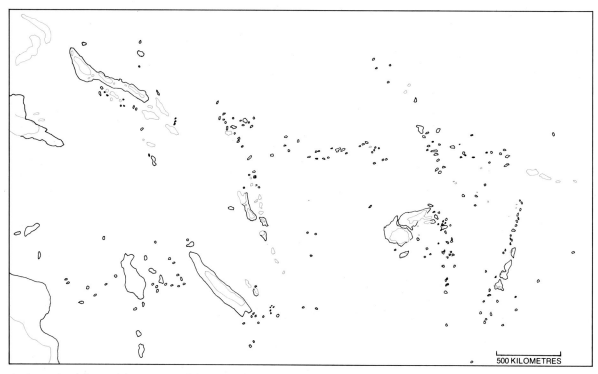

As the sea level dropped during parts of the Ice Ages, many new islands were formed. Colonisation of isolated groups by island-hopping was much easier than at present. (Islands as they are today are drawn in red, the exposed islands as they appeared in parts of the Ice Ages are drawn in black — based on a 120 metre drop in sea level.)

500 KILOMETRES

termed the Central Polynesian District. (It is, unfortunately, confusing that the correct geographical definition of Polynesia differs from that based on the distribution of the Polynesian race. Thus, Fiji, New Hebrides and Micronesia all have typical Polynesian faunas, but are not inhabited by a Polynesian people. To avoid confusion in this book I use the simpler "Fiji region" for the long-winded Central Polynesian District.) The isolation of the region has resulted in its large number of endemic forms and the relatively few species whose arrival can be traced as fairly recent. The land avifauna consists of eighty residents and a single regular migrant — the Long-tailed Cuckoo. Eleven introduced species are naturalised; one of these — the Jungle Fowl — was an aboriginal introduction brought by early Polynesians, and the remainder are post-European. Of the sixty-nine indigenous land birds thirty-nine (56 per cent) are endemic species and ten (14 per cent) of these are endemic genera or subgenera.

The high degree of endemism has meant that the exact origin and route of colonisation of most species cannot be traced with certainty, although the Papua New Guinea region, Australia — or both — supplied the ancestral stock of virtually all species. Recent stragglers in the region, such as the Glossy Ibis and White-faced Heron, have all come from the west. Despite the relative proximity of New Zealand, no species appear to have originated from this area. Climatical difference is the likely reason. (Table 2.)

It can be readily appreciated that the New Hebrides has acted as an important stepping-stone during the invasion and colonisation of the Fiji region. This group has acted as the apex of a funnel drawing species from both major source regions, and leading on to Fiji. Its geographical position and relative proximity to Australia and Papua New Guinea has resulted in it having a very different avifauna when compared to the Fiji region. Whilst the latter is rich in endemic species and poor in recent arrivals, the reverse holds for the New Hebrides, which has many recent arrivals and only two endemic species.

Within the Fiji region, the distribution of land birds is remarkably discontinuous. Many species are restricted to a single or to a few islands and yet, are absent from nearby similar

22

Table 2: The likely origin and route of colonisation of some birds of the Fiji region.

Origin	Papua and New Guinea	Australia	Either region
Route of colonisation	The Bismarks, Solomons and New Hebrides	New Caledonia and New Hebrides	Via New Hebrides
	White-throated Pigeon	Swamp Harrier	Reef Heron
	White-collared Kingfisher(?)	Fan-tailed Cuckoo	Mangrove Heron
	Pacific Swallow	Scarlet Robin	Pacific Black Duck
	Island Thrush	Golden Whistler	Wandering Whistling-duck
	Red-throated Lorikeet (close relative)	Grey-backed White-eye	Peregrine Falcon
		Cardinal Honeyeater	Banded Rail
	Niuafo'ou Megapode (close relative)	White-breasted Woodswallow(?)	White-browed Crake
		Vanikoro Broadbill (close relative)	Spotless Crake
			Purple Swamphen
		Blue-crowned Broadbill (close relative)	Barn Owl
			Grass Owl

ones; other species are widespread on all types of island in one part of the region, yet are totally absent in another part. Such distributions are found in many archipelagos throughout the world and have excited the attention of naturalists for many years, for they provide a natural playground for the consideration of principles of evolution, ecology and zoogeography. Thanks to the Whitney South Sea Expedition, we have an excellent basic knowledge of the distribution of species within the region. But the majority of islands have not been visited by ornithologists since, and it is probable that on some, species were missed by the expedition. Although a matter for conjecture, it is very likely that the distribution of some species change within a time-scale that we can observe.

One might consider the extinction of the Wandering Whistling-duck as a natural event. Much of the evidence for the presence of this species in Fiji comes from anecdotal accounts of early writers, but two specimens (one an immature) probably collected in the 1870s and presently in the Australian Museum, confirm its identification and status as a breeding bird in Fiji. It was not collected by the Whitney South Sea Expedition and despite a tentative report since [161] it is considered extinct in Fiji. This species is a well-known nomad or migrant throughout much of its range, and its disappearance from Fiji probably represents the loss of the descendants of a small group which wandered outside the normal range of the species to an area, too isolated for regular colonisation.

There are many factors which appear to be important in controlling the inter-island distribution of particular birds, but there is much that we do not understand. Important factors include the isolation of the island in question; its size and its altitude. Generally, isolation appears to be the least important of the three. The size and altitude usually control the "ecological diversity"—the number of plants it supports and the number of distinct habitat types. It is this ecological diversity which appears to be the most important factor controlling the number of bird species on an island. But it is too easy to generalise and use rather vague terms such as "ecological diversity" in equally vague statements. What is required is that the general terms be superseded by knowledge of the specific facets of an island's make-up which control the composition of its avifauna.

This requires prolonged and careful observation. In his last book *Island Biology,* one of the world's great ornithologists, David Lack, with typical simplicity summed up a fundamental difference in the methods currently used to study this ecological problem.

The 'distant' view depends on *a priori* ideas, mathematical analyses and selected examples, and in the hands of masters has led to outstanding advances. But it has two weaknesses in lesser hands, first a tendency to concentrate on numbers of species rather than the particular species involved, and secondly, because nature is so various, one can with diligence find examples to illustrate almost any new idea. The 'close' view, in contrast, depends on the intensive study of a particular situation in all its aspects, from which conclusions are later drawn.

Lack strongly advocated the "close" view and without any reservations I whole-heartedly support his bias.

A great deal has been written about the intra-island distribution of birds, especially when considering the effects of habitat and altitude. My own brief discussion of these will be confined to the island of Viti Levu, Fiji, where I have had the most experience.

Viti Levu, together with Vanua Levu, the two largest islands of the Fiji region, are of sufficient size to maintain large areas of distinct habitats, and have decidedly drier leeward sides which support more open country, much of which is under agriculture. Three broad habitats eclipse all others in their extent and ornithological importance on Viti Levu today; the largest is rain forest, followed by the man-modified habitat complex (urban, suburban, and agricultural land) and of smaller extent, but similar importance, the intermediate zone habitat, a mosaic of reed-grassland and dry forest.

The structure of the rain forest is of great complexity; whilst the majority is mature, very little is primeval. Stratification leads to imponderable complications which in my experience are ornithologically meaningless. Because altitude is often an important determinant of forest type my comment extends to this variable as well. It will possibly come as a surprise that altitude and forest type have apparently little or no effect on bird distribution on Viti Levu, but it is a considered opinion. More intensive research is needed to confirm it, and I am sure will uncover subtle preferences of forest type by certain species.

Within this broad framework one can stratify birds as to their habitat preferences. This is summarised in Table 3 for Viti Levu birds (pigeons to passerines only). All the native birds, except for the Pacific Swallow which is a coastal, estuarine or riverine species, are found in forest. Only twelve have been able to invade suburban habitats through agricultural land. The introduced species, on the other hand, are essentially birds of man-modified habitats, although the two mynahs — more especially the Jungle Mynah — will venture into forested areas on occasions whilst the Red-vented Bulbul is seen regularly in forest.

The introduced birds have often been accused of preventing the indigenous species from using man-modified habitats and "driving them into the bush". There is no evidence for this, and it is more likely that it is the inability of the majority of the forest adapted birds to adjust to the vastly different man-modified habitats, which has led to their absence from town and villages.

By comparison with Hawaii and New Zealand, the Fiji region has escaped fairly lightly from the blight of introduced species. Luckily many introductions died out and at present eleven species are naturalised. Most of these are confined to the larger islands of the Fiji group, but it is probable that they will slowly spread their range. The majority of the introduced species arrived in the era of European settlement; some, such as the two mynahs, were deliberate introductions brought in for specific purposes. Others were brought for sentimental reasons. The history of bird introduction is, however, far older. The early Polynesian people brought the Jungle Fowl along with the pig, the dog, and possibly the Polynesian rat. At a later date, Tongans probably introduced Fiji's Red-breasted Musk Parrot to the islands of Tongatapu and 'Eua, thus saving themselves the hazardous journey to Fiji to trade for its red feathers, which were highly prized. The Samoans, for the same reason, took the Collared Lory back to Samoa but it never apparently established itself in the wild.

In conclusion, a brief word must be written on the sea birds and waders, two groups which have not yet been discussed. The sea birds found within the group are — with one exception

—widespread tropical species; many of them have been noted as breeding in the region and others are thought to do so. Tonga appears to have the most suitable breeding habitats, but a great deal of research needs to be carried out throughout the region. The exceptional species found in the area is MacGillivray's Petrel, which is known only from the single fledgling taken from Gau, Fiji, in 1855.

A checklist of fourteen waders from the region is without doubt a considerable under-estimate of the number which do pass through, although it may well be representative of regular migrants.

Table 3: Habitats of the land birds of Viti Levu, Fiji.

Pigeons to passerines only. Asterisks = very occasional observations.

	Rainforest	Intermediate vegetation zone	Agriculture	Suburban
18. White-throated Pigeon	•	•	•	
20. Friendly Ground-dove	•	•		
22. Peale's Pigeon	•	•		
24. Many-coloured Fruit-dove	•	•		*
26. Golden Dove	•	•	*	
29. Collared Lory	•	•	•	•
30. Red-throated Lorikeet	•			
32. Yellow-breasted Musk Parrot	•	•		
34. Fan-tailed Cuckoo	•	•	•	
36. Barn Owl	•	•	•	•
37. Grass Owl		?		
39. White-rumped Swiftlet	•	•	•	•
40. White-collared Kingfisher	•	•	•	•
42. Pacific Swallow			•	•
43. White-breasted Woodswallow	•	•	•	•
45. Island Thrush	•	•		
47. Polynesian Starling	•	*		
52. Fiji Warbler	•	•	•	
53. Long-legged Warbler	?			
54. Spotted Fantail		•		
57. Slaty Flycatcher	•	•	*	
59. Fiji Shrikebill	•	•	•	
60. Black-faced Shrikebill	•	*		
61. Vanikoro Broadbill	•	•	•	•
62. Blue-crested Broadbill	•	*		
64. Scarlet Robin	•	•	*	
65. Golden Whistler	•	•		
67. Polynesian Triller	•	•	•	•
69. Layard's White-eye	•	•	•	
70. Grey-backed White-eye	•	•	•	•
72. Orange-breasted Honeyeater	•	•	•	•
74. Wattled Honeyeater	•	•	•	•
76. Giant Forest Honeyeater	•			
78. Red-headed Parrotfinch	•	•	•	•
79. Pink-billed Parrotfinch	•			
Introduced birds				
10. Swamp Quail			•	
17. Feral Pigeon			•	•
19. Spotted Turtle-dove	*	•	•	•
33. Red-breasted Musk Parrot			•	
44. Red-vented Bulbul	•	•	•	•
49. Common Mynah	*	*	•	•
50. Jungle Mynah	•	•	•	•
80. Red Avadavat	*	•	•	•
81. Java Sparrow			•	•

ECOLOGICAL ISOLATION
OF CLOSELY RELATED LAND BIRDS

In recent years great interest has been shown in the many ways by which closely related species avoid competition when they occur together. The principle of competitive exclusion states that two complete competitors cannot co-exist in the same habitat.

It is generally recognised that isolation can be maintained in one or more of three ways:

1. Distinct ranges; for instance, members of a competing pair are confined to different islands in a group.
2. Occupation of different habitats; although living on the same island they occupy distinct habitats.
3. Feeding differences; although occupying the same habitat, closely related species feed on different foods. They may do this because of marked size differences or due to differing feeding strategies.

Archipelagos are especially useful in demonstrating this principle because all three methods of isolation can be readily utilised. The large number of islands give scope for range differences, whilst the characteristic broad niches of island birds, mean that habitat and/or feeding differences tend to be accentuated.

In the Fiji region there are seventeen* groups of indigenous, closely related, land birds, involving forty species (Table 4). The majority (fourteen) involve pairs of species; three consist of a triplet (fantails, broadbills and flycatchers), and one consists of five species — the fruit-doves. Amongst the seventeen groups are thirty-two possibly competing pairs. Of these twenty (63 per cent) are separated by differences in geographical distribution. I do not consider any to be isolated by distinct habitat occupation and consequently the remainder are presumed to differ in their feeding ecology. A lot of research is still needed to demonstrate this, however. One strategy appears to be prevalent; there exists a "generalist" species with a broad ecological tolerance, together with a "specialist" species having a limited habitat tolerance and/or a specialist feeding technique. Four (and possibly five) pairs can be distinguished on this basis, they are the two trillers in Western Samoa and the two broadbills, white-eyes and parrotfinches of Fiji; the shrikebills and fruit-doves are also possibly separated by this strategy. One pair — the starlings in Samoa — are separated by an obvious size difference.

Of great interest is the existence of the two *Mayrornis* flycatchers on Ogea Levu, a very small island in the Southern Lau group of Fiji. The Versicolour Flycatcher is confined to this island, whilst the Slaty Flycatcher is a widespread species throughout the Fiji group and occurs in two distinct subspecies. The Versicolour and Slaty Flycatchers are very closely related and there is some evidence of hybridisation. The Versicolour Flycatcher is a slightly smaller bird and it is interesting to find that of the two subspecies of the Slaty Flycatcher, it is the larger which is found on Ogea Levu.

* One pair, the Barn Owl and Grass Owl is not considered here. The Grass Owl is known only from four specimens collected from Viti Levu, Fiji, in the 1860-1870s. It has not been identified since.

26

Table 4: Ecological isolation of closely related indigenous land birds.

Group	Species involved	Number of competing pairs	Range	Habitat	Size	Generalist/specialist	Uncertain
					Isolating strategy — Feeding differences		
Pigeons	Peale's Pigeon and Pacific Pigeon	1	(?)	(?)			*
Fruit-doves	Flame Dove, Golden Dove, Whistling Dove, Many-coloured Fruit-dove, Crimson-crowned Fruit-dove	10	* = 6			* = 4	
Lories	Collared Lory and Blue-crowned Lory	1	*				
Parrots	Yellow-breasted Musk Parrot and Red-breasted Musk Parrot	1	*				
Kingfishers	White-collared Kingfisher and Flat-billed Kingfisher	1	*				
Trillers	Polynesian Triller and Samoan Triller	1				*	
Starlings	Samoan Starling and Polynesian Starling	1			*		
Fantails	Samoan Fantail, Kadavu Fantail and Spotted Fantail	3	* = 3				
Flycatchers	Slaty Flycatcher and Versicolour Flycatcher	1					*
Shrikebills	Fiji Shrikebill and Black-faced Shrikebill	1			(?)	*?	
Broadbills	Samoan Broadbill, Vanikoro Broadbill and Blue-crested Broadbill	3	* = 2			*	
Whistlers	Samoan Whistler and Golden Whistler	1	*				
White-eyes	Samoan White-eye, Grey-backed White-eye and Layard's White-eye	3	* = 2			*	
Honeyeaters	Orange-breasted Honeyeater and Cardinal Honeyeater	1	*				
Honeyeaters	Wattled Honeyeater and Kadavu Honeyeater	1	*				
Honeyeaters	Giant Forest Honeyeater and Mao	1	*				
Parrotfinches	Red-headed Parrotfinch and Pink-billed Parrotfinch	1			(?)	*	

Summary

Number of Competing Pairs   32
Separated by range   20
Separated by habitat   0
Separated by feeding   12— Size 1, Generalist/specialist 9, Uncertain 2

The two large *Ducula* pigeons are to some degree separated by range. The Pacific Pigeon being found on the smaller islands of the whole region, whilst Peale's Pigeon is confined to the larger islands of the Fiji group. However, they do occur together on many of the medium-sized islands of Fiji, and the Pacific Pigeon is found on the two large Samoan islands of Savai'i and Upolu in the absence of Peale's Pigeon. It seems, therefore, that the Pacific Pigeon—which is a nomadic species and well known for its inter-island wanderings—is not excluded from large islands because of habitat specialisation. At the same time it appears that it may not be excluded by Peale's Pigeon because they occur together on some islands. An interesting suggestion[108] is that the Pacific Pigeon may be particularly susceptible to predation by hawks and this is why it is found on the large islands of Samoa, but is not found on the large and many medium-sized islands of Fiji where two hawks—the Fiji Goshawk and the Swamp Harrier—are found. Despite this correlation, it is more probable that in Fiji it is the vegetation diversity of the islands which is the controlling factor, whilst in Samoa, the Pacific Pigeon has expanded its niche in the absence of its close competitor.

The five fruit-doves form the largest group of closely related species. Taxonomically they belong to two groups, the *Ptilinopus luteovirens* or *Chrysoenas* group containing the Golden, Orange and Whistling Doves, and the *P. purpuratus* group with the Many-coloured and Crimson-crowned Fruit-doves. The Many-coloured Fruit-dove is an aggressive, gregarious canopy feeder, found throughout the region on the larger and medium-sized islands. It co-exists with each of the other four fruit-doves. The latter despite differing taxonomic affinities are ecological counterparts and have separate distributions. In general, they are not gregarious and feed below the forest canopy.

There exists one other interesting situation involving a closely related pair. Two species of mynah were introduced to Fiji almost simultaneously in the late nineteenth century. They exhibit differences in foraging behaviour and gregariousness, but appear to have a wide ecological overlap in the man-modified habitats that they occupy.[219]

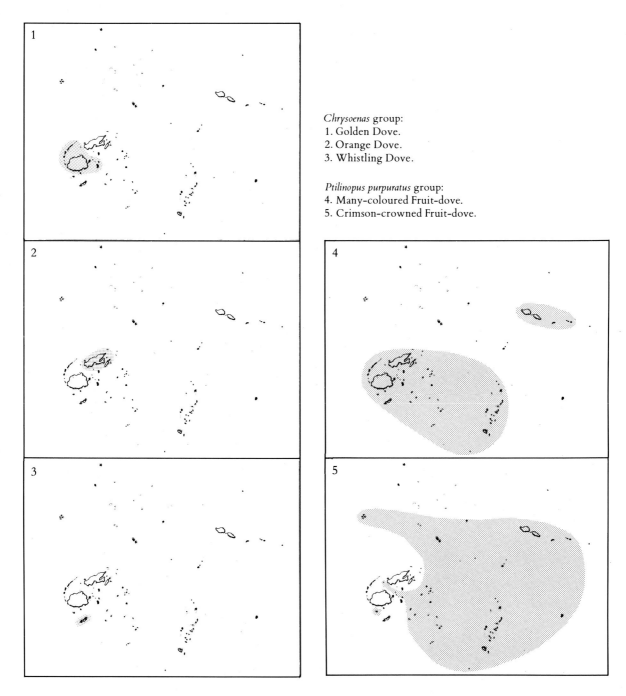

Chrysoenas group:
1. Golden Dove.
2. Orange Dove.
3. Whistling Dove.

Ptilinopus purpuratus group:
4. Many-coloured Fruit-dove.
5. Crimson-crowned Fruit-dove.

BREEDING AND MOULT

This section gives a brief summary of our knowledge of the breeding and moult seasons of Fijian land birds. Existing breeding records are so few and fragmentary that a detailed account is not possible, especially in the case of the sea birds, and any attempt to draw conclusions for this group would be misleading. Consequently, I have confined myself to land birds and, a few comments apart, to Fiji's land birds.

About half of nearly 500 breeding records of Fijian birds that I have accumulated, come from the Whitney South Sea Expedition. The members of this expedition noted whether the birds they collected were breeding or not, and they also recorded the size of each bird's gonads. In the large series of some species collected by the expedition, the proportion of birds with enlarged gonads in each month is a useful indication of breeding seasons, and this was used to corroborate actual breeding records. It is important to appreciate, however, that whilst the Whitney Expedition was in the region for two years and in Fiji for over half of this period, it only paid brief visits to each island. Nowhere were they able to obtain records over a complete annual cycle. Consequently, conclusions drawn from such a source might be regarded as suspect, although the overall results clearly indicate that there is a distinct seasonal pattern in both breeding and moult for many species.

Naturalists distinguish two distinct factors which control the timing of breeding cycles in birds. The ultimate (or distant) factor has been evolved to ensure that birds breed at the most suitable time, thereby raising the most offspring which, in their turn, breed at that same time. Breeding at other times is generally unsuccessful so that the trait for breeding at the most suitable time is maintained in the population. The proximate (or near) factor ensures that birds anticipate or commence breeding at the right time. For most birds throughout the world, the ultimate factor is the food supply needed to raise the young, most commonly insect or animal food. In temperate areas, increasing day length is generally considered to be the most important proximate factor, but in tropical areas where the day length varies not at all, or by only a small amount, this factor is usually discounted. However, very few places have a completely aseasonal environment, so there are always clues by which birds can anticipate the optimum season in which to breed.

In an ensuing section the climate of the region is described, pointing out the seasonal pattern of rainfall. For the most part this seasonality is regular, even though comparative rainfall figures from various localities differ greatly, and it is the regular seasonal rainfall which appears to be the controlling influence of the breeding cycles. The wetter months are from November to March, whilst May to September is regarded as the dry season. In general, primary productivity is greatest during the months of highest rainfall, when there is a concurrent increase in insect abundance, taking advantage of the flush of new vegetation. Most birds breed at that time to take advantage of the increased abundance of insects, although fruit, nectar, and grain-eating species are sometimes — but not always — exceptions. Thus, the majority of land birds in Fiji and Tonga, but less clearly in Samoa, start breeding at the end of the dry season and continue through the first half of the wet season — from August to January.

Table 5: Breeding records of Fijian land birds.

Confirmed breeding seasons are indicated with a solid line.

Bird number and species	J	F	M	A	M	J	J	A	S	O	N	D
1. Reef Heron							•	•			•	
2. Mangrove Heron								•				
3. Pacific Black Duck	•	•	•									
5. Fiji Goshawk		•			•		•	•		•	•	
6. Swamp Harrier										•	•	•
7. Peregrine Falcon								•				
9. Jungle Fowl							•	•		•		•
11. Barred-wing Rail										•		
12. Banded Rail										•	•	
15. Purple Swamphen	•	•	•				•			•		
18. White-throated Pigeon	•						•	•	•	•	•	
19. Spotted Turtle-dove	•				•		•	•	•	•		•
20. Friendly Ground-dove							•	•	•	•	•	
21. Pacific Pigeon							•	•	•		•	•
22. Peale's Pigeon				•			•	•	•			
24. Many-coloured Fruit-dove							•	•	•	•	•	•
25. Crimson-crowned Fruit-dove					•		•	•	•	•	•	
26. Golden Dove			•	•		•	•	•				
27. Orange Dove						•	•	•	•			
28. Whistling Dove										•	•	
29. Collared Lory							•					
31. Blue-crowned Lory						•		•				
32. Yellow-breasted Musk Parrot							•	•	•			
33. Red-breasted Musk Parrot				•		•		•				
34. Fan-tailed Cuckoo		•	•								•	•
36. Barn Owl			•	•		•					•	
39. White-rumped Swiftlet			•								•	
40. White-collared Kingfisher	•	•						•		•	•	
42. Pacific Swallow						•	•	•	•	•	•	•
43. White-breasted Woodswallow					•	•						•
44. Red-vented Bulbul	─	─								─	─	─
45. Island Thrush	•					•				•	•	
47. Polynesian Starling	•						•	•		•	•	•
49. Common Mynah	─	─	─	─						•	─	─
50. Jungle Mynah	─	─	─	─							─	─
51. Silktail						•		•	•			
52. Fiji Warbler	•	•				•				•	•	•
54. Spotted Fantail				•		•	•	•		•		•
55. Kadavu Fantail										•		
57. Slaty Flycatcher						•	•	•	•	•		
59. Fiji Shrikebill							•	•	•	•		•
60. Black-faced Shrikebill								•			•	•
61. Vanikoro Broadbill	─								─	─	─	─
62. Blue-crested Broadbill									•	•	•	
64. Scarlet Robin	•					•	•			•	•	•
65. Golden Whistler	•	•				•	•	•	•	•		•
67. Polynesian Triller	•						•	•	•	•		•
69. Layard's White-eye							•				•	•
70. Grey-backed White-eye	•						•		•		•	
72. Orange-breasted Honeyeater				•	•			•	•			
73. Cardinal Honeyeater											•	
74. Wattled Honeyeater	•	•				•	•	•		•		•
75. Kadavu Honeyeater									•		•	
76. Giant Forest Honeyeater												
78. Red-headed Parrotfinch	•					•	•	•			•	•
79. Pink-billed Parrotfinch								•				
80. Red Avadavat			•		•	•						
81. Java Sparrow			─	─	─	─	─					

30

Table 5 summarises the known monthly breeding records of Fijian land birds. In the preparation of this table a breeding record was defined as (1) a nest being constructed; (2) an occupied nest; (3) a fledgeling; or from the Whitney South Sea Expedition collection, birds labelled as (1) breeding, (2) nesting, (3) about to lay. Such a broad definition will tend to lengthen the actual breeding season of each species. Extended observations in the more open habitats of western Viti Levu, indicate that a general breeding season from the end of the dry season through to January or February, is normal, but many forest birds were not included in these observations. Species which have been regularly noted as breeding at other times of the year are five graminivorous species — the Spotted Turtle-dove, the Feral Pigeon, the Red Avadavat and the Java Rice Sparrow (all introduced) and the indigenous Red-headed Parrotfinch. These species probably take advantage of the large increase in seeds after the growth of annual plants during the wet season. They may, in fact, experience a food shortage during the wet season, since most seeds from the previous year will be germinating and a fresh supply will not have been produced. The nectivorous Wattled Honeyeater is also frequently found breeding during the dry season, but this species appears to breed during the wet season as well. The Golden Dove, and probably other fruit-doves as well, also breed in the dry season and, somewhat surprisingly, the Pacific Swallow is a regular breeder at this time.

In Samoa, there is far less evidence for a specific breeding season. Its more northerly latitude and less seasonal rainfall may be important differences, but more intensive field research is required to see if there is indeed a distinct breeding season.

For most small birds the physiological demands of the moult and of breeding are such that the two cannot be undertaken simultaneously by any individual. Consequently, the majority of small birds breed and moult at different times of the year. Whilst these seasons may overlap in the population, it is rare for breeding individuals to moult, although there is evidence that both the Wattled Honeyeater and Fiji Shrikebill are able to do this. In Fiji, the normal moult season of small birds follows the breeding season, as it does in most temperate regions. There are very few moult records in the literature and the evidence for seasonal moult, which is summarised in Table 6, comes from an examination of all the land birds collected by the Whitney Expedition. Only those species collected in sufficient number throughout the year were considered in the preparation of this table.

Table 6: Moult records of Fijian land birds.

Birds which appear to have a distinct moult season.			*Birds which appear to have no specific moult season.*
32. Yellow-breasted Musk Parrot	Nov–Feb		24. Many-coloured Fruit-dove
33. Red-breasted Musk Parrot	Nov–Feb		52. Fiji Warbler
44. Red-vented Bulbul	Jan–May		70. Grey-backed White-eye
45. Island Thrush	Jan–April		
47. Polynesian Starling	Nov–April		
49. Common Mynah	Feb–May		
50. Jungle Mynah	Feb–May		
57. Slaty Flycatcher	Dec–May		
59. Fiji Shrikebill	Jan–May	Breeding birds moult	
60. Black-faced Shrikebill	Jan–May	??	
61. Vanikoro Broadbill	Dec–April		
62. Blue-crested Broadbill	Dec–April		
64. Scarlet Robin	Jan–May	??	
65. Golden Whistler	Oct–May		
67. Polynesian Triller	Jan–April		
72. Orange-breasted Honeyeater	Oct–Feb		
74. Wattled Honeyeater	Oct–Feb	Breeding birds moult	
76. Giant Forest Honeyeater	Oct–Feb	??	

CONSERVATION, SPECIES LOST AND RARE OR ENDANGERED BIRDS

The region is indeed fortunate in that, by comparison with some island groups such as Hawaii, the Seychelles or the Mascarenes, the number of extinct or gravely threatened species is remarkably few. Only one species is almost certainly extinct — the Samoan Wood Rail — whilst two others might still survive. This enviable position is not, however, a result of judicious conservation; in fact ecological conservation in the region is negligible. It is only because of hitherto low environmental pressure that the present *status quo* of many species has been maintained. In the face of rapidly increasing habitat destruction through deforestation, the cream of the avifauna is threatened and immediate and effective steps are now required for their conservation, otherwise we will be joining Hawaii and the Seychelles in last-ditch attempts to save endangered species.

The loss of the Samoan Wood Rail is virtually certain, despite the large tracts of undisturbed mountainous forest which remain on Savai'i, the only island from which it has been recorded with certainty. First collected by J. Kubary in 1869, only a dozen or so specimens have ever been collected, and it has not been positively identified this century. The only member of its genus, it had remarkably aberrant habits — if early accounts of its behaviour are to be believed.

Although considered probable, it is not certain that the Barred-wing Rail and the Grass Owl are extinct in Fiji. The former — a large, weak flying species recorded from Viti Levu and Ovalau — was probably always rare, although early accounts are somewhat confusing on this matter. Only a handful of specimens have ever been collected, all in the late nineteenth century. However, there was an unconfirmed report of this bird by an experienced ornithologist who visited Fiji in 1973. Further research in the area is required, as is also needed to confirm the status of the Grass Owl. This species is only known from four specimens collected in the 1860-1870s. In appearance it is similar to the Barn Owl and it is possible that it might be present but is being overlooked. In contrast with the Barred-wing Rail, which is an endemic species with only one close relative — Woodfords Rail *Nesoclopeus woodfordi*, from the Solomons, the Grass Owl is a widespread owl ranging in tropical and subtropical areas throughout the Old World.

There exists a perennial question as to whether a megapode ever existed in Fiji. There are several anecdotal accounts of such a bird which have been amplified but not confirmed by early visiting ornithologists.[8, 240] No specimens have ever been procured and there is not sufficient evidence to confirm its status. It is very probable that the bird described as a megapode was none other than the Barred-wing Rail, for descriptions given could equally apply to either bird and the Fijian name Sasa (correctly the Barred-wing Rail) has been recorded for them both.

MacGillivray's Petrel is the only sea bird endemic to the region, and is known solely from a single fledgling collected in 1855 from Gau, Fiji. It has not been recorded since but it is doubtful if any ornithologists have visited the island since the Whitney South Sea Expedition visited Gau in 1924. They did not find it. If it is a true species and not an aberrant individual of Bulwers Petrel, as one author has proposed, there is no immediately obvious reason why it should not still be present on the island or elsewhere.

The most exciting ornithological discovery in the region over the last few decades was the finding, in 1974, of a subspecies of the Long-legged Warbler on Vanua Levu, by Fergus Clunie and his associates. The nominate form of this bird, from Viti Levu, has long been considered extinct, without real evidence. It is more than likely that it still survives in some isolated areas and there have been two unconfirmed reports of its existence in the last fifteen years.

The Pink-billed Parrotfinch and Red-throated Lorikeet are two Fijian birds not commonly seen but they are certainly in no immediate danger of extinction and more research is required to elucidate the reasons for their rarity. In Samoa, the remarkable Tooth-billed Pigeon is not uncommon on the island of Savai'i, but is restricted to a few well forested gorges on Upolu. The survival of this species and many other Samoan endemics will depend on the preservation of some undisturbed areas of mature forest.

The status of many other species, whilst in no immediate danger, must be considered precarious. Foremost amongst these are birds found on only a single or a few islands, such as the Versicolour Flycatcher, the Tongan form of the Golden Whistler and Kadavu's endemic Fantail, Honeyeater and Whistling Dove. Of special interest is the Niuafo'ou Megapode, the only megapode found in the region where it is confined to the small isolated island of Niuafo'ou. It breeds in association with volcanic soil close to thermal vents. A population of 100 birds in 1968 may have been an underestimate,[244] while a figure approaching 2,000 in 1969 is certainly too high.[229] The most recent and detailed research, undertaken in 1976, indicated a population of between 200-400 individuals.[214]

Kadavu Honeyeater *Xanthotis provocator*,
by William Belcher.
Courtesy of the Fiji Museum.

One bird, the Yellow-breasted Musk Parrot, has been widely reported as being rare or threatened with extinction. In fact, this large and beautiful species is very common in the forests and intermediate zone vegetation of Viti Levu, Fiji. It is by no means restricted to mature or mountain forest, as it is commonly seen in secondary bush areas and will sometimes venture into agricultural habitats. However, it breeds only in sizeable areas of mature forest, and these are required for its survival.

Whilst ecological conservation in the region is still in its infancy and no managed reserves are established, great service was done in protecting the avifauna by former colonial governments. By a rigorous export ban on all wildlife, and more important by preventing the widespread use of firearms, they curtailed a trade in such sought-after avicultural favourites as the Musk Parrots and Collared Lory. Restrictions on the possession and use of firearms have meant that hunting pressure in the region has — with one or two island exceptions — been light or negligible, and is not likely to endanger any species.

In 1873, the mongoose *Herpestes auropunctatus,* was introduced to the Fijian islands of Viti Levu and Vanua Levu in an effort to control rats, which were causing damage in the sugarcane fields. Events have shown that the consequences of this introduction have been little short of devastating. If not the sole cause, the mongoose must bear the major responsibility for the virtual extinction of all ground nesting species on the two islands where it is established. These include the Banded Rail, White-browed Crake and the Spotless Crake, all of which may still survive but in small relict populations; the Purple Swamphen and the Jungle Fowl which are

Slaty Flycatcher *Mayrornis lessoni,*
by William Belcher.
Courtesy of the Fiji Museum.

now restricted to islands free of the mongoose; and possibly, it accounts for the extinction of the Barred-wing Rail and Grass Owl. The Pacific Black Duck appears to be far less numerous now than in former times. Once regarded as an excellent sporting bird it is now no longer common enough to be categorised thus. Other animals have also been affected. The scarcity of terrestrial lizards, the land crab, the two indigenous frogs and possibly the Banded Iguana on Viti Levu and Vanua Levu, can all be attributed to the ravages of the mongoose and feral cats.

It is fortunate that, with the exception of the Barred-wing Rail, the birds affected by the mongoose are widespread species found elsewhere in the Pacific or Indo-Australasian region. However, its depredations have provided a vivid demonstration of the damage that can be done to island ecosystems by the introduction of exotic animals. It is too late to save the affected fauna on Viti Levu and Vanua Levu, but hopefully a drastic lesson has been learnt and the spread of the mongoose will be prohibited, and the future introduction of any exotic species be rigorously screened—if indeed they have to come at all.

There is no doubt, however, that the major threat to the region's avifauna comes from habitat destruction through deforestation. This threat, hitherto unimportant, is now real and pressing; it is also irreversible, and to all intents and purposes unchecked with regard to the region's wildlife. With only one or two exceptions the endemic land birds of the region are forest species; the majority are totally unable to adapt to open or man-made environments. Their fate can be considered sealed unless there is a drastic change in attitude on the part of the various governments of the region. Carefully selected, representative areas of mature forest must be set aside and managed as National Parks. It is not sufficient to point out that the rugged mountainous terrain will always ensure that a sizeable proportion of forests (i.e. 30 per cent in Viti Levu) be classified as "protection forest" and will not be logged. Fragmentation of the forests into isolated patches will, in the end, be equivalent to total deforestation. It is disheartening to note that not a single National Park in the region has been set up as a result of competent ecological surveys. Of late there has been a great deal of talk upon the subject, and one can only hope that action will ensue. This cannot be guaranteed; conservation efforts in the region lack the political punch of well organised or powerful naturalist groups; the region lacks any birds with sufficient popular appeal to draw immediate support from the public; and there are no great rarities to interest international bodies. The immediate situation is not hopeless, but the outlook is grim indeed.

THE FIJI REGION

A common avifauna is one of only a few features which serve to identify the island groups of the Fiji region as a discrete unit.

Politically, the islands (nearly 500 in number) are divided into six countries — Fiji, Western Samoa, American Samoa, Tonga, Niue and the French Territories of Wallis and the Iles de Hoorn.

Physically, they are dispersed in over a million square kilometres of the South Pacific and may be grouped into three island types based upon the origin of their formation. The larger, higher islands, are of volcanic origin, while those of coral or limestone formation are generally small, low islands.

The people of the region afford most striking contrasts. Fijians are of Melanesian stock with many Polynesian characteristics, whilst to the east, even within the Fijian group itself, the Polynesian influence grows stronger and predominates in Tonga and Samoa. Even "pure" Tongans and Samoans, though, have Melanesian characteristics when compared with the Polynesians of Tahiti or Hawaii. Fiji may well be called the modern crossroads of the Pacific, but there is an abundance of evidence to show that the inhabitants of the region have been crossing its waters for many years before the arrival of the Europeans.

All the large and many of the small islands of the region are "high" islands of volcanic origin.

The Fiji Islands dominate the region, if for no other reason than because of their size and number. Over 300 islands straddle the 180° meridian, two of which, Viti Levu (10,386 square kilometres) and Vanua Levu (5,535 square kilometres), together constitute 86 per cent of the groups total land mass. Both are rugged, volcanic islands with mountainous interiors which are for the most part forest clad and deeply dissected by streams. Viti Levu is roughly circular with its highest mountain, Mount Victoria, rising to 1,323 metres. Vanua Levu is narrower with a single mountainous spine and shorter rivers. To the east of Vanua Levu lies the fertile island of Taveuni (435 square kilometres), the largest of Fiji's "small" islands. Despite its small size it has an impressive contour and Mount Uluigalau rises to nearly 1,300 metres. The isolated island of Kadavu, to the south of Viti Levu, is only slightly smaller (407 square kilometres) and its richly forested hills are dominated by the abrupt cone of Cape Washington (830 metres) on its western seaboard.

The "low" islands of coral formation are found mainly in the Fijian Lau group and in the Tongan archipelago.

Palmerston Atoll lies between Tonga and the Cook Islands, few atolls in the region match its perfect configuration.

Limestone islands are usually rugged and inhospitable, with jagged outcrops, deep fissures and undercut cliffs, features which often afford good protection for nesting birds.

Fiji supports a population of just over half a million. Indentured labour from India, brought to work on plantations around the turn of the century, introduced a population of ethnic Indians to Fiji, who are now numerically dominant, comprising 51 per cent of the population.

The small island group of Rotuma lies nearly 400 kilometres to the north-west of Viti Levu. Although part of the Dominion politically, its people are Polynesian, which together with its isolation separate it from Fiji. The small, isolated, volcanic islands of Uvea (Wallis Island) and Futuna and Alofi (Iles de Hoorn) lie 250 kilometres north-east of Vanua Levu. Administered by France, they have a population of about 8,500.

The topography of Samoa bears a strong resemblance to the larger Fijian islands although on a smaller scale. Savai'i (1,820 square kilometres) has a central core of volcanic peaks, one of which, Mount Silisili, rises to 1,875 metres and is the highest peak of the region. The interior is rugged and forest clad except in a few areas where recent lava flows have scoured their way to the sea. Upolu (1,100 square kilometres) has a chain of volcanic peaks running east to west across the island, with coastal plains lying on either side. To the east, American Samoa comprises seven small volcanic islands of which Tutuila (150 square kilometres) is the largest and rises to 702 metres. The population of Western Samoa is nearly 160,000 and that of American Samoa just over 30,000, almost all of whom are Polynesian.

The Tongan archipelago consists of over 150 islands, situated in three circumscribed groups — Tongatapu and 'Eua to the south, the central Ha'apai group and the northern Vava'u group. Less than a third of them are permanently inhabited. Further to the north, and in fact closer to Samoa, are the islands of Tafahi (Boscawen Island) and Niuatoputapu (Keppel Island) whilst the isolated volcanic island of Niuafo'ou lies to their west. The islands of Tonga lie roughly in two parallel lines. The eastern chain has more islands, all of which are "low" and are of coral formation. The western chain from 'Ata to Niuafo'ou consists of larger "high" islands of volcanic origin. Three of these — Tofua, Fonualei and Niuafo'ou are still volcanically active. The small island of Kao rises dramatically out of the sea to 1,125 metres, in an impressive cone. Tongatapu is the largest and most densely populated island of the group, with a population of over 50,000 living on 260 kilometres (in 1966). At the same time fewer than 25,000 were scattered throughout the remainder of the group.

The isolated island of Niue, which is administered by New Zealand, lies 480 kilometres east of Tonga. It is a raised coral outcrop of 258 square kilometres, dominated by a central, saucer-shaped plateau which rises to about 60 metres. It has a population of nearly 4,000 but nearly as many Niueans now live in New Zealand.

The climate of the region is maritime and hence equable. During the winter months the steady South-east Trade Winds blow, but as the inter-tropical convergence zone swings south during the summer, wind direction becomes more variable and hurricanes regularly pass through the region.

Altitude is the most important variable determining rainfall — the higher rainfall being at the higher altitudes. However, on the larger islands of Fiji and Samoa, the windward coasts facing the prevailing Trades receive more rainfall than the leeward coasts which lie in the rain shadow. Throughout the region there is seasonal variation in rainfall with most occurring in the summer months. In Fiji, this seasonality is most pronounced on the leeward coasts and distinct climatic zones can be distinguished:

1. "Wet Zone" — on windward side. Rainfall is high, and seasonal variation small. Humidity is high and daily temperature range small.
2. "Dry Zone" — on leeward side. Rainfall is lower with marked seasonal variation. Humidity is lower and daily temperature range greater.
3. The small low islands. Rainfall is similar to that of the Dry Zone but seasonal variation is less. The daily temperature range is similar to that of the Wet Zone.

The interior of Viti Levu, Fiji, is rugged and mountainous, for the most part covered in thick tropical rain forest.

Lake Tagimaucia on Taveuni, Fiji, lies amidst thick forest in an old volcanic crater. The forests of Taveuni still retain the ground-living birds which have suffered greatly as a result of the introduction of the mongoose to the islands of Viti Levu and Vanua Levu in Fiji.

Most of the smaller islands have a more arid climate than the larger islands and their natural vegetation has in many cases given way to a grass or scrub climax.

The natural vegetation of the islands is related mainly to rainfall and island type. The high, volcanic islands are generally more fertile and their natural vegetation is a lush tropical forest stretching from seashore to mountaintop. In the "Dry Zone" of Fiji this probably gave way to a monsoon forest, but none of this remains. Soil fertility and abundance varies considerably on the small coral islands, the majority having a shortage of good soil. Atolls, for instance, which rise only a few metres above the sea have a shallow sandy soil which can support little but coconut palms, pandanus and a limited scrub growth. Tongatapu is exceptional in being remarkably fertile, but this is because of an overlying accumulation of volcanic dust. Today, much of the natural vegetation has been lost throughout the region. Only the tropical forest on the large islands and the mangrove stands still survive. It is doubtful if any of the tropical forest can be classed as primary. Modification of the natural forest started long before the Europeans arrived.

A dense tropical forest is the natural vegetation of the large islands.

Tree Ferns *Cyathea* sp. are prominent members of the forest community.

Extensive stands of mangroves lie at the mouth of Fiji's major rivers.

In Fiji, the use of fire in the "Dry Zone" reduced the dry forest to a reed and grass dominated landscape. Between this and the windward forested side, lies a distinct intermediate vegetation zone, which consists of a mosaic of light forest, bamboo, reed and grassland. Many of the smaller islands were denuded at an early stage, and the arrival of the Europeans merely accelerated the change. The characteristic beach forest on many small islands and on parts of the larger islands, gave way to coconut plantations on an unprecedented scale. In Fiji, the coastal plains of Viti Levu and Vanua Levu were found to be suitable for growing sugar cane and an industry soon developed.

Only the rain forest in the rugged interior was little affected, and it may even have benefited from the arrival of the Europeans for there are extensive areas of mature secondary forest which are attributable to wide-scale felling in pre-contact periods. The Europeans brought disease and a new type of warfare, which caused a dramatic fall in the population during the nineteenth century, and probably pre-empted the possibility of a larger and more industrious population in the inland regions of Viti Levu and Vanua Levu than is found at present.

Fire keeps the hills of the drier leeward sides of Viti Levu
and Vanua Levu, Fiji, under a reed-grassland climax. Lying
between this habitat and the dense forests to the east is the
intermediate vegetation zone, which is a mosaic of light
forest, stands of bamboo and grassland.

Coconut plantations have taken over much of the land formerly under beach forest. This now remains in isolated patches on the larger islands and on the more rugged and inaccessible of the smaller islands.

The coastal plains on the dry leeward sides of Viti Levu and Vanua Levu, Fiji, are the growing areas for the sugar industry.

The rain forest of the region varies considerably in composition and cannot be stratified by broad classifications. None of the mountains are high enough to support an "Alpine" zone, and many of the trees found on the mountain tops are also found by the sea. An elfin forest does occur on the higher ridges and peaks but it is very limited in extent. A characteristic beach forest did occur, but now only remnants remain. Between these extremes the coniferous genera of *Agathis*, *Podocarpus* and *Dacrydium* are characteristic species.

The larger islands of Fiji and Samoa still retain large vistas of forest (over 50 per cent of the land area) but these are being exploited rapidly for timber. The timber extraction is often followed by clear felling for alternative land use, and there can be no doubt that within a decade the character of much of the forests will be irreversibly altered. Only isolated islands of forest terrain will survive.

The countries of the region have an economy which is based upon agriculture, although American Samoa is an exception in having a thriving fishing industry. Sugar is Fiji's major export and agricultural crop; the growing areas are on the coastal plains of the drier leeward sides of the two major islands. Over 4,500 hectares are presently under cane with an annual production of two million tonnes of sugar cane.

For many years copra has been important as an agricultural crop throughout the region, and Fiji, Tonga and Samoa have large copra industries. Production in recent years has been affected by many diverse factors including the depredations of the Rhinoceros Beetle, together with a widely fluctuating world price. The Rhinoceros Beetle is now being controlled by the introduction of a virus; world economics are less satisfactorily controlled!

Bananas, once an important export from the region, have suffered from disease problems and now, only Tonga has a significant industry. Agricultural development in the region faces difficult problems. In Fiji, only about 12 per cent of the land is reasonably flat and suitable for mechanised farming, whilst a further 20 per cent may be cultivated by hand. In Samoa, the rocky composition of the soil is a serious handicap for mechanical cultivation. These factors compounded by transport costs and low overall production, in comparision with other primary producers, makes many agricultural export crops economically marginal.

Timber extraction on the larger islands of Fiji and Samoa is being undertaken at a rapid and increasing rate. Deforestation for alternative land use often follows, and within a short time only isolated islands of forest on the most rugged terrain will survive.

Copra production is the most widespread agricultural industry in the region, for many of the inhabitants of the small islands it is the only source of regular income.

PART TWO
Colour Plates

PLATE 1

Reef Heron (1)
Egretta s. sacra

Grey phase   White phase   Mottled phase

Mangrove Heron (2)
Butorides striatus diminutus

Wandering Whistling-duck (4)
Dendrocygna arcuata

Jungle Fowl (9)
Gallus gallus

Pacific Black Duck (3)
Anas superciliosa pelewensis

Eastern Curlew (119)
Numenius madagascariensis

Bristle-thighed Curlew (118)
Numenius tahitiensis

Eastern Bar-tailed Godwit (120)
Limosa lapponica baueri

PLATE 2

51

Swamp Harrier (6)
Circus a. approximans

Juvenile

Fiji Goshawk (5)
Accipiter rufitorques

Female

Peregrine Falcon (7)
Falco peregrinus nesiotes

Barn Owl (36)
Tyto alba lulu

Grass Owl (37)
Tyto capensis walleri

Yellow-breasted Musk Parrot (32)
Prosopeia personata

Long-tailed Cuckoo (35)
Eudynamis taitensis

Australian Magpie (38)
Gymnorhina tibicen

P.t. atrogularis

Red-breasted Musk Parrot (33)
Prosopeia tabuensis splendens

PLATE 3

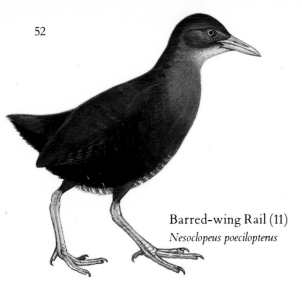

Barred-wing Rail (11)
Nesoclopeus poecilopterus

White-browed Crake (13)
Poliolimnas cinereus tannensis

Samoan Wood Rail (16)
Pareudiastes pacificus

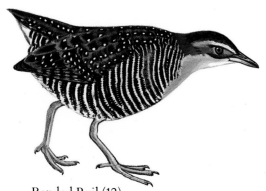

Banded Rail (12)
Gallirallus philippensis sethsmithii

Swamp Quail (10)
Synoicus ypsilophorus

Spotless Crake (14)
Porzana t. tabuensis

Niuafo'ou Megapode (8)
Megapodius pritchardii

Purple Swamphen (15)
Porphyrio porphyrio samoensis

PLATE 4

53

Peale's Pigeon (22)
Ducula latrans

Pacific Pigeon (21)
Ducula p. pacifica

White-throated Pigeon (18)
Columba vitiensis castaneiceps

Female — brown phase

Friendly Ground-dove (20)
Gallicolumba stairii

Male

Spotted Turtle-dove (19)
Streptopelia chinensis tigrina

Tooth-billed Pigeon (23)
Didunculus strigirostris

Feral Pigeon (17)
Columba livia

 PLATE 5

Crimson-crowned Fruit-dove (25)
Ptilinopus p. porphyraceus

Female

Male

Many-coloured Fruit-dove (24)
Ptilinopus perousii mariae

Male

Female

Golden Dove (26)
Ptilinopus luteovirens

Orange Dove (27)
Ptilinopus v. victor

Male

Male

Female

Whistling Dove (28)
Ptilinopus layardi

Female

PLATE 6

55

Pacific Swallow (42)
Hirundo tahitica subfusca

White-rumped Swiftlet (39)
Collocalia s. spodiopygia

White-breasted Woodswallow (43)
Artamus leucorhynchus mentalis

White-collared Kingfisher (40)
Halcyon chloris vitiensis

Flat-billed Kingfisher (41)
Halcyon recurvirostris

Blue-crowned Lory (31)
Vini australis

Collared Lory (29)
Phigys solitarius

Red-throated Lorikeet (30)
Charmosyna amabilis

Adult

Juvenile

Adult — melanistic phase

Fan-tailed Cuckoo (34)
Cacomantis pyrrophanus simus

Red-vented Bulbul (44)
Pycnonotus cafer bengalensis

Island Thrush (45)
Turdus poliocephalus layardi

Polynesian Starling (47)
Aplonis tabuensis vitiensis

European Starling (46)
Sturnus vulgaris

Common Mynah (49)
Acridotheres tristis

Samoan Starling (48)
Aplonis atrifusca

Jungle Mynah (50)
Acridotheres fuscus

PLATE 8

57

Silktail (51)
Lamprolia v. victoriae

Fiji Warbler (52)
Vitia r. ruficapilla

Long-legged Warbler (53)
Trichocichla r. rufa

Spotted Fantail (54)
Rhipidura spilodera layardi

Kadavu Fantail (55)
Rhipidura personata

Samoan Fantail (56)
Rhipidura n. nebulosa

Versicolour Flycatcher (58)
Mayrornis versicolor

Scarlet Robin (64)
Petroica multicolor pusilla

Male

Female

Slaty Flycatcher (57)
Mayrornis l. lessoni

Male

Female

Blue-crested Broadbill (62)
Myiagra a. azureocapilla

Samoan Broadbill (63)
Myiagra albiventris

Male

Female

Male

Female

Vanikoro Broadbill (61)
Myiagra vanikorensis rufiventris

Golden Whistler (65)
Pachycephala pectoralis torquata

Female

Male

Samoan Whistler (66)
Pachycephala flavifrons

Female

Male

Fiji Shrikebill (59)
Clytorhynchus v. vitiensis

Black-faced Shrikebill (60)
Clytorhynchus n. nigrogularis

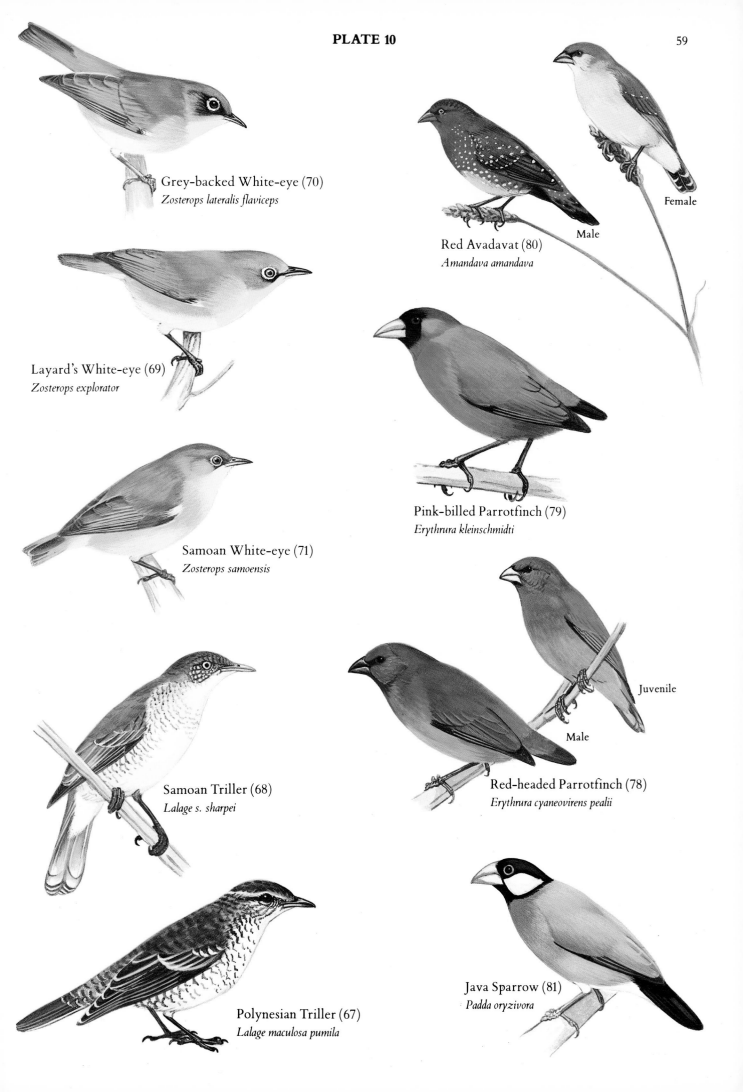

PLATE 10 59

Grey-backed White-eye (70)
Zosterops lateralis flaviceps

Red Avadavat (80)
Amandava amandava

Male

Female

Layard's White-eye (69)
Zosterops explorator

Pink-billed Parrotfinch (79)
Erythrura kleinschmidti

Samoan White-eye (71)
Zosterops samoensis

Juvenile

Samoan Triller (68)
Lalage s. sharpei

Male

Red-headed Parrotfinch (78)
Erythrura cyaneovirens pealii

Java Sparrow (81)
Padda oryzivora

Polynesian Triller (67)
Lalage maculosa pumila

Wattled Honeyeater (74)
Foulehaio c. carunculata

Female

Male

Cardinal Honeyeater (73)
Myzomela cardinalis nigriventris

M.c. chermesina

Kadavu Honeyeater (75)
Xanthotis provocator

Female

Male

Orange-breasted Honeyeater (72)
Myzomela jugularis

Giant Forest Honeyeater (76)
Gymnomyza v. viridis

Mao (77)
Gymnomyza samoensis

PLATE 12

61

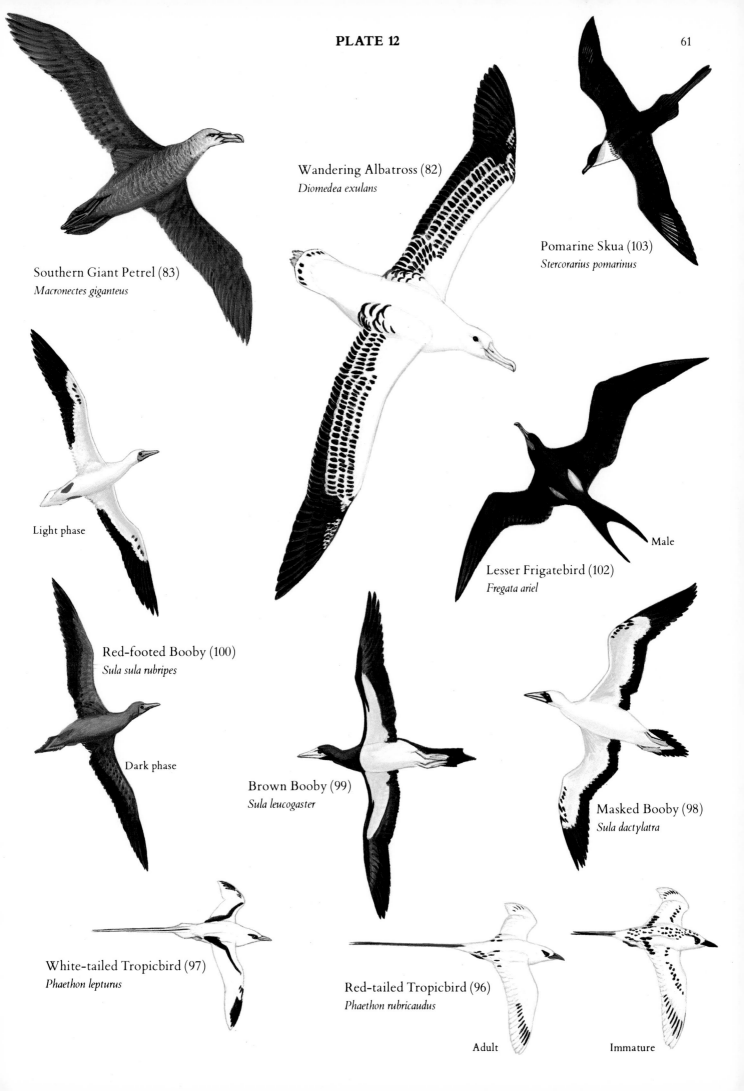

Wandering Albatross (82)
Diomedea exulans

Pomarine Skua (103)
Stercorarius pomarinus

Southern Giant Petrel (83)
Macronectes giganteus

Light phase

Lesser Frigatebird (102)
Fregata ariel

Male

Red-footed Booby (100)
Sula sula rubripes

Dark phase

Brown Booby (99)
Sula leucogaster

Masked Booby (98)
Sula dactylatra

White-tailed Tropicbird (97)
Phaethon lepturus

Red-tailed Tropicbird (96)
Phaethon rubricaudus

Adult

Immature

Audubon's Shearwater (95)
Puffinus lherminieri

Short-tailed Shearwater (94)
Puffinus tenuirostris

Wedge-tailed Shearwater (93)
Puffinus pacificus

Phoenix Petrel (85)
Pterodroma alba

Herald Petrel (87)
Pterodroma arminjoniana heraldica

Cape Petrel (84)
Daption capense

Black-bellied Storm-petrel (92)
Fregetta tropica

White-winged Petrel (88)
Pterodroma leucoptera brevipes

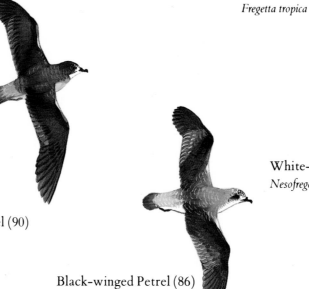

White-throated Storm-petrel (91)
Nesofregetta albigularis

Bulwers Petrel (90)
Bulweria bulwerii

Black-winged Petrel (86)
Pterodroma nigripennis

PLATE 14

63

Grey-backed Tern (107)
Sterna lunata

White Tern (113)
Gygis alba candida

Crested Tern (109)
Sterna bergii

Grey Noddy (110)
Procelsterna cerulea

Black-naped Tern (108)
Sterna sumatrana

Black Noddy (112)
Anous tenuirostris minutus

Common Tern (104)
Sterna hirundo

Common Noddy (111)
Anous stolidus

Sooty Tern (105)
Sterna fuscata

Bridled Tern (106)
Sterna anaethetus

PLATE 15
(All birds in non-breeding plumage)

Little Stint (125)
Calidris ruficollis

Wandering Tattler (121)
Heteroscelus incanus

Double-banded Plover (116)
Charadrius bicinctus

Mongolian Plover (115)
Charadrius mongolus

Lesser Golden Plover (114)
Pluvialis dominica fulva

Sanderling (124)
Calidris alba

Sharp-tailed Sandpiper (126)
Calidris acuminata

Terek Sandpiper (122)
Xenus cinereus

Ruddy Turnstone (123)
Arenaria interpres

Knot (127)
Calidris canutus

PART THREE
The Land Birds

1. REEF HERON
(Eastern Reef Heron, Pacific Reef Egret)

Egretta sacra sacra
(Gmelin, 1789)

Fiji: BELO.
Samoa: MATŪ'U.
Tonga: MOTUKU (MOTUKUTEA, white phase; MOTUKU'ULI, dark phase),
Motuka.

Identification Plate 1. 60 cm. The Reef Heron is found in three distinct colour phases in the region. The white phase is pure white, the grey (or blue) phase is entirely slate-grey with a white chin, whilst the mottled phase has a variable plumage of blue-grey and white. The beak is heavy; dark in grey phase birds and a dull yellow in white phase and mottled birds. Immature white birds are sometimes mottled with grey feathers, occasionally extensively, and may be confused with mottled adults.

Flight Slow and rather ponderous with the neck withdrawn. Courtship flights, where two or three birds may be involved, are more lively with speedy pursuits and rudimentary acrobatics.

Voice Generally silent, but sometimes utters a deep "kraak", especially during courtship flights.

Food A bird with a catholic diet, which includes fish, crustacea and molluscs. Prey items are generally captured after a stealthy approach, followed by a lightning strike or on occasions after a clumsy pursuit through shallow water.

Breeding Reef Herons usually roost communally in large trees or on isolated rocks, and their breeding is also communal, generally in loose colonies, although solitary breeding pairs are not uncommon. The large untidy nests of bare twigs and sticks are normally constructed in trees or on rock ledges in caves and occasionally on the ground on rocky islets. Three — but sometimes two or four — pale green eggs are laid.

Habitat and Range May be found in any aquatic habitat from an exposed reef to a small inland stream in thick forest. The Reef Heron has a wide range from the eastern Indian Ocean through South-east Asia, north to Japan and south to southern Australia and New Zealand. In the Pacific it is a characteristic species extending as far west as the Society Islands.

Remarks and Allied Species The Reef Heron is common throughout the region, although less frequently encountered in Samoa. The grey phase predominates, but there is great variability in the proportion of the three phases. The white phase is very rare in Samoa and the mottled phase is confined to the Lau group and Tonga, where it is the least common of the three phases. A subject of folk-lore and mythology, the Reef Heron has been accorded reverence in some parts of Fiji and some early ornithologists were unable to collect it in certain districts for this reason. No such considerations apply in Tonga where the Reef Heron is sometimes eaten.

The White-faced Heron *Ardea novaehollandiae,* is a rare vagrant to Fiji, it may easily be confused with grey phase Reef Herons, but is paler, has a conspicuous white face and whilst in flight the white underwing markings are diagnostic. Another vagrant from Australia which has been recorded in the region and may associate with Reef Herons is the Glossy Ibis *Plegadis falcinellus.* Except at close quarters, when it displays an iridescent green sheen, this bird appears wholly black, the strong down-curved bill is unmistakable.

The White-faced Heron, a rare vagrant.

2. **MANGROVE HERON**
(Striped, Little, Green, Green-backed, Striated)

Butorides striatus diminutus
Mayr, 1940

Fiji: VISAKŌ, VUSUKEWA (Macuata), Sakosakō (Kadavu group), Sakō.

Identification Plate 1. 35 cm. A small, rather secretive dark heron. Upperparts are grey-brown with a black crown, underparts grey with rufous-brown streaking. The throat has a white patch with a central black stripe. The bill is long with the upper mandible black and lower mandible yellow. The legs and feet are olive with bright yellow soles. Immature birds are heavily streaked black and brown above.

Flight Direct and rather fast always close to the ground or water.

Voice Rather vocal, the call being a short nasal "aahrk".

Food Fish and probably crustacea, usually caught in shallow pools in the mangroves and on adjoining mudflats at low tide; it may well supplement this diet — as it does in other parts of the world — with lizards and insects. Unlike the Reef Heron, it generally remains motionless, waiting for its prey to come within striking distance.

Breeding The nest, constructed of bare twigs, is generally built fairly low down in the mangroves. Two or three mottled pale blue eggs are laid.

Habitat and Range As its name suggests, it is restricted to the vicinity of mangrove stands but it will sometimes feed well out on the reef. The Mangrove Heron has a tropical distribution in the Indian and Pacific Oceans and South-east Asia. In the region it is confined to Fiji.

Remarks and Allied Species A shy bird, but not uncommon wherever there are suitable stands of mangroves. The Mangrove Heron is not readily observed unless looked for, and then usually only a glimpse as it slips, with its bright yellow soles flashing, into the thick of a mangrove stand, or occasionally as it flies between stands. When seen at rest it has a characteristic hunched-up appearance.

The heavily streaked juvenile is conspicuously different from the adult Mangrove Heron.

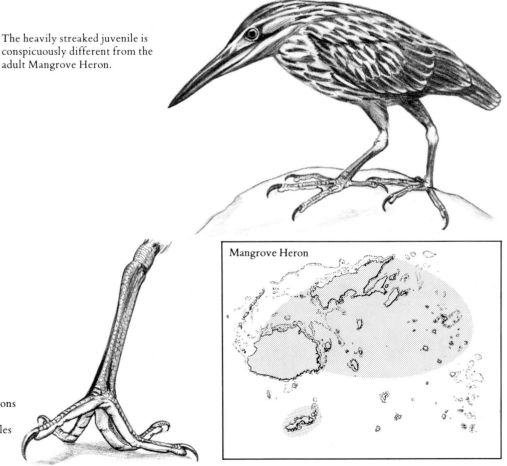

As Mangrove Herons scuttle away, the flashing yellow soles are sometimes conspicuous.

Mangrove Heron

3. PACIFIC BLACK DUCK
(Australian Grey, Grey)

Anas superciliosa pelewensis
Hartlaub & Finsch, 1872

Fiji: GA, GA LOA, GA NI VITI, GA NI VEIKAU.
Samoa: TOLŌA.
Tonga: TOLŌA.

Identification Plate 1. 50 cm. The only duck likely to be seen in the region. A dark brown duck with indistinct scaling, a paler head and a conspicuous black eye stripe between two white stripes. The speculum is bright iridescent green, and the legs and feet orange. The sexes are similar.

Flight Typical duck flight, showing conspicuous white underwing patches.

Voice Ubiquitous nasal "quack" usually delivered in flight.

Food Both animal and vegetable matter, generally procured by "up-ending" or dabbling.

Breeding Often nests far from water, the nest being found on the ground in thick vegetation or low down in a tree hollow. Five to ten pale green eggs are laid.

Habitat and Range The Pacific Black Duck may appear in any freshwater or estuarine locality throughout the region, and it can be seen commonly on the seaboard. It is not common in Samoa.

Remarks and Allied Species A widespread species but never particularly abundant, usually encountered in pairs or small flocks. Generally very quick in locating new pools after rain and will readily take up temporary residence in rice paddies, where it sometimes causes a little damage through its "muddling" activities. Never a sedentary species, local movements are normal and small flocks readily fly between islands. In Fiji, the Pacific Black Duck has probably suffered from the depredations of the introduced mongoose on the islands of Viti Levu and Vanua Levu. Early accounts describe it as an abundant and favourite sporting bird, a description which is not tenable today. The passage of the newly hatched ducklings from the nest site to the water must be the vulnerable stage, and one rarely sees more than two or three ducklings surviving from a clutch.

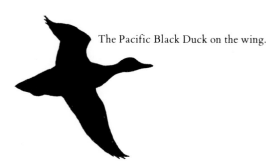

The Pacific Black Duck on the wing.

In flight Wandering Whistling-ducks have a characteristic silhouette with trailing legs, short rounded wings, and the head and long neck held depressed.

4. WANDERING WHISTLING-DUCK
(Whistling Tree Duck, Water Whistle-duck)

Dendrocygna arcuata
(Horsfield, 1824)

Fiji: GA DAMU.

Identification Plate 1. 55 cm. A typical Whistling-duck, with an upright stance, long neck and long legs. Upperparts dark brown with light chestnut barring, paler on the throat, almost pure black on the lower back. Crown very dark. Underparts bright chestnut contrasting with white undertail coverts. Legs and feet blue-grey.

Flight No white on the underwing, in contrast to the Australian Black Duck. In flight the short rounded wings, long extended neck and trailing legs are characteristic.

Voice Constant shrill whistling in flight.

Habitat and Range A coastal or subcoastal species throughout much of its range, which extends from northern Australia through Indonesia to the Philippines.

Remarks and
Allied Species The Whistling-duck is almost certainly extinct in Fiji, the only island group in the region where it has been recorded. However, there was an unconfirmed report in 1959.[161] Much of the evidence for the existence of this species comes from anecdotal accounts of early writers, or reports to ornithologists. These indicate that it was a migratory or a nomadic species. Two specimens, one of which was a juvenile, collected before 1870 from Nadi Bay (a location which could be either west Viti Levu or southwest Vanua Levu), confirm its status in Fiji.

In Australia, the Wandering Whistling-duck is a renowned nomad whilst in the Solomons it is regarded as migratory. Either Fiji was once within its migratory range — which is unlikely — or else it was colonised by vagrants at one stage, and the population subsequently died out.

The Green Tree Skink is a frequent prey item of the Fiji Goshawk.

5. FIJI GOSHAWK

Accipiter rufitorques
(Peale, 1848)

Fiji: REBA, TUITUI, Latui, Waituitui, Rebakamukamu
and Rebalago — immature birds.

Identification Plate 2. Male 30 cm, female 40 cm. Both adults have ash-grey upperparts with a vinaceous-pink collar and underparts. The cere, iris and feet are orange-yellow, the bill black. Immature birds are distinctively different with dark earth-brown upperparts, and buff-white underparts, strongly streaked with brown.

Flight When pursuing prey, fast and manoeuverable, but at other times rather leisurely with a combination of flapping flight and brief glides. Occasionally soars on outstretched wings. During courtship flights, a pair pursue one another, uttering a high-pitched piping sound and making shallow stalling dives with the tail arched, so that they assume a striking "U" shape.

Voice A strident "ki...ki...ki..." and a repeated "weit-weit-weit-weit". They are noisy in the vicinity of the nest.

Food A wide variety of prey items are taken, including medium-sized and small birds especially Mynahs and occasionally larger species such as Peale's Pigeon. Insects form a large proportion of the diet and lizards are frequently taken together with rodents.

Breeding A crude nest, composed of large twigs is constructed high in a lightly foliaged tree, often the Rain Trees *Samanea saman* and *Albizzia lebbeck*. Two to four pale eggs with dark red-brown blotches are laid.

Habitat and Range A wide-ranging bird which may be encountered in any habitat including urban parks. The favoured habitat is open woodland or well-wooded agricultural areas. Endemic in Fiji, it has a curious discontinuous distribution among the larger and medium-sized islands.

Remarks and Allied Species A common bird, but less frequently observed than the larger Swamp Harrier. Its presence when resting is frequently betrayed by the mobbing antics of the Vanikoro Broadbill or other small birds and when in flight it is boldly harassed by Woodswallows. At other times the ringing alarm calls of Wattled Honeyeaters and Red-vented Bulbuls leave no doubt as to its whereabouts. Generally, with a docile disposition that allows a close approach, the Fiji Goshawk fiercely defends its nest.

6.   **SWAMP HARRIER**   *Circus approximans approximans*
Peale, 1848

Fiji: TUIVUCILEVU, MANULEVU, TAISENI
         (Lau group), Reba levu; Tuitoga levu, Tuitoga,
         Takelu (all central Viti Levu), Takubu.
Tonga: TAISENI.

Identification   Plate 2. 55 cm. A large, dark bird of prey with the typical harrier silhouette of long tail and long broad wings. There is great variability in the plumage but most adults have dark brown upperparts with a paler rump, that is sometimes white, and generally pale buff underparts which are heavily streaked. In some individuals the underparts are dark, and these resemble the juvenile bird. The bill is black; the cere, iris and feet yellow.

Flight   A characteristic flight, slowly quartering open ground with pronounced wingbeats and short glides. During the latter, the wings are often held above the back, producing a distinctive V-shaped silhouette. Sometimes soars to great heights and the display flights with their rudimentary acrobatics often take place so high as to be barely discernible to the naked eye.

Voice   Generally silent, but very vocal when displaying. Its high-pitched mewing scream can be heard from afar.

Food   Very catholic in its diet, the Swamp Harrier is partial to small birds, especially nestlings and fledglings, rodents, large insects and a proportion of carrion in addition to the occasional lizard and snake. Locally they become adept anglers and snatch *Tilapia* sp. from shallow water.

Breeding   Nests on the ground, in the dense reeds or sedges of marshy areas. Up to seven white eggs form the clutch. The nests are difficult to find.

Habitat and Range   The Swamp Harrier prefers open country, but is commonly seen over the forest. In the region it has a patchy distribution in Fiji, and is found on two islands in Tonga (Tofua and Kao), but is absent from Samoa. Elsewhere it occurs in Australia, New Zealand, New Caledonia, New Hebrides and there is an introduced population in the Society Islands.

Remarks and Allied Species   The Swamp Harrier is common, and frequently observed because of its large size, active hunting method and preference for open habitats.

   Its colonisation of Tonga is relatively recent and the Swamp Harrier may well be expanding its range. It spread rapidly in the Society Islands after its introduction in 1883 to control rats.

   In parts of Fiji, the Swamp Harrier undertakes local movements and large numbers sometimes congregate in areas of high food density. Similarly they are often absent from some areas, occasionally for extended periods.

In flight the Swamp Harrier often holds its wings in a characteristic "V".

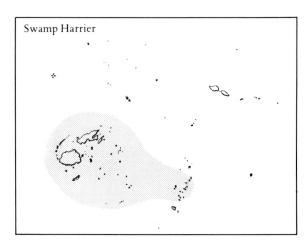

7.	PEREGRINE FALCON	*Falco peregrinus nesiotes*

7. PEREGRINE FALCON

Falco peregrinus nesiotes
Mayr, 1941

Fiji: GA NI VATU.

Identification   Plate 2. Male 40 cm, female 50 cm. The only falcon found in the region. Adults are very dark, almost black above, with a black head and cheeks. The breast is cream or rufous-buff, the flanks and thighs grey with black barring. Immatures have similar upperparts to adults, but their underparts are heavily streaked with black. The feet and cere are yellow, the iris is dark brown and the bill black.

Flight   The long pointed wings and long tail are distinctive. The flight consists of alternating rapid flapping and long glides with wings held swept back, in a sickle-like silhouette. The passage of a Peregrine arching through the sky with partly folded wings as it stoops in pursuit of prey; is a memorable sight.

Voice   The tiercel (male) has a lower pitched call than its mate, which is usually a harsh "kew". A variety of chattering and mewing calls have also been recorded, and intruders are mobbed with a harsh "airk-airk-airk".

Food   A wide variety of birds varying in size from finches to large pigeons. In some areas the staple diet is the Flying Fox, Fruit Bats of the *Pteropus* genus. In other environments sea birds are frequently taken and Peregrines hunt several kilometres out to sea.

Breeding   The eyrie is generally placed on inaccessible cliff ledges, either inland or near the coast. Peregrines lay three or four white eggs with olive-brown blotches.

Habitat and Range   The occurrence of suitable nesting cliffs possibly dictates the distribution of the Peregrine in the region and it may be found hunting over any habitat in their vicinity, even urban environments. It is known to breed only in Fiji but has been recorded from Samoa. Elsewhere in the world it has a cosmopolitan distribution.

Remarks and Allied Species   The Peregrine Falcon is not common, but is well known to Fijians and in some inland districts it has, in the past, been revered by some tribes.

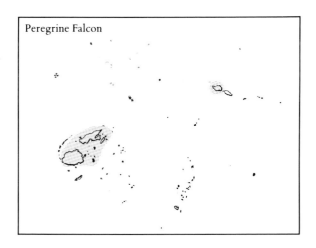

Peregrine Falcon

Flying foxes *Pteropus* sp. form the staple diet of some inland Peregrine Falcons.

8. NIUAFO'OU MEGAPODE
(Malau, Pritchards Megapode)

Megapodius pritchardii
Gray, 1864

Tonga: MALAU.

Identification   Plate 3. 28 cm. Uniformly dark slate-grey with a paler nape and rufous-brown rump and wings. The tail is short and the orange-yellow legs are distinctively sturdy. The head appears disproportionately small with a strong yellow bill. Immature birds are brown above with dark tan markings, and pale buff below.

Flight   A reluctant flier, but will do so if surprised, with deliberate wingbeats and intermittent glides.

Voice	The alarm call is a loud "creek". A three syllable call followed by an ascending trill has also been recorded.
Food	Scratches amongst leaf litter for insects, worms and grubs. Also feeds on fruit and other vegetable matter and occasionally on snails and small crabs.
Breeding	Megapodes are well known for their aberrant breeding behaviour. The Niuafo'ou Megapodes lay their eggs in loose soil associated with warm volcanic vents. The female burrows to depths of one or two metres before laying a single egg, then carefully refills the burrow. The buff coloured eggs are strongly eliptical and large for the size of the bird. Breeding is continuous with a peak in April and May.

The "nests" are not attended by adults, the young birds making their own way to the surface where they are immediately independent and able to fly.

Habitat and Range	An endemic species on Niuafo'ou Island, Tonga; recently introduced to Tafahi.

Remarks and Allied Species

One of the most interesting birds of the region whose nearest relative is in the New Hebrides. How it arrived and why it is restricted to Niuafo'ou is enigmatic, although its specialised breeding requirements may well be a crucial factor.

The Niuafo'ou Megapodes have been thought to be in danger of extinction, but, a volcanic eruption apart, there appears to be no immediate fear of this occurring. Although officially prohibited, the collection of eggs is regularly carried out, but a few nesting sites are never visited because of their inaccessibility. A report of over 1,000 birds and possibly even 2,000 in 1969 was almost certainly an over-estimate.[229] A study in 1976 indicated a population of between 200 and 400.[214]

In 1968, six adult birds and three immature birds were introduced to the island of Tafahi in an attempt to start a new breeding colony. Its outcome has not yet been reported, but this is soon to be investigated.

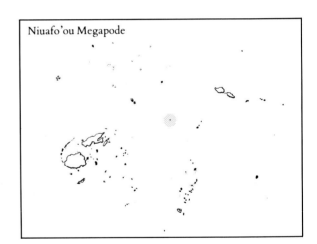

Niuafo'ou Megapode

9. JUNGLE FOWL
(Feral Fowl)

Gallus gallus
Linnaeus, 1758

Fiji: TOA, TOA NI VEIKAU.
Samoa: MOA'AIVAO, MOA.
Tonga: MOAKAIVAO.

Identification

Plate 1. Male 65 cm, female 45 cm. The Jungle Fowl can only be confused with domestic chickens, with which it readily interbreeds, and as a consequence the plumage of many of them—especially females—show strong traces of domestic strains. The wild type male has a beautiful iridescent, multi-coloured plumage with bright orange neck and rump hackles, a maroon mantle and glossy blue wing coverts. The lustrous green tail has long arching feathers. The female is an inconspicuous brown bird with buff and black vermiculations. The chicks are buff with disruptive black markings on the back.

72

Flight	Reluctant to take to the air, but has a strong gliding flight when forced to do so.
Voice	The cocks are noisy birds and their unmistakable crowing resound through the forests in areas where they occur.
Food	Omnivorous, Jungle Fowls feed on any fruits, insects or grains.
Habitat and Range	The Jungle Fowl inhabits mature forest, scrub and thick reed breaks and is found on many of the larger islands in the region, excluding Viti Levu and Vanua Levu in Fiji where it is now extinct. In Tonga it probably only remains on the smaller uninhabited islands such as 'Ata. The Jungle Fowl was an aboriginal introduction whose ancestral stock came from South-east Asia.
Remarks and Allied Species	The early Polynesians took semi-domesticated Jungle Fowls with them on their colonising voyages and on many islands in the Pacific they became feral and formed naturalised populations. In Fiji, Jungle Fowls were common on Viti Levu and Vanua Levu, before the introduction of the mongoose, but have since been lost to these islands as a result of its depredations. On some of the smaller islands they are heavily trapped by Fijians and in danger of extinction. They are shy birds and soon retreat in the face of encroaching agriculture. Their presence is usually betrayed by the ringing crow of the cocks whose strong aggressive instincts allow them to be easily decoyed into a trap by the presence of semi-domesticated cocks tethered in suitable locations.

Chicks of the Jungle Fowl have a characteristic "camouflage" colouration.

10.   **SWAMP QUAIL**
             (Brown Quail)

Synoicus ypsilophorus
(Bosc, 1792)

Fiji: Moa.

Identification	Plate 3. 18 cm. A small brown quail which lacks distinctive features. Both sexes are brown with chestnut and black mottling, the underparts are greyer and heavily streaked with black. The throat is pale buff.
Flight	Flies only under duress and then briefly before dropping down to the ground again. Relatively broad, rounded wings.
Voice	An extended rising whistle.
Food	Mainly grass and weed seeds.
Breeding	A ground nester which constructs a meagre nest of grass or leaves usually under thick cover. In Australia, seven to eleven dull white eggs with brown freckling are laid.

<table>
<tr><td>Habitat and Range</td><td>The Swamp Quail was introduced and is found only on the dry, leeward sides of Viti Levu and Vanua Levu in Fiji. It inhabits scrub and grassland, especially in and around the extensive sugar-cane growing districts. Originally from Australia, the Swamp Quail has also been successfully introduced to New Zealand.</td></tr>
<tr><td>Remarks and Allied Species</td><td>The date of the Swamp Quail's introduction is not known but it was almost certainly after the introduction of the mongoose, whose presence it has been able to survive. However, it is a rare bird and in Viti Levu may well have declined in recent years.</td></tr>
</table>

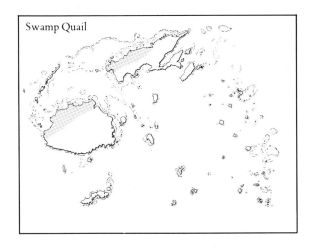

Swamp Quail

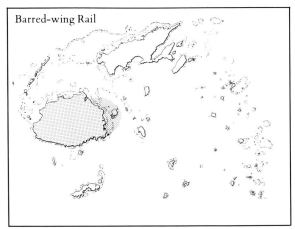

Barred-wing Rail

11.   BARRED-WING RAIL

Nesoclopeus poecilopterus
(Hartlaub, 1866)

Fiji: Sasa, Bidi.

<table>
<tr><td>Identification</td><td>Plate 3. 33 cm. A large drab rail. The upperparts are brown tinged with rufous and the underparts grey, paler on the throat. The flight feathers are distinctively barred black and rufous. The stout bill is yellowish and slightly paler than the legs and feet.</td></tr>
<tr><td>Flight</td><td>Although believed by some authors to be flightless, this is almost certainly incorrect. Early anecdotal accounts indicate that it had weak powers of flight and preferred to run; the size of the wings certainly do not negate the probability of flight.</td></tr>
<tr><td>Voice, Food</td><td>Not recorded.</td></tr>
<tr><td>Breeding</td><td>The eggs have been described as "a warm brown-cream colour, marked throughout with irregularly shaped and sized blotches of indistinct pale purple and dry blood colour".</td></tr>
<tr><td>Habitat and Range</td><td>Only recorded from the islands of Viti Levu and Ovalau in Fiji, where it was said to have inhabited swamps and thick taro gardens.</td></tr>
<tr><td>Remarks and Allied Species</td><td>The Barred-wing Rail is known only from less than a dozen specimens collected in the mid-nineteenth century, and from the accounts of early naturalists. Its only close relative is the rare Woodfords Rail N. woodfordi, of the Solomon Islands. Generally considered to be extinct as a result of the depredation of the mongoose. It is, however, possible that a few may still survive in swampy inaccessible areas and there was an unconfirmed report of a sighting in 1973.[107] There is some evidence to indicate that the Barred-wing Rail was rare even before the introduction of the mongoose and that it was regularly hunted with dogs.</td></tr>
</table>

The perennial question as to whether a megapode once existed in Fiji, probably stemmed from anecdotal descriptions of the Barred-wing Rail.

The wing of the Barred-wing Rail bears a short spur on the carpal joint.

12.   BANDED RAIL
(Buff-banded)

Gallirallus philippensis
(Linnaeus, 1766)

Fiji: BICI, Bidi, Bisi (Lau group), Kuma (Vatulele Island).
Rotuma: Vea.
Samoa: VE'A.
Tonga: VEKA.
Niue: VEKA.

Identification   Plate 3. 25 cm. A medium-sized rail with a smart appearance, if it allows itself to be closely observed. The upperparts are dark ochraceous brown with white spangling especially on the lower back. The throat is grey and the underparts finely banded dark brown and white, with the flanks more strongly barred. The crown, nape and eye stripe are chestnut-brown contrasting strongly with the greyish white eyebrow. The flight feathers are barred rufous and white. The stout bill is light brown and the legs and feet variable. Immature birds have a similar plumage but are duller, whilst the precocious young have black down.

Flight   Flies ponderously with dangling legs.

Voice   A creaking rattle.

Food   Small insects and grubs, snails and crustacea, also fruit and plant material such as leaf and flower buds.

Breeding   A flimsy nest is generally built in thick vegetation, or under the protection of overhanging branches or tree limbs. Four to six heavily blotched pinkish brown eggs are laid.

A Banded Rail, soon after hatching.

Habitat and Range   A widespread species in the region, the Banded Rail may be found on almost any island including small islets with no fresh water, but it is probably absent, certainly very rare, on Viti Levu and Vanua Levu in Fiji. On the larger islands it prefers secondary scrub and rank vegetation. It is commonly seen in native gardens.
   Races of the Banded Rail are found on islands in the west Indian Ocean, through South-east Asia, north to the Philippines and south through Australia to the sub-Antarctic islands off New Zealand. In the Pacific, the Fiji region marks the eastern border of its range.

Remarks and Allied Species   Unlikely to be confused with any other rail, it is the commonest and most frequently observed rail of the region. Usually it is seen as it scampers across a road or scuttles into thick vegetation. It can also be encountered on the foreshore, nervously picking its way through tidal debris, constantly flicking its tail; and commonly on mangrove verges at low tide. It is most active in the early morning and evening.

Subspecies   Three races are currently recognised in the region, but they have no major distinguishing features which would be apparent in the field. In addition to *G.p. sethsmithi*, which is the Fijian and Rotuman representative, *G.p. goodsoni* is found in Samoa and *G.p. ecaudata* in Tonga and Niue.

13.   WHITE-BROWED CRAKE
(Grey Rail or White-browed Rail)

Poliolimnas cinereus tannensis
(Forster, 1844)

Fiji: Gigi.
Samoa: VAI, Poipoi.

Identification   Plate 3. 18 cm. A small grey-brown rail with relatively long legs. The upperparts are grey-brown, rather darker on the lower back and rump. The dark grey eye stripe below a white eyebrow produces a prominent head pattern. The underparts are light grey-brown with a chestnut wash on the flanks. Immature birds are brown and lack the distinctive facial pattern.

Flight   Quick and always brief before dropping into thick vegetation.

Voice	Recorded variously as "i-kiu" or a repeated "chu-chi, chu-chi..." delivered in rapid bursts and a double "krek-krek".
Food	Small aquatic animals.
Breeding	Not recorded in the region, although it is a resident breeding bird. In Australia, it lays three to seven buff-coloured eggs in an insubstantial, loosely-constructed nest, lined with fine grass and generally placed over water in a clump of reeds or other vegetation.
Habitat and Range	Usually found in coastal or inland swamps, but has also been reported from rank secondary vegetation away from water. In the Fiji region it is absent from Tonga, but is found throughout Samoa, whilst in Fiji it has been recorded only from Viti Levu, Ovalau and Gau. A careful search would probably extend this range in Fiji.
Remarks and Allied Species	The White-browed Crake is distinctly smaller than the Banded Rail, and this, together with its light underparts, and longer legs, makes confusion difficult. It is a timid, retiring species and difficult to observe, and in many places probably overlooked. Despite the presence of the mongoose it survives in at least two large swampy areas on Viti Levu and may well exist in other similar places.

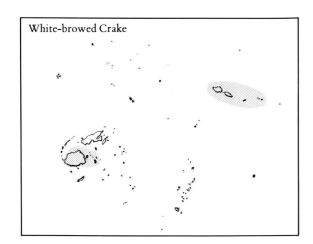

White-browed Crake

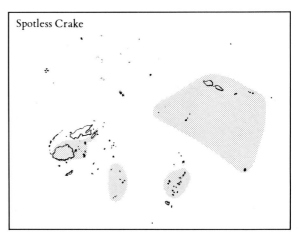

Spotless Crake

14. SPOTLESS CRAKE
(Sooty Rail)

Porzana tabuensis tabuensis
(Gmelin, 1789)

Fiji: MO, Mu.
Tonga: MOHO.
Niue: MOHO.

Identification	Plate 3. 15 cm. A small rail, appearing entirely black at first glance. On closer observation the grey wash to the neck, head and underparts and dark brown mantle and wings, are noticeable. Also conspicuous are the red iris and legs, whilst the bill is black. Immature birds have white marks on the chest and abdomen.
Flight	A reluctant flier, but when forced to do so the dangling red legs are conspicuous.
Voice	A vocal bird with a variety of calls ranging from a mechanical clicking to a "low crooning", and including chirping whistles.
Food	Small aquatic animals and vegetable matter.
Breeding	The nest is usually constructed close to water and consists of loosely interwoven sedge or grass. Three to six buff-coloured eggs blotched with brown are laid.

| Habitat and Range | Liable to turn up in almost any habitat so long as the vegetation is rank, usually near water though. The Spotless Crake has a wide distribution in the region, being found in all three island groups and on many of the isolated islands. Outside of the region it has a wide distribution in the Pacific extending as far east as Ducie Island and westward through Australia to South-east Asia; to the south it is found in New Zealand. |

Habitat and Range Liable to turn up in almost any habitat so long as the vegetation is rank, usually near water though. The Spotless Crake has a wide distribution in the region, being found in all three island groups and on many of the isolated islands. Outside of the region it has a wide distribution in the Pacific extending as far east as Ducie Island and westward through Australia to South-east Asia; to the south it is found in New Zealand.

Remarks and Allied Species Its dark plumage and small size make the Spotless Crake unmistakable but it is a secretive, crepuscular bird and is generally overlooked. Yet it has remarkable powers of dispersal and colonisation as is demonstrated by its distribution in the Pacific. As with the White-browed Crake, it is possible that it may survive in some isolated swamps of Viti Levu and Vanua Levu, despite the presence of the mongoose. At present it has not been recorded from Vanua Levu.

15. PURPLE SWAMPHEN

Porphyrio porphyrio
(Linné, 1758)

Fiji: TERI, Tiri, Kitu (Lau group, Kadavu group, Nadroga), Qala, MAYĀ (Vanua Levu and Taveuni).
Rotuma: Kale.
Samoa: MANU ĀLI'I, MANU SĀ.
Tonga: KALAE.
Niue: KALE.

Identification Plate 3. 37 cm. The large size, together with its conspicuous purple-blue plumage, red bill and frontal shield and long red legs, make the Purple Swamphen unmistakable. The precocious chicks are black.

Flight It will readily fly when disturbed, but often waits to the last moment before exploding out of thick vegetation. Noticeably ponderous in flight, it allows its legs to dangle over short distances but they are held up and trail behind the tail on longer flights.

Food The mixed diet includes insects, worms and other invertebrates, and plant material consisting of seeds, fruit, young shoots and tubers. It has also been recorded as a predator, killing and eating a wounded Wandering Tattler. Its damage to bananas, plantains, taro and cassava frequently bring it into confrontation with farmers.

Breeding The nests are often built far from water in suitable thick vegetation, usually on the ground but sometimes low in bushes. Three or four buff-coloured blotched eggs constitute the normal clutch.

Habitat and Range Despite its common name, the swamphen is frequently encountered away from water, sometimes in mature forest, but usually in thick secondary vegetation or overgrown native gardens. The Purple Swamphen has a wide distribution in the region, but because of the depredations of the mongoose it is probably extinct on Viti Levu and Vanua Levu in Fiji.

Remarks and Allied Species Nowhere a very common bird, but nevertheless widespread on even small islands with thick cover. The Purple Swamphen is most active at dawn or dusk and is partly nocturnal in its habits. When picking its way through vegetation, its hesitant step and rapidly flicked tail which displays the white undertail coverts, give it a characteristic nervous appearance.

Subspecies Two subspecies are distinguished in the region which are based on minor differences, *P.p. vitiensis* is found in Fiji and Tonga, and *P.p. samoensis* in Samoa.

The conspicuous red frontal-shield of the Purple Swamphen.

16. SAMOAN WOOD RAIL

Pareudiastes pacificus
Hartlaub & Finsch, 1871

Samoa: PUNA'E.

Identification Plate 3. 25 cm. A sooty or olive-black rail with a slightly blue-tinged throat and breast. The bill, frontal shield and legs are reddish-orange.

Flight Generally considered to be flightless, its wings are noticeably short and rounded.

Voice, Food, Breeding Not known.

Habitat and Range Recorded with certainty only from the island of Savai'i in Western Samoa, although there are reports of its existence on other islands in Samoa.

Remarks and Allied Species A remarkable bird belonging to an endemic monotypic genus. Unfortunately it is almost certainly extinct (for unknown reasons). It has not been seen in this century and the last specimen was collected by George Brown and given to the naturalists of the Challenger Expedition, which visited Samoa in 1874. At the present time only eleven skins are held by museums around the world.

Early accounts — if they are to be believed — indicate that the Samoan Wood Rail had remarkably aberrant habits which included living in burrows. Of the latter, this may well be a case of mistaken identity with nesting shearwaters or petrels.

17. FERAL PIGEON

Columba livia
Gmelin, 1789

Identification Plate 4. 30 cm. A variety of plumage types exist of which the commonest is a uniform grey, lighter on the back and wings and with an iridescent dark blue-grey head, neck and belly. A double dark wing bar is conspicuous on the folded wing.

Flight Swift and steady, most birds displaying white underwings and rump.

Voice A variety of subdued coos.

Food Seeds, especially grains.

Breeding Breeds in towns, on ledges or under eaves, or in makeshift dovecotes.

Habitat and Range Common in some of the larger towns of the region, it rarely moves into agricultural areas and has not reverted to the wild state by colonising islands or sea cliffs.

Remarks and Allied Species Although the date of its introduction has not been recorded, it has only recently appeared in ornithological literature from the region. Yet, it is not a recent arrival, for it was certainly present soon after the turn of the century and there is evidence that it may have first arrived with missionaries as early as the 1840s.

18. WHITE-THROATED PIGEON
(Chilli Pigeon)

Columba vitiensis
Quoy & Gaimard, 1830

Fiji: RUVE, SOQE LOA.
Samoa: FIAUĪ.

Identification Plate 4. 40 cm. A large pigeon, which at a distance appears uniformly black. The upperparts and wings are sooty grey with a green iridescent wash. The underparts are rufous and the flanks grey. Males have a conspicuous white throat, which is usually less distinct in females and inconspicuous in young birds. The plumage of the latter is duller than that of the adults.

Flight Generally ponderous with deep deliberate wingbeats

Voice A slowly delivered and carrying "oo-oooo". Normally rather quiet except during courtship and breeding.

Food Mainly small fruits and berries, especially those of Prickly Solanum *Solanum torvum,* and wild chillis. May also be found feeding on the ground on seeds and young shoots.

Breeding	A rudimentary platform of bare twigs serves as the nest. One or two pure white eggs are laid.
Habitat and Range	The White-throated Pigeon is a bird of immature secondary habitats and although it may be occasionally encountered in true forest it is not the preferred habitat. It is usually seen in clearings in forest, village gardens or on the periphery of agricultural land. Although not recorded from Tonga, the White-throated Pigeon is widespread throughout the rest of the region. Samoa marks the eastern boundary of its range. To the west of the region its range extends to eastern Australia, and north-west to Papua New Guinea, the Philippines and Japan.
Remarks and Allied Species	A conspicuous and common pigeon which is generally encountered in pairs or small flocks. Not a sedentary species, it undertakes irregular local movements in search of food. In the early morning, it may frequently be observed taking grit from gravel roads.
Subspecies	Two subspecies are found in the region, *C.v. vitiensis* from Fiji and *C.v. castaneiceps* from Samoa. The latter lacks the rufous underparts of *C.v. vitiensis*, theirs being slate-grey and similar to the upperparts, and it has an indistinct purple-chestnut crown.

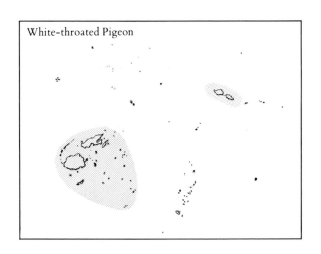

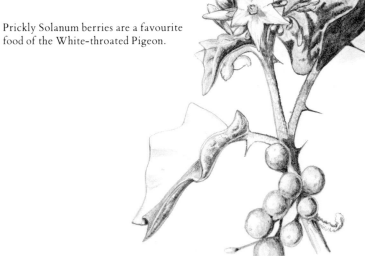

Prickly Solanum berries are a favourite food of the White-throated Pigeon.

19.   SPOTTED TURTLE-DOVE
(Malay Turtle-Dove)

Streptopelia chinensis tigrina
(Temminck, 1810)

Fiji: KUKURU.

Identification	Plate 4. 30 cm. A delicate, brown dove with black mottling on the back and wings. The underparts are vinaceous, lighter on the belly. A striking black collar spangled with silver-white is diagnostic.
Flight	Swift and agile. Spotted Turtle-doves rise from the ground with a clap of wings and on landing frequently spread the tail displaying the conspicuous white tips to the outer tail feathers.
Voice	A variety of two or three syllabled coos, "koo-kru-koo", or "ko-koo".
Food	Weed seeds and grain form the bulk of the diet but young shoots and exposed cassava tubers are also eaten. They can become a serious pest of sorghum or lodged rice, though of the latter they more commonly feed on fallen grain after harvest.
Breeding	The Spotted Turtle-dove has a distinctive courtship, being very vocal with a conspicuous display flight. This is initiated with a near vertical rising flight by the male, accompanied by several wing claps, followed by a stall and then a spiral glide on stiffly spread wings and tail down to a perch near his mate. This may be followed by the male rapidly hopping from branch to branch around the female, making stiff bows. The nest is a fragile looking platform of small twigs and one or two white eggs form the clutch.

Habitat and Range The Spotted Turtle-dove is usually encountered in suburban gardens, villages and agricultural land, although it sometimes ventures into grass clearings in forested areas. Confined to Fiji it is found on the larger islands, and some of the smaller islands close by.

Remarks and Allied Species An introduced bird, the Spotted Turtle-dove was first recorded as being established in 1923. It is now a very common species in most man-modified habitats.

Kosters Curse was a very serious weed in Fiji before it was brought under an effective biological control. It invades forested areas and its berries are eaten by the Friendly Ground-dove.

Friendly Ground-dove

20. FRIENDLY GROUND-DOVE
(Friendly Quail Dove)

Gallicolumba stairii
(Gray, 1856)

Fiji: Qilu, Gila, Ruve ni qele, Soqe loa.
Samoa: TU 'AIMEO, Tu 'autifa (male), Tu 'aimeo (female).
Tonga: TŪ.

Identification Plate 4. 26 cm. A medium-sized brown ground-dove. Males have rufous-brown upperparts with a bronze-green iridescence, the crown and nape are grey and the wings rufous with a purplish lustre. The tail is dark brown. The abdomen and belly are dark brown olive, whilst the breast shield is vinaceous pink with a white border. Female Friendly Ground-doves are dimorphic in Fiji, but not in Tonga or Samoa where only the pale phase occurs. The brown phase has complete tawny underparts with no breast shield, whilst the pale phase is similar to males but rather duller. Immature birds are similar to adults but are uniformly brown.

Flight Friendly Ground-doves prefer to escape by running, but when forced to fly do so with an explosive start, accompanied by a clatter of wings and a swift agile flight through the substage of the forest.

Voice A resonant, mournful coo, monotonously repeated, "coo-a-coo, coo-a-coo, coo-a-coo", etc.

Food Seeds, fruit, buds and young leaves and shoots taken on the ground or in the substage.

Breeding An insubstantial nest of interwoven twigs, vine stems and rootlets, is constructed, usually between one and three metres from the ground. One or two pure white eggs are laid.

Habitat and Range May be found in any forest type including bamboo thickets and gallery forest, but it does not venture beyond the forest fringe. The Friendly Ground-dove is an endemic species in the region with an interesting discontinuous distribution in the three archipelagos.

Remarks and Allied Species The Friendly Ground-dove has a most inappropriate common name, since far from being friendly it is a timid, wary bird, the usual sighting being a brief glimpse of a brown bird flying swiftly away. Overall, it is not a common species although it may be locally common for no apparent reason. It survives in Fiji despite the presence of the mongoose, but probably suffers some predation from it. When perching in low trees or shrubs it is noticeably clumsy, and when alerted on the forest floor it often holds its tail cocked up above its back.

Subspecies Some authorities recognise two races in the region, *G.s. stairii* from Samoa and *G.s. vitiensis* from Fiji and Tonga. Although the former is a slightly smaller bird, the differences are minimal and they may be safely united.

The flowers of the Makasoi contain an aromatic oil and are used in the region for making necklaces or scenting cocount oil. The fruits are much sought after by all the fruit-eating pigeons and the Pacific Pigeon may well have helped to spread this tree between islands.

21. PACIFIC PIGEON

Fiji: SOQE.
Samoa: LUPE.
Tonga: LUPE.
Niue: LUPE.

Ducula pacifica pacifica
(Gmelin, 1789)

Identification Plate 4. 40 cm. A large grey-brown pigeon with a rather long square-ended tail. The head, neck and upper mantle are a uniform grey merging into a glossy olive-brown over the remaining upperparts. The underparts are vinaceous with a paler chin and greyer flanks. The underwing is dark slate, this and the tawny chestnut undertail coverts together with the enlarged black cere are diagnostic of the Pacific Pigeon. Females are similar to males and also display the swollen cere, the latter is lacking in the duller immature birds.

Flight Leisurely but deceptively fast.

Voice A harsh barking call and a variety of subdued coos.

Food A true frugivore, the Pacific Pigeon feeds mainly on the fleshy fruits of large trees. Favoured fruits include those of Makasoi *Cananga odorata*, *Guettarda*, *Dysoxylum*, *Scaevola* and *Rhus* sp. On occasions it also feeds on the ground.

81

Breeding	A single white egg is laid on a platform of bare twigs. The nest is usually constructed well up in a large tree.
Habitat and Range	Throughout much of its range the Pacific Pigeon is a bird of dry beach forest and scrub, but in Samoa it is found in mountain forest on the larger islands. In other localities— indeed throughout much of the Pacific and Fiji in particular—it is found only on the smaller islands including islets.
Remarks and Allied Species	One of the characteristic birds of the region, which in Tonga and Samoa figures prominently in folklore. This may be attributed to its former abundance, gregarious nature and nomadic habits. Flocks of Pacific Pigeons regularly move between islands in search of fruiting trees and such visits are annual events where the tree species fruits seasonally.

There seems little doubt that the arrival of Europeans has had an adverse effect on the numbers of the Pacific Pigeon and this is generally attributed to the introduction and widespread use of firearms. This may well be true, but in former times Samoans and Tongans captured enormous numbers of Pacific Pigeons. They devised intricate traps and snares to capture them and sometimes whilst hunting, whole villages slept in the bush, near flocks which were feeding on a particular fruiting tree. In Samoa especially, the numerous proverbial expressions (muagagana) relating to pigeon catching indicate how popular and important the occupation once was. It seems very likely that the widespread and severe loss of beech forest habitat, because of its conversion to coconut plantations, has been a major cause of the decline of the Pacific Pigeon. It is a factor which is commonly overlooked and demonstrates the need for habitat conservation in the region.

The Pacific Pigeon is similar in appearance to Peale's Pigeon — the following species, under which distinguishing features are given.

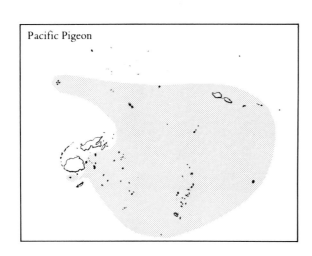

Pacific Pigeon

Only the larger fruit pigeons, such as Peale's Pigeon — are able to swallow the fruit of the Nutmeg.

22.	**PEALE'S PIGEON** (Barking Pigeon)	*Ducula latrans* (Peale, 1848)

Fiji: SOQE, SOQE DAMU, COQE, Soqe dina.

Identification	Plate 4. 40 cm. A large pinkish-grey pigeon with a long square-ending tail. The upperparts are ash-grey with a vinaceous wash, darker towards the rump; tail and wings are dark brown. The underparts are pale vinaceous grey, and the undertail coverts a dark buff. The underwing is chestnut. The bill is black (with no enlarged cere, cf., Pacific Pigeon), the feet and legs dull red. Immature birds are duller.
Flight	Sometimes swift and agile, closing its wings for brief periods, or on other occasions leisurely and rather ponderous.
Voice	A resounding "woof", something between a cough and a bark, is the usual call and may be delivered singly but more frequently twice in quick succession. Also, a wide variety of quieter snarls and squawks.

Food Like the Pacific Pigeon, Peale's Pigeon is a true frugivore feeding on large fleshy fruits especially those of Makasoi *Canaga odorata, Dysoxylum richii, Endospermum macrophylum* and Nutmegs *Myristica* sp.

Breeding An insubstantial platform of twigs built in the fork of a lateral branch. A single white egg is the normal clutch.

Habitat and Range A forest pigeon which is generally restricted to extensive tracts of mature forest. Peale's Pigeon is endemic on the larger islands of Fiji.

Remarks and Allied Species In appearance Peale's Pigeon may be readily confused with the Pacific Pigeon, but it lacks the enlarged cere and its undertail coverts are buff, as opposed to the rich tawny colour of the Pacific Pigeon. In overhead flight, the different underwing colours may be apparent. By far the best distinguishing feature is their separate range. With a few exceptions in the Lomaiviti and Lau groups, Peale's Pigeon is found on the larger islands, and Pacific Pigeon on the smaller islands. The exceptions are islands of intermediate size where there may be subtle habitat differences. With this situation in mind it is interesting to note that the Pacific Pigeon is found at high elevations on the large Samoan islands, in the absence of Peale's Pigeon.

Peale's Pigeon was first collected and is named after Titian Ramsay Peale, a naturalist and artist of the United States Exploring Expedition, which visited Fiji in 1840. The expedition made excellent collections of both Fijian and Samoan birds, despite its brief stay in the region. Peale was responsible for publishing the ornithological work and for his work on Samoan birds, he must certainly be regarded as the father of Samoan ornithology.

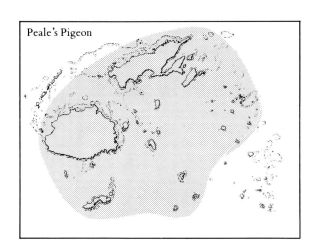

Peale's Pigeon

The extraordinary bill of the Tooth-billed Pigeon led some early ornithologists to believe it was related to the extinct Dodo of Mauritius.

23. **TOOTH-BILLED PIGEON** *Didunculus strigirostris*
(Jardine, 1845)

Samoa: MANUME'A.

Identification Plate 4. 38 cm. A large dark pigeon with a distinctive bill. The head, neck and mantle are glossy blackish green, and the back, rump, tail and wing coverts chestnut-brown. The flight feathers are dark brown. The underparts are blackish-brown merging into chestnut undertail coverts. Females are similar to the male but duller. Immature birds are strongly barred black and chestnut, with a deep rufous tail. The most striking feature of the Tooth-billed Pigeon is its peculiar orange-yellow bill which is reminiscent of that of a parrot; the upper maxilla is compressed and overlays the shorter lower mandible which bears a notch on the cutting edge. Immatures have a black bill.

Flight A rather ponderous flight through the substage of the forest follows a noisy start with a clattering of wings. The flight often finishes with an extended glide.

Voice A single drawn out "oooo".

Food	A frugivorous pigeon feeding particularly on Nutmegs *Myristica* sp., and the fruits of *Dysoxylum* sp.
Breeding	Not recorded.
Habitat and Range	A forest pigeon which is restricted to tracts of mature forest on the islands of Upolu and Savai'i in Samoa where it is endemic.
Remarks and Allied Species	An extraordinary bird without close relatives anywhere; its origin is an enigma. The Tooth-billed Pigeon has excited the curiosity of ornithologists ever since its discovery by Titian Peale of the United States Exploring Expedition which visited Samoa in 1839. Since then it has been variously described as a close relative of the extinct Dodo, similar to a parrot, a terrestrial pigeon running like a rail and a true frugivorous pigeon. Despite such statements, no study of the Tooth-billed Pigeon has been undertaken, something which is urgently required if effective measures for its conservation are to be proposed. At the present time it is not rare on the large, relatively undisturbed island of Savai'i, but it is scarce on Upolu and confined to a few rugged gorges.

Fruits of various Figs are sought after by all the fruit-doves.

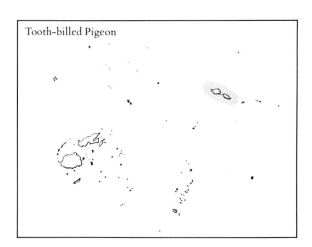

Tooth-billed Pigeon

24.	**MANY-COLOURED FRUIT-DOVE** (Nutmeg, Rainbow or Painted Dove)	*Ptilinopus perousii* Peale, 1848

Fiji: KULUVOTU, Kolavula, Sanakulu, Bune soluve, Saukula.
Samoa: MANULUA (male), MANUMĀ (female).
Tonga: MANUMA'A.

Identification	Plate 5. 23 cm. The *Ptilinopus* doves are all small, compact birds and to those unfamiliar with them not immediately apparent as doves either in flight or when foraging. The male Many-coloured Fruit-dove is a striking bird, but this is only apparent on close inspection when it can be seen to be a truly multi-coloured bird defying an accurate brief description. In flight, or high in the canopy, the male appears creamy-yellow with darker hindparts. The female is less conspicuous being a drab olive-green with pale yellow underparts, a greyish breast with dark indistinct spotting and a magenta cap. The immature bird is dull green.
Flight	Swift and direct with rapid whirring wingbeats.
Voice	A distinctive call which is more accurately described as an accelerating diminuendo or with more licence as similar to water being poured out of a bottle, "koo-koo-ko-ko-kokokokoko".
Food	An active, gregarious feeder on small fruits and berries, generally in the canopy. Favourite fruits include *Ficus* sp. (especially the Strangling Fig *F. obliqua*), Makasoi *Canaga odorata, Bischoffia javanica* and *Dysoxylum* sp.
Breeding	One or two pure white eggs are laid on a small fragile platform of twigs, often fairly high off the ground and in small terminal branches or on the crotch of a branch.

Habitat and Range	The Many-coloured Fruit-dove is an endemic bird in the region, found only on the larger and medium-sized islands. It is primarily a forest bird, and rarely encountered away from large tracts of mature forest, but locally it may be found in isolated stands of favoured fruiting trees, and in some parks and gardens. It also occurs on some small islands which have only scrub forest habitat.

Remarks and Allied Species	The female is readily confused with both sexes of the Crimson-crowned Fruit-dove, but the latter have bright yellow undertail coverts which contrast with their darker underparts. In addition the two species may be distinguished by behavioural characteristics and in Fiji they occupy different ranges over much of the archipelago.

The Many-coloured Fruit-dove is a gregarious species generally feeding in small flocks of up to twenty birds; they are aggressive and tend to dominate the canopy. However, in the presence of human observers they are timid, and when alarmed remain motionless. Despite their bright colour the males are extremely difficult to see in the canopy against the open sky. Frequently one scans a tree without seeing a single bird, only to lower one's binoculars and watch a dozen or more Many-coloured Fruit-doves trail out in pairs or small groups.

Subspecies	Two races are recognised in the region, *P.p. perousii* is restricted to Samoa; it has yellower upperparts than *P.p. mariae* which is found in Fiji and Tonga and whose upperparts are almost white.

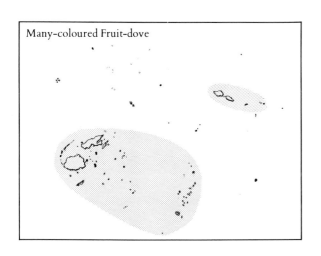

Many-coloured Fruit-dove

The rusty-coloured fruits of *Dysoxyllum richii* are eaten by all the frugivorous pigeons and doves.

25. CRIMSON-CROWNED FRUIT-DOVE
(Purple-crowned)

Ptilinopus porphyraceus
(Temminck, 1821)

Fiji: KULUVOTU, Kolavalu.
Rotuma: Ku ku.
Samoa: MANUTAGI.
Tonga: KULUKULU.
Niue: KULUKULU.

Identification	Plate 5. 23 cm. The only fruit dove of the region in which the sexes are similar. They both strongly resemble the female Many-coloured Fruit-dove. The upperparts, wings and tail are dark green merging into a light grey on the head and neck. The conspicuous magenta cap has an indistinct yellow border to it. The grey-green breast becomes dark green on the belly which contrasts with the yellow undertail coverts. There is an obscure purplish abdominal patch and a light yellow subterminal bar on the tail, both of which are poor field characters. Immatures are entirely green.

Flight	The same as the Many-coloured Fruit-dove — fast and direct with whirring wingbeats.

Voice	A rather high-pitched cooing of two or three notes.

Food	Although there is overlap, the Crimson-crowned Fruit-dove is not a gregarious canopy feeder like the Many-coloured Fruit-dove; rather it tends to feed solitarily or in pairs and usually beneath the canopy in small trees, shrubs or on vines.
Breeding	It is recorded as laying a single pure white egg on an insubstantial twig platform, normally built low down in bushes or small trees.
Habitat and Range	An endemic in the region, the Crimson-crowned Fruit-dove is widespread in Tonga and Samoa, but in Fiji is restricted to the islands of the Lau group and also Vatulele, Rotuma, Makogai, Wakaya and Yadua.
Remarks and Allied Species	May be confused with the female Many-coloured Fruit-dove, but the latter lacks the bright yellow undertail coverts. It is generally assumed that the restricted distribution of the Crimson-crowned Fruit-dove in the Fiji islands is due to ecological exclusion by the Many-coloured Fruit-dove. However, both species exist together on many islands in Samoa and Tonga as well as a few in Fiji. It is more likely that its distribution is due to competitive exclusion by the three doves of the *Ptilinopus luteovirens* group, all of which are essentially non-gregarious and subcanopy feeders similar to the Crimson-crowned Fruit-dove. Their ranges in the Fiji archipelago do not overlap.
Subspecies	Three races are recognised in the region, *P.p. porphyraceus* found in Fiji, most of Tonga, Rotuma and Niue. *P.p. fasciatus* is restricted to Samoa and *P.p. graeffii* to Uvea, Futuna and Niuafo'ou. Their differences are not apparent in the field.

Fruits of *Bischoffia javanica* are eaten by fruit-doves and bulbuls.

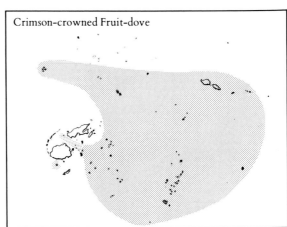

Crimson-crowned Fruit-dove

26.	**GOLDEN DOVE** (Lemon Dove)	*Ptilinopus luteovirens* (Hombron & Jacquinot, 1841)

Fiji: BUNEDROMO, KŌ (Nadroga, Navoha), Bunekō (Ovalau), Bune, Bune karawa (female).

Identification	Plate 5. 20 cm. The male is bright lemon-yellow with olive-green streaking. The head and chin are darker as are the flight and tail feathers. The female is uniformly green but rather lighter below. The fleshy parts of both sexes are emerald green. Juveniles are similar to females.
Flight	Fast and direct with whirring wingbeats.
Voice	The male delivers a sharp yapping sound, frequently repeated at intervals and similar to a dog's bark heard at a distance. It has a strong ventriloquial quality. At close quarters various chortles and growls are sometimes heard.
Food	The Golden Dove is predominantly an active and agile subcanopy feeder of small berries and fruits. Common foods include various *Ficus* species, Prickly Solanum *Solanum torvum,* and Koster's Curse *Clidemia hirta.*

Breeding	A flimsy nest of bare twigs and vine tendrils is constructed fairly low down in a thick shrub or amongst a tangle of vines. A single white egg is laid.
Habitat and Range	Confined to Viti Levu and several islands of the Lomaiviti and Yasawa groups in Fiji. The Golden Dove is particularly common in the intermediate vegetation zone where it frequents light forest, secondary scrub and gallery forest, but it is also regularly seen in mature forest.
Remarks and Allied Species	The male is a striking bird and most conspicuous when flying, but, as with the Orange and Whistling Doves, it blends subtly into the foliage when at rest and is most difficult to locate, even at close quarters. The yapping call of the male is a characteristic sound of many parts of Viti Levu; it is far more often heard than the dove is seen.
Taxonomy	Previously, the Golden, Orange and Whistling Doves were separated into a distinct genus (correctly *Chrysoenas*) on the basis of their characteristic feather structure and distinctive plumage. They are currently placed in the large *Ptilinopus* genus as three geographical representatives of the *Ptilinopus luteovirens* superspecies.

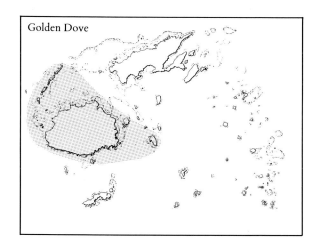

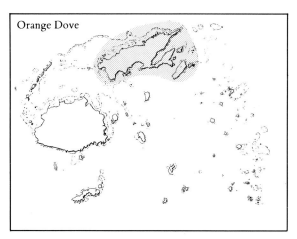

27. ORANGE DOVE
(Flame Dove)

Ptilinopus victor
(Gould, 1871)

Fiji: BUNEDAMU, Bunedromo, Bulidamu, Borabora tana (male), Bune karawa (female).

Identification	Plate 5. 20 cm. The male is unmistakable with a vivid orange plumage and greenish-yellow head. The back is slightly darker and the flight feathers have an olive-grey tinge. The female is uniformly dark-green with a pale olivaceous head, yellow undertail coverts and dark flight feathers. The bill, cere and legs are green. Juvenile birds are uniformly green and the male assumes a sub-adult plumage which closely resembles the female.
Flight	Fast and direct, with whirring wingbeats.
Voice	A penetrating "tock" frequently repeated and probably only given by the male.
Food	Similar feeding habits to the Golden Dove.
Breeding	A single white egg is laid on a typically flimsy platform of bare twigs.
Habitat and Range	The Orange Dove has a restricted range on Vanua Levu, Taveuni and their off-shore islands, and similar habitat requirements to the Golden Dove.
Remarks and Allied Species	A fairly common bird throughout its range, but more often heard than seen.
Subspecies	There are two races currently recognised, *P.v. victor* is found throughout the range except on the island of Qamea where the brighter *P.v. aureus* is found.

28. WHISTLING DOVE
(Yellow-headed, Velvet, Green)

Ptilinopus layardi
(Elliot, 1878)

Fiji: SOQEDĀ, Kanedromo, Sokulu, Bune karawa (female).

Identification   Plate 5. 20 cm. The male is uniformly green, although slightly darker on the back but with a yellowish-green head, a white belly and yellow undertail coverts. The female is similar to the male but lacks the distinctive head plumage.

Flight   Fast and direct with whirring wingbeats.

Voice   A single mellow whistle which is immediately followed by a short trill, the latter only heard at close quarters.

Food   Similar to the two preceding species.

Habitat and Range   Confined to the Kadavu group in Fiji, the Whistling Dove is generally found in the well-forested areas but may also be encountered in village gardens. Principally forages below the canopy.

Remarks and Allied Species   The Whistling Dove was collected first by naturalists from the Challenger Expedition which visited Fiji in 1874. It was named after Edgar Layard, the acting British Consul at the time and one of Fiji's pioneering ornithologists.

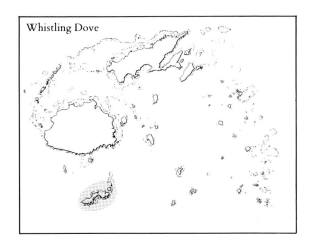

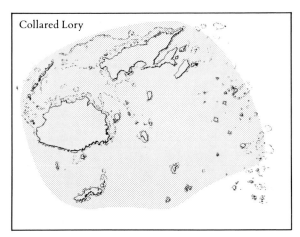

29. COLLARED LORY

Phigys solitarius
(Suckow, 1800)

Fiji: KULA, Kakakula.
Samoa: Sega'ula, Segafiti.

Identification   Plate 6. 20 cm. One of Fiji's most striking birds. The dark purple-black cap contrasts strongly with the scarlet throat and cheeks and the vivid green upperparts, which are broken by a scarlet band across the back. The wings and rather stubby tail are darker green, the breast and belly scarlet, and the lower abdomen and thighs purple-black. The bill and legs are orange. Immature birds are similar to adults.

Flight   Swift and direct with rapid indistinct wingbeats.

Voice   A penetrating, mechanical screech, uttered both on the wing and whilst feeding.

Food   The Collared Lory has a brush tongue with highly developed papillae, — ideally suited for its diet of nectar and pollen which it finds from the flowers of a wide variety of tree species. It is an agile and acrobatic feeder commonly using its beak to hold on to branches.

Habitat and Range   An endemic bird of the region, which is found throughout the Fiji Islands except in the Southern Lau group. It is not restricted to any particular habitat and may be encountered anywhere there are suitable flowering trees.

Remarks and Allied Species — Conspicuous birds, usually seen in groups of five to fifteen, calling attention to themselves with their penetrating screeches. The Collared Lory is a common bird in the forests and in the wetter, windward areas of Viti Levu and Vanua Levu, but is less frequently found in the open agricultural areas of the leeward coasts. They are a highly mobile, nomadic species and soon find any large concentrations of flowering trees. In the Sigatoka Valley of Viti Levu, Collared Lories are normally rare, but in the months of August and September they suddenly appear in large numbers as soon as the Drala *Erythrina indica*, blooms.

The scarlet feathers of the Collared Lory used to be prized highly by the Samoans and Tongans. They were used for edging mats, and a considerable trade existed, not only in their feathers but also in live birds which the Samoans used to keep alive and periodically pluck. Escaped Lories were often seen in Samoa, but never managed to establish themselves. The trade was officially prohibited at the beginning of the century, but has continued intermittently. Today the Fijians still call the wool which has substituted feathers for decorating the edges of mats — kula (the Fijian name for the Collared Lory), while the Tongans call it kulasi, but when red feathers alone are used it is termed kula.

Flocks of Collared Lory's travel long distances to visit *Erythrina* trees during its short flowering season.

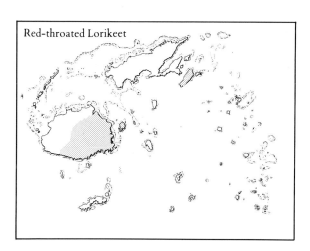

Red-throated Lorikeet

30. RED-THROATED LORIKEET

Charmosyna amabilis
(Ramsay, 1876)

Fiji: Kula wai, Vuni as, Drē, Tikivili.

Identification — Plate 6. 18 cm (includes the long tail). A small and delicate lorikeet, entirely green but for its red cheeks, throat and thighs. The red throat is bordered with yellow whilst the undertail and tail tips are a mustard yellow. The sexes are similar and have an orange bill and legs. Immature birds have purplish thighs and are duller than adults.

Flight — Direct, but the rapid wingbeats produce a fluttering quality.

Voice — Brief, high-pitched squeaks are uttered whilst feeding or in flight.

Food — Nectar and probably pollen.

Breeding — Not recorded.

Habitat and Range — The Red-throated Lorikeet is found only in mature forest on the islands of Viti Levu, Taveuni and Ovalau in Fiji, where it is endemic.

Remarks and Allied Species — A rare bird, which when encountered is usually found in small flocks feeding high in the canopy of trees. The reasons for its rarity are unknown.

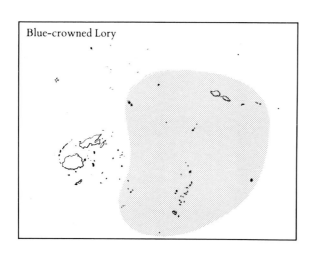

Blue-crowned Lory

Coconut flowers are a common feeding site of the Blue-crowned Lory.

31. BLUE-CROWNED LORY

Vini australis
(Gmelin, 1788)

Samoa: SEGA, SEGAVAO.
Tonga: HENGA, Lohanga.
Niue: HENGA.

Identification Plate 6. 19 cm. A bright emerald green lory with a conspicuous red throat and abdominal patch. The crown, lower abdomen and thighs are purple-blue, the crown being faintly streaked. The bill and feet are orange. Immatures are duller and lack the purple-blue plumage on the thighs and abdomen.

Flight Steady and direct with rapid wingbeats.

Voice A shrill screech delivered in flight and whilst feeding.

Food Nectar, pollen and soft fruit.

Breeding Normally nests in holes in trees, but has been recorded as digging burrows in earth banks. One or two white eggs are laid.

Habitat and Range One of the region's endemic species, the Blue-crowned Lory is widespread, except in Fiji where it is found only in the Southern Lau group. It may be encountered in any habitat where there are suitable flowering trees.

Remarks and Allied Species A pleasant, likeable species which is common through much of its range. In Tonga it is apparently decreasing in numbers and is no longer found on several islands from which it has previously been recorded. Elsewhere, however, it has a discontinuous distribution and has never, for instance, been recorded in Tutuila, Samoa. Such interruptions in its range may not be permanent for the Blue-crowned Lory is well known as an inter-island nomad. Its absence from most of the Fiji islands, on the other hand, is probably due to competitive exclusion by the Collared Lory, for their ranges do not overlap.

The Blue-crowned Lory is an aggressive bird, usually seen in small flocks of six to a dozen. During the breeding season these break down and birds are generally encountered in pairs.

32. YELLOW-BREASTED MUSK PARROT

Prosopeia personata
(Gray, 1848)

Fiji: KŌKĪ, Vaqa, Kakā, Kabote, Kā.

Identification Plate 2. 47 cm. A bright green parrot with a striking orange-yellow breast and belly. The head is darker and towards the beak merges into a sooty black. The tail and flight feathers have a heavy blue suffusion. The bill and feet are black. Males are slightly larger with heavier bills than females, immature birds are similar to adults but have horn-coloured bills.

90

Flight	Appears rather ponderous because of its heavy wingbeats; the long tail and short blunt head is characteristic. The flight is generally slow with gentle undulations and brief glides; when flying in and amongst trees it is surprisingly agile.
Voice	A wide variety of raucous, penetrating squawks and screeches, uttered both in flight and when perched.
Food	Fruits, flowers and seeds.
Breeding	Nests in holes or fissures of forest trees, two rounded white eggs are laid.
Habitat and Range	Restricted to mature forest and the secondary forest associations of the windward and intermediate vegetation zones of Viti Levu, Fiji, where it is frequently seen in the vicinity of village gardens. It is possible that it formerly occurred on Ovalau.
Remarks and Allied Species	The yellow underparts immediately distinguish this parrot from the Red-breasted Musk Parrot. In the past, the Yellow-breasted Musk Parrot has been considered rare and threatened with extinction. It is, in fact, a common species and in no danger of extinction. Although not restricted to mature forest, fairly large tracts of such habitat are required for breeding. At present, there is no shortage of this on Viti Levu, but it is being rapidly felled or fragmented.

A noisy parrot; its raucous screeches are one of the natural alarm calls of the forest. Birds frequently form loose, noisy flocks around fruiting trees and they occasionally damage cultivated fruits.

The strong, musky odour of this species, which is not unlike that of a billy goat, is a natural condition and not — as sometimes reported — a product of captivity. The Red-breasted Musk Parrot has only a slight, almost imperceptible, smell but both members of the genus *Prosopeia,* which is endemic to Fiji, derive their name from it.

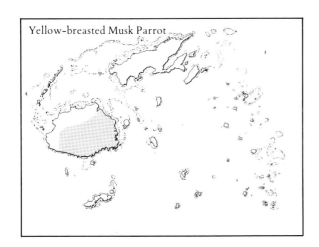

Yellow-breasted Musk Parrot

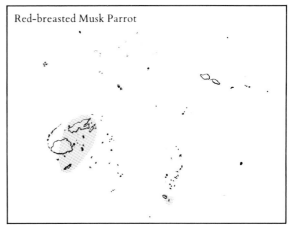

Red-breasted Musk Parrot

33. RED-BREASTED MUSK PARROT
(Red Shining Parrot)

Prosopeia tabuensis
(Gmelin, 1788)

Fiji: KAKĀ, KŌKĪ, Ka damu, Ka kula.
Tonga: KAKĀ, KŌKĪ.

Identification	Plate 2. 45 cm. Head and upperparts scarlet-crimson; a broad blue collar extends across the lower neck and the wings; back and rump are bright green. The flight feathers and tail are green, strongly suffused with blue. The bill and feet are black, the sexes are similar although the bill of males is generally considerably larger.
Flight	Rather slow and ponderous with a noticeably long tail and short blunt head. Occasionally undertakes rudimentary acrobatics.
Voice	A dry rattle or variety of raucous squawks and screeches are given either singly or in series. In captivity, the Red-breasted Musk Parrot is easily taught to speak.
Food	Fruit and seeds.

Breeding	Nests in excavated holes in rotten wood or in enclosed tree fissures at any height from the ground. Two (but three have also been recorded) rounded white eggs are laid.
Habitat and Range	Primarily a bird of forest or secondary scrub associations, the Red-breasted Musk Parrot is also commonly seen in village gardens and on the outskirts of villages on some islands. At present it is found on the six largest islands of the Fiji group (excluding Ovalau), and on 'Eua in Tonga.
Remarks and Allied Species	The scarlet underparts readily distinguish this species from its close relative the Yellow-breasted Musk Parrot; both species may be encountered together, only on the island of Viti Levu. There is little doubt that the range of the Red-breasted Musk Parrot has been extended by human agency. As with the Collared Lory, there was a considerable trade with the Samoans and Tongans for its red feathers and there is documented evidence of live parrots being taken to Tonga in the eighteenth century. Either it was purposely introduced to the islands of 'Eua and Tongatapu there, or escaped birds became naturalised there. The population on Tongatapu has died out with the widespread clearance of natural habitat for agriculture, but it still thrives on 'Eua. In Fiji, the Kadavu race was introduced to Viti Levu and to the Yasawas, possibly by Europeans but equally probably at an earlier date by Fijians. Early accounts suggest that it was much more common on Viti Levu than it is today, and possibly it may be declining.

Throughout its natural range, the Red-breasted Musk Parrot is a common and conspicuous species, often aggregating into small noisy parties at favoured feeding sites.

Subspecies	Five subspecies are recognised. *P.t. splendens,* which is described above, is restricted to Kadavu and the nearby island of Ono (contrary to a popular Fijian legend). It is also the form introduced to Viti Levu. Whilst the other races have maroon underparts, those of *P.t. splendens* are bright scarlet. The distinguishing features of the remaining four subspecies are not apparent in the field, being dependent on slight differences in size and details of plumage. *P.t. atrogularis* is found on Vanua Levu and its offshore islands, *P.t. taviunenesis* is restricted to Taveuni and Qamea; *P.t. koroensis* is confined to Koro and *P.t. tabuensis* is found on Gau and in Tonga.
Taxonomy	There is some uncertainty attached to the taxonomy of this species. The type specimen was collected by Captain Cook's naturalists from the introduced population in Tonga. This population cannot be safely distinguished from that on the island of Gau and they are classified as the same race. It seems unlikely, however, that the Tongan birds are the descendents of Gau birds alone; it is more probable that both populations which form the nominate subspecies are in fact a mixture of two or more races.

34. FAN-TAILED CUCKOO

Fiji: Doti, Tode.

Cacomantis pyrrophanus simus (Peale, 1848)

Identification	Plate 7. 24 cm. The normal adult plumage of this cuckoo is dark sooty to olive-brown upperparts with light rufous brown underparts. The tail is long with conspicuous barred white markings, especially on the outer tail feathers. The broad bill and legs are black. A rarer melanistic phase occurs with uniform sooty black plumage with terminal white markings on the tail. Immature birds have a more complicated set of plumages, the majority have finely barred black and white underparts and an unmarked tail, whilst others have varying degrees of solid black and barred underparts, which in some cases approach the fully melanistic phase.
Flight	A rather furtive flight, generally of brief duration, through foliage or the substage.
Voice	Generally silent but when pursued utters a strident series of brief screams "ki-ki-ki-ki". The advertising call is usually delivered from high in a tree and consists of a two occasionally three syllable wavering whistle — "Towtee" monotonously repeated. It sometimes sings at night.
Food	Insects, especially caterpillars.
Breeding	A typical cuckoo which parasitises small birds, especially Fiji Warblers and Fantails.

| | Primarily a resident of forest or heavily wooded areas, but also seen in more open immature habitats, and occasionally in agricultural land. The Fan-tailed Cuckoo is confined to the larger and a few of the smaller islands in Fiji; other races are found in Australia and intervening island groups to the west of the region. |

Habitat and Range Primarily a resident of forest or heavily wooded areas, but also seen in more open immature habitats, and occasionally in agricultural land. The Fan-tailed Cuckoo is confined to the larger and a few of the smaller islands in Fiji; other races are found in Australia and intervening island groups to the west of the region.

Remarks and Allied Species The Fan-tailed Cuckoo is a fairly common but inconspicuous bird. Originally it was described as two species because of its plumage variation, and it was also thought to be migratory. This was possibly because a post-breeding period of dispersal occurs and takes many birds into more open habitats. Certainly in the agricultural areas of western Viti Levu and in the Sigatoka Valley, Fan-tailed Cuckoos are rarely seen except between February and May when juveniles especially, are regularly observed.

On alighting, Fan-tailed Cuckoos normally fan or gently bob their tails, but for most of the time they remain quietly perched on low branches. They are readily mobbed by small birds and are regularly forced to flee from the aggressive attacks of the Wattled Honeyeater.

Superficial observation may confuse the Fan-tailed Cuckoo (especially melanistic individuals) with the Red-vented Bulbul, but its lack of a white rump is noticeable in flight and absence of a red vent can be seen when at rest.

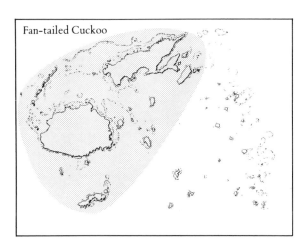
Fan-tailed Cuckoo

35.   LONG-TAILED CUCKOO

Eudynamis taitensis
(Sparrman, 1787)

Fiji: Bici vuka i lagi, Kawa kasa.
Samoa: 'ALĒVA.
Tonga: KALEVA, KALEVALEVA, KALIVA.
Niue: KALUE.

Identification Plate 2. 40 cm. A long-tailed, slender bird which can be readily confused with a small raptor. The upperparts and tail are dark brown, barred with rufous; the wings, back and head have white markings and there are white stripes above and below the eye. The underparts are white with black streaking, as are the long thigh feathers which are visible when the bird is perched.

Flight A strong flapping flight with occasional brief glides. The long tail is conspicuous.

Voice The call is described as a long, harsh screeching, sometimes given at night but not recorded from the region.

Food A varied diet, consisting mainly of large insects, but crab and fish remains have even been recorded.

Habitat and Range The Long-tailed Cuckoo is a migrant to the region, coming from its breeding quarters in New Zealand. It may be encountered on any island, even small islets, and in any habitat, although principally in wooded areas.

| *Remarks and*
Allied Species | The Long-tailed Cuckoo is readily confused in flight with the immature Fiji Goshawk, although the cuckoo's silhouette is more like a falcon. When at rest it is mobbed by small birds in a similar manner to raptors. |

The Long-tailed Cuckoo is readily confused in flight with the immature Fiji Goshawk, although the cuckoo's silhouette is more like a falcon. When at rest it is mobbed by small birds in a similar manner to raptors.

The Fiji region and its environs is the principal wintering area of the Long-tailed Cuckoo, although it does disperse over much of the South Pacific. It is the only regular land migrant which arrives in large numbers in the region; most birds arrive in April and depart in September or October, but some individuals remain through to December. There are no substantiated records of birds remaining the whole year.

36. BARN OWL

Tyto alba lulu
(Peale, 1848)

Fiji: LULU.
Rotuma: RURU.
Samoa: LULU.
Tonga: LULU.
Niue: LULU.

Identification Plate 2. 35 cm. Upperparts grey-buff mottled with dark brown and white. The underparts are silky white with fine black spots on the sides. The prominent facial disc is white with buff margins. The bill and feet are light creamy-brown.

Flight The wings are conspicuously long and broad. The silent flight is light and bouyant.

Voice Harsh screeching, but rarely the blood curdling screams which are characteristic of some races of the Barn Owl.

Food Rats form the staple diet, but small birds and insects are also taken.

Breeding Breeds in holes in trees or in caves; three to five white eggs are laid.

Habitat and Range The Barn Owl is found throughout the region, in any habitat from montane forest to suburban gardens. The Barn Owl is found on every continent except Antarctica and probably has the widest distribution of any land bird.

Remarks and Allied Species A widespread species in the region and locally abundant. It is not restricted to the larger islands and certainly moves between islands in some areas. The Barn Owl is not usually active during the day; it prefers to remain silently perched in a thickly foliaged tree or in a cave, hoping to escape the attention of small birds which persistently mob it.

The Barn Owl is similar to the Grass Owl in appearance, and they cannot be distinguished with certainty in flight.

37. GRASS OWL

Tyto capensis walleri
(Diggles, 1866)

Identification Plate 2. 36 cm. The upperparts are dark brown with large orange-buff markings and fine white spots. The facial disc is pale buff and the underparts white with scattered black spots. The wing and tail are barred dark brown and orange-rufous. The legs are very long and the feet light brown.

Flight, Voice, Food Not recorded.

Breeding Grass Owls breed on the ground in long grass or reeds.

Habitat and Range Only recorded from the island of Viti Levu in Fiji. Other races are found to the west of the region in New Caledonia, Australia and through tropical Asia to Africa.

Remarks and Allied Species The Grass Owl is known from only four specimens collected in the last century. It is presumed extinct but this is by no means certain. Without being able to collect specimens it is almost impossible to distinguish this species from the Barn Owl and there are no breeding records. However, owls can occasionally be disturbed from thick reed tracts in the intermediate zone of Viti Levu, but their specific identity is not known.

38. AUSTRALIAN MAGPIE

Gymnorhina tibicen
(Latham, 1801)

Identification Plate 2. 42 cm. A large black and white bird which cannot be mistaken for any other species. Both the White-backed and Black-backed races are present and freely interbreed; the hybrids have a variable proportion of white on the back.

Voice Melodic whistling calls and a harsh "crark-crark".

Food A mixed feeder which includes a large proportion of insects in its diet as well as fruit, domestic scraps, carrion, grubs and worms; it occasionally turns predator on small animals.

Breeding The nests are substantial structures of bare twigs, built in the forks of large trees or in the crown of coconut palms. Two young are usually raised.

Habitat and Range In Fiji, it is restricted to the lowland, plantation areas of Taveuni, with occasional stragglers being seen on nearby Vanua Levu.

Remarks and Allied Species On Taveuni, the Australian Magpie is a common bird which was first introduced in the 1880s to control the Coconut Stick Insect *Graeffea crouani,* which can on occasions be a serious pest of coconut palms. There have been at least two and probably more separate introductions from Australia, one of which, in 1916, was organised by the Agriculture Department who charged planters £1 a pair. Some of these birds went to plantations on islands other than Taveuni, certainly to Vanua Levu and probably also to Viti Levu, but only on Taveuni are they established, although they are frequently seen on the southern coast of Vanua Levu.

The Australian Magpie was introduced to control the Stick Insect, a serious pest of coconut palms.

39. WHITE-RUMPED SWIFTLET

Collocalia spodiopygia
(Peale, 1848)

Fiji: LAKABA, KAKABA, Kabalata, Kabalamodrau, Lala kairo, Kakabace, Lalamakadrau.
Samoa: PE'A PE'A.
Tonga: PEKEPEKA, Pekepekatea, Pekapekatea.
Niue: PEKA PEKA.

Identification Plate 6. 10 cm. An unmistakable, delicate black swiftlet with a subdued grey wash on the underparts and a conspicuous white rump. The tail has a central notch.

Flight The long, thin sickle-shaped wings and erratic flight with quick shallow wingbeats and intermittent glides are diagnostic. In a steady wind, swiftlets will glide almost continuously but the course remains erratic.

Voice A high-pitched twitter, most commonly heard when used for echo-location in the dark caves where they breed and roost. A distinct clapping of bills may be heard whilst feeding.

Food Insects.

Breeding The White-rumped Swiftlet will sometimes nest under cliff overhangs or in boulder screes, but normally in caves. Although most nests are built in the twilight zone of such caves, swiftlets are capable and commonly do nest in areas of total darkness where they navigate by echo-location. The nest consists of a small platform with a matrix of moss, lichen, *Casuarina* needles or other fine material, cemented with the swiftlet's own saliva. One or two white eggs are laid.

Habitat and Range Widespread in the region, the White-rumped Swiftlet is an ubiquitous aerial feeder which may be found above any habitat at any elevation. It feeds not only above the canopy but also under trees and close to the ground. Outside the Fiji region, the White-rumped Swiftlet is found throughout Melanesia and in north Australia.

Remarks and
Allied Species

The White-rumped Swiftlet is easily distinguished from the only other resident aerial feeder of comparable size — the Pacific Swallow, by the swiftlet's white rump and darker underparts, but its erratic flight and distinctive silhouette are better field characteristics. More difficulty may be encountered in distinguishing it from the migratory Spine-tailed Swift *Chaetura caudacuta,* for which there is single record from Fiji. The Spine-tailed Swift lacks a white rump and its white chin and undertail coverts are diagnostic.

The abundance of the White-rumped Swiftlet, together with its ceaseless activity, makes it one of the most commonly observed birds in the region. It never lands except at the nest or in the roosting caves and activities such as drinking and collecting nesting material are done on the wing. Rain does not deter the swiftlet and it can be seen battling against the heaviest showers. It is frequently seen far from caves in the twilight hours and some birds probably sleep on the wing.

The White-rumped Swiftlet is closely related to the swiftlets whose nests are used for preparing "Birds Nest Soup". These contain much less fibrous material than those of the White-rumped Swiftlet, which for this reason cannot be used.

Subspecies

Each of the three archipelagos in the region have their own race of the White-rumped Swiftlet, the differences are not apparent in the field. *C.s. spodiopygia* is found in Samoa, *C.s. assimilis* is restricted to Fiji, and *C.s. townsendi* to Tonga.

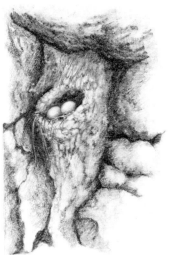

The nest of the White-rumped Swiftlet consists of a matrix of fibres cemented with the swiftlet's own saliva.

Grasshoppers are a staple in the diet of the White-collared Kingfisher.

40. WHITE-COLLARED KINGFISHER
(Mangrove Kingfisher)

Halcyon chloris
Scopoli, 1786

Fiji: LESI, SESE (Viti Levu), SECALA (Lau, Kadavu groups), HECALA (Vatulele Island), SEASEA, LELEWAI, SESEWAI (Vanua Levu), Lele, Levecagi.
Samoa: Tuitala (Tutuila Island).
Tonga: SIKOTĀ, Gikota.

Identification

Plate 6. 21 cm. The upperparts are turquoise blue, rather greenish on the rump and head; the underparts are white, suffused with tawny-chestnut on the flanks. There is a narrow white eyebrow extending from the bill right around the nape where it is ochraceous, the lores and eye stripe are blackish green and, like the eyebrow, extend round to the nape. It is separated from the turquoise upperparts by the narrow eye stripe above, and below by an indistinct white collar which runs from the white underparts across the shoulder. Females have little or no tawny-ochre in their plumage. The conspicuous, long pointed bill of both sexes is black.

Flight

Fast and direct with rapid wingbeats. The long bill is conspicuous in flight.

Voice

Most frequently a rising crescendo "ki-ki-ki-ki-ki — i-i-ee", occasionally a monotonous "ki-ki-ki-ki" and also a variety of hisses and gurgles.

Food

Predominantly large insects such as grasshoppers and crickets, also lizards, young birds and crabs.

Breeding	Nests in holes burrowed into termite mounds, earth banks or rotten trees. Four to six white eggs are laid.
Habitat and Range	The White-collared Kingfisher exhibits a broad habitat tolerance and may be encountered anywhere from montane forest to urban centres, or foraging on the reef. It is a member of a genus which contains primarily woodland birds and is not associated with aquatic habitats. The White-collared Kingfisher is found in over forty races stretching from Africa through southern Asia, Indonesia and northern Australasia, to the Fiji region, where it is widespread — although not found in Western Samoa.
Remarks and Allied Species	A common bird which usually reveals its presence by its loud, penetrating call or the flash of blue as it pounces on an unsuspecting insect and then carries it back to its elevated perch. It is often mobbed by small birds, but pays little attention to them. Although it rarely manages to take one, its undue attention to chicks does not endear it to the majority of farmers.
Subspecies	In the Fiji region, the White-collared Kingfisher is separated into seven subspecies all of which are confined to separate islands or island groups. Size differences, the intensity of the blue on the back, the amount of brown on the underparts and eyebrow-nape stripe, and the absence of the lower white stripe on the collar, are the variable features.

H.c. vitiensis — Viti Levu, Vanua Levu, Taveuni and the Lomaiviti group, Fiji.
H.c. eximia — Kadavu group, Fiji.
H.c. marina — Lau group, Fiji.
H.c. sacra — Tonga archipelago.
H.c. regina — Futuna.
H.c. manuae — Manua Islands, Samoa.
H.c. pealei — Tutuila Island, Samoa.

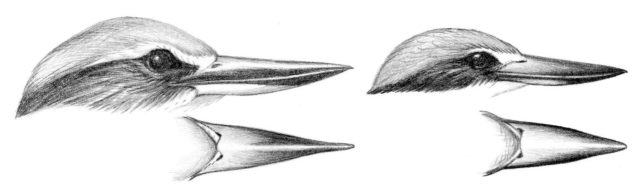

The bill of the White-collared Kingfisher (left) and the closely related Flat-billed Kingfisher (right).

41.   FLAT-BILLED KINGFISHER

Samoa: TI'OTALA (Western Samoa).

Halcyon recurvirostris
(Lafresnaye, 1842)

Identification	Plate 6. 18 cm. Similar to the White-collared Kingfisher, although smaller. The white eyebrow is reduced to a buff loral spot, the eye stripe is indistinct, but the white collar is broader and darker. The white underparts are heavily suffused with tawny brown.
Flight, Voice, Food, Breeding	In all respects very similar to the White-collared Kingfisher.
Habitat and Range	An endemic bird in Savai'i and Upolu, Samoa, where it may be found in all habitats.
Remarks and Allied Species	It is an enigma that this Kingfisher has been able to diverge into a full species, whilst its close relative — the White-collared Kingfisher — has over forty subspecies, which are geographically separated, in a range that stretches around half the world and encompasses that of the Flat-billed Kingfisher.

| 42. | PACIFIC SWALLOW | *Hirundo tahitica subfusca*
Gould, 1856 |
| | Fiji: Kakabe, Manumanu ni doa, Levelevecagi,
Manu ni cagi.
Tonga: PEKEPEKA, Pekepeka'uli'uli. | |

Identification Plate 6. 13 cm. The crown, back and rump are glossy bluish-black, whilst the wings and slightly forked tail are brownish-black. The throat is bright chestnut, and traces of this extend out to the lores and forehead. The underparts are uniform brownish-grey.

Flight A more direct, graceful flight than that of the White-rumped Swiftlet, rarely far above the ground or water.

Food Insects.

Breeding The Pacific Swallow builds a substantial nest of mud with a matrix of rootlets, grass stems or other fibres and lined with feathers. It often builds on the nest of a previous season. Two eggs form the normal clutch. The nests are generally built under the eaves of houses and under bridges; they may also be found at the mouth of caves, under cliff overhangs or occasionally under tree limbs.

Habitat and Range An aerial feeder which is restricted to coastal and estuarine habitats, although occasionally seen along rivers inland. In the Fiji region it is absent from Samoa and much of Tonga, but elsewhere in the Pacific it is widespread.

Remarks and Allied Species A locally common bird, the Pacific Swallow is partial to suburban areas near the coast or at the mouth of rivers. It is interesting to note that on Viti Levu there are only two aerial species feeding on small insects, whilst on Jamaica in the Caribbean—which has a similar land area and altitude—there are six comparable species.

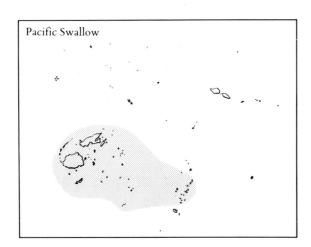

Pacific Swallow

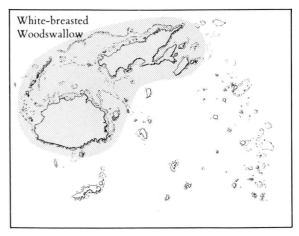

White-breasted Woodswallow

| 43. | WHITE-BREASTED WOODSWALLOW | *Artamus leucorhynchus mentalis*
Jardine, 1845 |
| | Fiji: HIKOHIKORERE (Nadroga, Navoha), SIKORERE,
Galamakadrau, Dree, Vutiase, Vukase, Vuase,
Leleve (Macuata and Bua), Vuevue. | |

The distinctive silhouette of the White-breasted Woodswallow is a familiar sight in most parts of Fiji.

Identification Plate 6. 17 cm. A robust black and white bird with a characteristic upright posture when perched, and a conspicuous aerial feeding behaviour. The head, throat, back, wings and white-tipped tail are black, contrasting strongly with the pure white underparts and rump.

Flight The White-breasted Woodswallow is a strong and efficient flier. Its normal rather leisurely flight, with brief bursts of rapid wingbeats alternating with stretches of gliding flight, belies its speed and agility, which it displays when pursuing insects or mobbing birds of prey. Occasionally it may be seen soaring to great heights.

Voice	The song is a soft medley of chortles and whistles which is infrequently heard. The normal call is a rapid chatter, and the alarm call is a metallic "wit-wit-wit".
Food	Woodswallows are insectivorous, catching their food on the wing, or pouncing on it from the air. Foraging birds are generally perched in a conspicuous position affording a good all-round view, and make diving swoops at insects such as grasshoppers or moths. After being caught in the bill, the prey items are transferred to the feet and carried back to the perch where they are eaten.
Breeding	White-breasted Woodswallows are group breeders with up to four birds being involved in nest construction and care of the young. The substantial nests are cup-shaped and constructed of small twigs and grass stems, often in branch forks in the tree canopy or in holes in cliffs. The normal clutch consists of three white eggs speckled with red, especially in a band around the maximum breadth.
Habitat and Range	The White-breasted Woodswallow is restricted to the islands of Viti Levu, Ovalau and the Yasawas, and to Vanua Levu, Taveuni and their offshore islands. It is more commonly found in open habitats especially on the drier western sides of the larger islands, but may, nevertheless, be regularly encountered hawking over forest at high elevations.

44. RED-VENTED BULBUL

Pycnonotus cafer bengalensis Blyth, 1845

Fiji: ULURIBI, ULURUA, ULUSUKU, TOBE, PAPILO, BULUBULU.
Samoa: MANU PA PALAGI, MANU FAISOPE.
Tonga: FUIVA (Tongatupu Island), MANUFO'OU.

Identification	Plate 7. 20 cm. A conspicuous bird, easily recognised by the combination of its dark, almost black plumage, black erectile crest, white rump, and scarlet vent. The tail is dark black-brown with white tips. Freshly-moulted birds are black but with a silvery sheen on the back and breast because of the white edges on the new feathers. Birds about to moult are much browner, especially the wing and tail feathers. The sexes are similar, but males are larger. The juvenile is brown and is distinguished from adults by its inconspicuous orange, as opposed to red, vent.
Flight	Bulbuls generally have a direct flight with rapid wingbeats, although they frequently undulate over short distances. They are often seen hawking especially in the evenings.
Voice	Bulbuls have a wide variety of calls, ranging from a fairly clear whistle to a harsh chatter. The usual call is a two or three syllable "pee-plo, pee pee-plo". A distinct variation of this, a more strident double syllable note, is used as an alarm call for avian predators, whilst ground predators are mobbed with a harsh scolding.
Food	Omnivorous. Although the bulk of the diet consists of fruits and berries, a small proportion of insects is always taken and this increases in the breeding and moulting seasons. The fruit of weed species such as Prickly Solanum *Solanum torvum,* Cape Gooseberry *Physalis angulata, Piper aduncum,* and Lantana *Lantana camara* are favoured foods. Flowers form a small but significant part of their diet—especially the reproductive parts of many legumes. They also frequently take nectar from many types of flower and small geckos and skinks are eaten on occasion. Bulbuls can become agricultural pests, feeding on tomatoes, egg plant and other soft fruits, although this role is over-emphasised.
Breeding	Bulbuls have a well-defined breeding season in Fiji — October to February — with late broods sometimes hatching in March. The breeding season is the same in Samoa. The nest constructed of rootlets, dry grass, pieces of vine and sometimes artificial fibres, is lined with softer grass or hair. It is built mainly by the female, generally in a conspicuous position from two to twelve metres high, in branch forks, amongst a tangle of vines or at the end of branches. Clutches of two or three are normal, the egg being white with red spots, especially around the broader end. Incubation is eleven to twelve days and the nestling period about two weeks. Individual bulbuls take about one hundred days to moult and the moult season follows the breeding season from January to May.

Habitat and Range Like most introduced birds, the bulbul is confined to man-modified habitats, and is common in suburban and agricultural areas, especially if they contain recently cleared land where its principal weed foods are likely to occur. Since these weed species are invasive weeds of almost any habitat, bulbuls may also be found in forested areas, but generally in association with river flood plains, or forest clearings. They do not penetrate mature forest to any great degree.

In Fiji the bulbul is common only on the main island of Viti Levu and its small adjacent islands. It is present at a reduced density on Ovalau and Wakaya and a small population exists on Taveuni. In Tonga it is found on Niuafo'ou, Tongatapu and 'Eua, whilst in Samoa it occurs on Upolu, Savai'i and Tutuila.

Remarks and Allied Species The Red-vented Bulbul is native to India, Nepal, Ceylon, Pakistan and Burma. The subspecies, *P.c. bengalensis,* is found in Nepal, Bengal and Uttar Pradesh. From the latter two areas most of Fiji's indentured labour was drawn at the end of the nineteenth century.

Because the bulbul was first noticed at the turn of the century, it is most likely to have arrived with the indentured migrants, for it was not deliberately introduced by any agent such as the Agriculture Department.

The bulbul holds a special place in Indian literature and folk-lore and was extensively used as a gaming bird in the subcontinent. During a fight, the adversaries were tethered to a T-shaped perch by a cord fastened to a soft string around the body to prevent escape. Although gaming is now prohibited in India, bulbul fighting still continues as a popular rural sport in some provinces. The sport is not practised in Fiji. Apart from Fiji, Tonga and Samoa, the bulbul has been introduced to Hawaii and is also found in the suburbs of Melbourne. A small population was successfully eradicated from New Zealand in the early 1950s, since it was considered an agricultural pest.

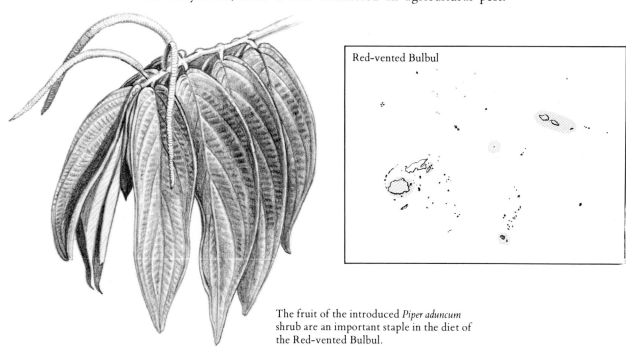

Red-vented Bulbul

The fruit of the introduced *Piper aduncum* shrub are an important staple in the diet of the Red-vented Bulbul.

45.   ISLAND THRUSH

Turdus poliocephalus
Latham, 1801

Fiji: Tola, Siwe, Natola.

Identification Plate 7. 22 cm. Adults have dark brown upperparts, wings and tail; the chin and throat are ashy-grey and the breast and flanks a rich tawny-chestnut with a white suffusion on the abdomen. Immature birds are a lighter uniform brown with black mottling. The bill and legs are a prominent orange.

Flight A distinctive, swift flight through the substage of the forest, with a flash of orange bill and legs often noticeable. Normally delivers the chattering alarm call in flight.

Voice	The alarm call is a penetrating chatter—"tchick-tchick-tchick" run together. Less often heard is the subdued song consisting of a melody of fluted whistles, usually delivered in the early morning or evening.
Food	A ground feeder that searches energetically for snails, worms and insects in loose leaf litter; also eats fruit.
Breeding	The Island Thrush builds a substantial nest of interwoven grass, vine tendrils and pliable twigs often incorporating leaves or shredded bark fibres. Sometimes the whole nest is covered on the outside with moss. Generally built fairly low down in forest regrowth or small trees. The eggs have a blue-green base colour and are heavily marked with small tawny-brown spots. One to three—but normally two—eggs are laid.
Habitat and Range	The Island Thrush does not venture beyond the forest fringe, being restricted to any well-wooded area with mature trees and a fairly open substage. It may be found at any altitude on the larger islands of Fiji and Samoa, but is absent from Tonga. Elsewhere the Island Thrush has a wide range, the Fiji region being on its eastern border, to the west it is found in all island groups from Norfolk Island in the south, through Indonesia to Formosa in the north.
Remarks and Allied Species	The habits of the Island Thrush ensure that there is unlikely to be any confusion over its identification despite the six very distinct subspecies found in the region. It is a shy bird whose presence is usually betrayed by its alarm call as it flies swiftly away through the substage of the forest. Patient observers may watch it foraging noisily on the forest floor, moving with deliberate hops or making brief sallies onto the lower branches.
Subspecies	Six very different races are found in the region:

T.p. layardi — Described above. Found on Viti Levu, Koro, Ovalau and the Yasawa group in Fiji.

T.p. vitiensis — The male is grey, darker on the back; the female is similar but the breast and belly is washed with chestnut. Found on Vanua Levu.

T.p. tempesti — A dark almost black bird, the male having a grey head and throat, which in the female is dark brown. Restricted to Taveuni, Fiji.

T.p. hades — A completely black bird which is confined to Gau, Fiji.

T.p. ruficeps — Dark black-brown, with a light tawny head and throat. Found in Kadavu, Fiji.

T.p. samoensis — An entirely dull black bird, but slightly lighter on the head and throat. Found on Savai'i and Upolu in Samoa.

T.p. hades from Gau, Fiji (left) and *T.p. ruficeps* from Kadavu, Fiji (below).

Island Thrush

46. **EUROPEAN STARLING**   *Sturnus vulgaris*
                                                             Linnaeus, 1758

Tonga: NGUTUENGA.

Identification Plate 7. 21 cm. A blackish bird with a metallic green and purple lustre. After moulting, the birds are richly spangled with buff spots. The bill is yellow during the breeding season, otherwise dusky. Immatures are uniform ashy-brown with a pale throat.

Flight Direct with quick shallow wingbeats and intermittent glides. The wings are distinctly triangular in silhouette.

Voice An accomplished mimic with a wide repertoire of sounds. An extended, descending whistle is characteristic.

Food Gregarious feeders. Starlings are omnivorous although primarily insectivorous.

Breeding Nests in a hole in a tree or more commonly around buildings. Four to seven pale blue eggs are laid in temperate countries.

Habitat and Range Prefers open areas in man-modified habitats, although commonly feeds on tidal flats. In the Fiji region, the European Starling is restricted to Tongatapu in Tonga and the islands of Vatoa and Ono-i-lau in Fiji.

Remarks and Allied Species A recent arrival in the region, it was first discovered in Fiji, in 1951. A subsequent attempt to eradicate it proved unsuccessful, but fortunately it has not spread as was first envisaged. The European Starling is a temperate species, it is probable that tropical conditions do not suit it and it will remain restricted to the southernmost islands of the region.

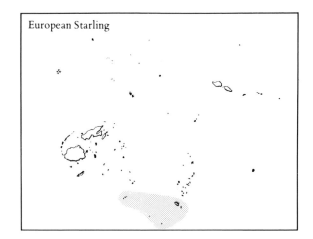
European Starling

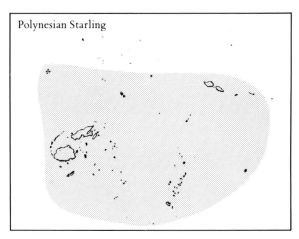
Polynesian Starling

47. **POLYNESIAN STARLING**   *Aplonis tabuensis*
                                                             (Gmelin, 1788)

Fiji: VOCEA (Lau and Kadavu groups), Kiro, Husila.
Rotuma: Husela.
Samoa: MITI VAO.
Tonga: MISI, Megi.
Niue: MISI.

Identification Plate 7. 19 cm. A medium-sized, rather dumpy, grey-brown bird. The upperparts are dark ashy-brown, darker with a faint gloss on the crown. The underparts are lighter grey-buff with distinct pale streaking. The lower abdomen and chin are pale buff, and the bill and feet are dark brown. The iris is brown or a conspicuous yellow, dependent on location.

Flight Rather quick and direct with rapid wingbeats; the broad rounded wings give the flight a slight fluttering quality.

Voice	The advertising call is a fluting, high-pitched double whistle "twee-wee", regularly repeated; also utters a variety of other whistles and a hissing trill.
Food	An active and sometimes acrobatic forager in the forest canopy and substage, feeding mainly on small fruits and berries but may frequently be seen gleaning for insects.
Breeding	The Polynesian Starling nests in holes in trees or rotten stumps, at any height above the ground. Two light blue eggs with brown speckling form the usual clutch.
Habitat and Range	The Polynesian Starling has a wide distribution throughout the region and may be found on even the smallest islet. Its habitat preference depends on the island's topography. On smaller islands it may be found in any habitat including villages and suburban areas, but on the larger islands of Fiji and Samoa it is primarily a forest species favouring the forest edge, clearings or well-wooded secondary habits. It is one of the characteristic species of the region, outside of which it is only found in the Santa Cruz Islands.
Remarks and Allied Species	No difficulty arises in distinguishing the Polynesian Starling from the Samoan Starling; the latter being far larger, an almost black bird with a long tail. The Polynesian Starling is a widespread, but nowhere particularly abundant bird, except on some of the smaller islands. It is generally gregarious, actively feeding in small loose flocks, but solitary birds attracting attention to themselves with their whistling call, are often difficult to locate. There are two distinct iris colours—yellow and brown—with very few intermediates. Geographical location determines which colour is found and only in the Northern Lau group in Fiji are both varieties commonly found together.
Subspecies	The Polynesian Starling is separated into nine subspecies in the region, most of which are indistinguishable in the field, but the very dark forms from American Samoa are conspicuously different.

        A.t. vitiensis — Is found throughout Fiji, with the exception of the southernmost islands of Ono-i-lau and Vatoa where the following race is found.

        A.t. tabuensis — Occurs in the Tongan groups of Tongatapu, Ha'apai and Vava'u, as well as Vatoa and Ono-i-lau in Fiji.

        A.t. tenebrosus — Niuatoputapu and Tafahi, Tonga.

        A.t. nesiotes — Niuafo'ou, Tonga.

        A.t. brunnescens — Niue.

        A.t. manuae — Manua Islands, Samoa.

        A.t. tutuilae — Tutuila, Samoa.

        A.t. brevirostris — Western Samoa.

        A.t. fortunae — Uvea, Futuna.

        A.t. rotumae — Rotuma.

The Iris of the Polynesian Starling may be either yellow or brown depending on location (as shown below). Y = yellow, B = brown and M = both yellow and brown occur.

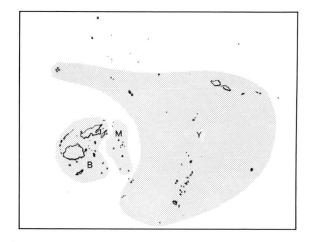

48. SAMOAN STARLING

Samoa: FUIA.

Aplonis atrifusca
(Peale, 1848)

Identification Plate 7. 30 cm. A large, entirely dark brown bird with a faint purple-green iridescence, the heavy black, slightly down-curved bill and long tail are characteristic. Immature birds are a dull brown.

Flight Slow and laboured with shallow undulations as the wings are briefly closed.

Voice The normal call is a harsh screech, but it also utters a variety of softer whistles.

Food Primarily fruit but also insects.

Breeding Nests in holes or fissures of large trees. The eggs are pale blue, the normal clutch size is not recorded.

Habitat and Range Endemic in Samoa where it may be found in any habitat.

Remarks and Allied Species Far larger and darker than the Polynesian Starling. It is also commoner and more conspicuous, frequently forming small garrulous parties whose raucous calls resound over the hills. It will be interesting to see if the Samoan Starling, which is an aggressive bird, in any way checks the spread of the recently introduced Jungle Mynah, on Upolu. Although the mynah is primarily a terrestrial and insectivorous species, the two will certainly compete for nesting holes.

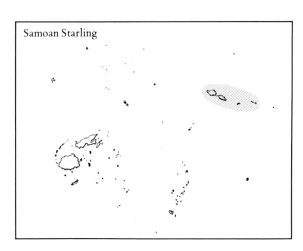

Samoan Starling

When in season, the Guava fruits prolifically and many birds, including the Samoan Starling, eat the fruit.

49. COMMON MYNAH
(Indian, House Mynah)

Fiji: MAINA.

Acridotheres tristis
(Linnaeus, 1766)

Identification Plate 7. 23 cm. A dark vinaceous brown bird with paler underparts, and a white abdomen and undertail coverts. The head, nape and throat are almost black with a slight gloss. The wings and tail are darker than the body with a white wing patch and white terminal bar on the tail. The bill and feet are yellow and there is a conspicuous patch of bare yellow skin below and behind the eye. The eye has a brown iris.

Flight The white wing patch and tail bar are very conspicuous in flight.

Voice	A noisy bird with a large repertoire of rather harsh unmusical sounds, although it does include some tuneful whistles. The normal call is a medley of gurgles, screeches and chattering squawks. Readily tries to mimic other species but is not an accomplished mimic.
Food	A ground feeder which is essentially insectivorous but the Common Mynah readily feeds on any fruit, grains or domestic waste.
Breeding	Common Mynahs nest under the eaves of houses, in thatched roofs and occasionally in holes in trees. They accumulate a considerable quantity of assorted nesting material, but are particularly fond of plastic bags or polythene strips. Three or four pale blue eggs are laid. The nests are usually heavily infested with the mite *Liponyssus bursa*.
Habitat and Range	Common Mynahs are restricted to the proximity of human dwellings, and they may be considered true commensals of man. They are native to India, and have been introduced to and have become naturalised to many places in the tropics and subtropics, especially islands. In the Fiji region, they are restricted to the larger islands of the group and some of those close offshore, as well as Vatulele and Lakeba.
Remarks and Allied Species	The Common Mynah was introduced to Fiji in about 1890 to control insect pests of the emerging sugar industry. It is a very common bird throughout its range in the region, and because of its close association with man and its garrulous nature, it is probably the most conspicuous bird. The Common Mynah is generally seen stalking across garden lawns in pairs, or at midday quietly chortling under the eaves of a house. They are strongly territorial birds and pair for life. Frequently boundary disputes precipitate an incident in which both pairs may be involved. Usually in an open area, the adversaries jump at one another in a flurry of yellow feet and black and white wings, trying to grasp the opposing bird and pin it to the ground. All the appearances of an avian wrestling match, but something which is usually reported as a dance.

The Common Mynah, together with other introduced birds, is frequently accused of driving the indigenous birds "into the bush". Such an accusation is somewhat unfair and it is far more likely that it is the inability of the native birds to adapt to man-modified habitats which restricts them to forested areas.

The Common Mynah may be easily confused with the following species—the Jungle Mynah — under which distinguishing characters are given.

The nasal tuft of the Jungle Mynah (left) and the patch of bare yellow skin behind the eye of the Common Mynah (right) serve to distinguish the two species.

50.　JUNGLE MYNAH
(Hill, Buffalo, Field Mynah)

Acridotheres fuscus
(Wagler, 1827)

Fiji: MAINA.

Identification	Plate 7. 21 cm. A dark sooty-grey bird with paler grey underparts, which have a distinct vinaceous suffusion on the abdomen. The wing and tail markings are identical to those of the Common Mynah. The conspicuous, black nasal tuft is diagnostic. The bill and feet are orange-yellow, and the conspicuous iris yellow.
Flight	Same characteristics as the Common Mynah.
Voice	A rather less varied repertoire than the Common Mynah, with more strident penetrating notes.
Food	Primarily insectivorous, feeding mainly on the ground and normally seeking the company of horses or cattle, on which they readily perch; but only for a vantage point, as they do not remove parasites. They frequently feed on fruit and also on nectar especially from the flowers of the African Tulip Tree *Spathodea campanulata*.

Breeding — The Jungle Mynah nests in holes, usually in trees, but also excavated burrows in large epiphytic ferns, and will readily nest in buildings if allowed to do so by the Common Mynah. Two to four pale blue eggs are laid.

Habitat and Range — A bird of man-modified habitats, despite its common name. The Jungle Mynah favours rough pasture and lightly wooded areas, but small flocks will quite frequently be seen on forays into forested areas, and they are common in parks and gardens in urban areas.

The native range of the Jungle Mynah is in India and across to the Malay Peninsula. It has a restricted distribution in the Fiji region where it is found only on Viti Levu and its offshore islands and on Vanua Levu — although on the latter island it is very rare — in Fiji, and on Upolu in Samoa.

Remarks and Allied Species — The Jungle Mynah may be readily confused with the Common Mynah, although it is a smaller bird, black rather than brown. The distinguishing features are the black nasal tuft and yellow iris of the Jungle Mynah, whilst the Common Mynah has a bare patch of yellow skin below the eye which has a brown iris. The former is also the more gregarious species and readily associates in fairly large loose flocks. Jungle Mynahs were introduced to Viti Levu in about 1900, but not until after 1938 did they become established on Vanua Levu, where they have not flourished. It was purportedly introduced to control Armyworm, which can be a serious pest to many crops. In Samoa Jungle Mynahs arrived in about 1970.

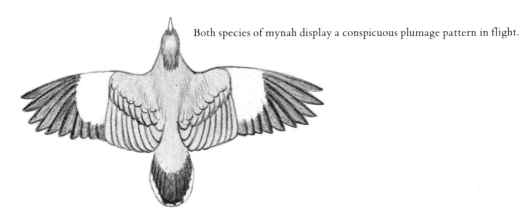

Both species of mynah display a conspicuous plumage pattern in flight.

51.   SILKTAIL
(Satin Flycatcher)

Lamprolia victoriae
Finsch, 1873

Fiji: Sesi, Kaya, Sasa, Wali na koli, Siya.

Identification — Plate 8. 12 cm. A striking bird, deep velvet black with metallic blue spangling on the head, nape, throat and breast. The rump is silky white, extending over the greater part of the tail.

Flight — A restless bird, with a swift darting flight, usually in the substage of the forest. The rounded wings and flashing white rump are distinctive.

Voice — A short, sharp twitter is the normal call.

Food — An insectivorous bird which energetically gleans small insects from the substage of the forest and often descends to the ground or makes aerial sallies after slow flying insects.

Breeding — A rather substantial nest for such a delicate bird, composed of pliable fibres, rootlets, shredded bark and vine tendrils; the outside is often covered with green leafy liverworts and the inside is generally lined with feathers. A single pale pink egg, with indistinct lilac and purple blotches, forms the clutch.

Habitat and Range — Restricted to mature forest on Taveuni and parts of Vanua Levu (probably only the Natewa Peninsula) where it is endemic. The Silktail forages almost exclusively in the substage of the forest, rarely ascending to the canopy.

Remarks and Allied Species An enigma, the Silktail has excited the curiosity of ornithologists since it was first described by Professor Otto Finsch in 1873, who named it after Victoria, Crown Princess of Germany. He was unable to assign it any specific taxonomic affinities and conservatively placed it in the Saxicolinae, a move which initiated considerable conjecture that has not yet been resolved. Some ornithologists have since placed it with the Birds of Paradise, whilst others maintained that it is a Warbler or a Chat-thrush. More ambitiously, and possibly more correctly, several taxonomists created new families or subfamilies to include the Silktail with several other aberrant species. At the present time there can be little doubt that the Silktail remains where E. Mayr placed it in 1945 — "Uncertain Family"[153]

A charming bird, the Silktail, is by no means uncommon on Taveuni, but only locally common on Vanua Levu. It is imperative that its status be carefully monitored and it is not allowed to die out through loss of habitat, for want of a few conservation measures.

Subspecies The Silktail from Taveuni and Vanua Levu were originally described as separate species, but are better classified as subspecies. *L.v. victoriae* on Taveuni and the slightly smaller more richly coloured *L.v. kleinschmidti* from Vanua Levu. Both birds were first collected by one of Fiji's pioneer ornithologists, Theodore Kleinschmidt (see the Pink-billed Parrotfinch for a biographical note).

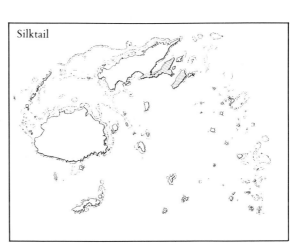

Silktail

The nest of the Fiji Warbler is surprisingly large and bulky for such a small and secretive bird.

52.   FIJI WARBLER

Vitia ruficapilla
Ramsay, 1876

Fiji: MAIA, Manu ni sala.

Identification Plate 8. 12 cm. A small, delicate warbler with olive-brown upperparts, a rufous cap and a white eyebrow above a dark eye stripe. The underparts are pale greyish-buff with brownish flanks. The bill is horn-coloured, thin and pointed.

Flight Rarely seen in sustained flight, usually glimpsed as it darts close to the ground between stands of thick vegetation.

Voice	Unmistakable, the duet of the Fiji Warbler is one of the characteristic sounds of the Fijian bush. The duet consists of a run-together crescendo of whistling notes often starting with a longer note, delivered by one bird and a sharp "tsic-tsic" reply by the other member of the pair. The answering call is often so prompt and consistent that one bird is thought to be responsible for both calls. Occasionally the order is reversed or a single bird can be heard delivering the "tsic-tsic" call.
Food	Entirely insectivorous, gleaning small insects in thick vegetation in the substage.
Breeding	The large, rather crude nest is domed with the entrance hole above mid-height, on one side. Two uniform red-chocolate eggs form the normal clutch.
Habitat and Range	The Fiji Warbler may be encountered in thick undergrowth in mature forest, secondary bush and even agricultural land. The Fiji Warbler is endemic on the four largest islands of the Fiji group.
Remarks and Allied Species	It is a rare occasion when one is able to get a good view of the Fiji Warbler. It is a retiring species that remains in thick vegetation and is frequently overlooked—even by experienced ornithologists. Yet the Fiji Warbler is one of the commonest of Fiji's small insectivorous species, which soon becomes apparent when one becomes familiar with its penetrating duet. In some localities it is the subject of local superstition and its call may be either a good or bad omen, depending on the occasion.
Subspecies	Each of the four islands in the Fiji Warbler's range maintain separate subspecies with rather different plumages. The description given above is *V.r. badiceps* from Viti Levu. *V.r. ruficapilla* from Kadavu has a more extensive rufous plumage, especially on the crown, and it lacks the pale eyebrow. *V.r. castaneoptera,* confined to Vanua Levu, has a buff eyebrow and a browner plumage, whilst the most distinctive race is the larger and very dark *V.r. funebris* from Taveuni, which also has a pale eyebrow.

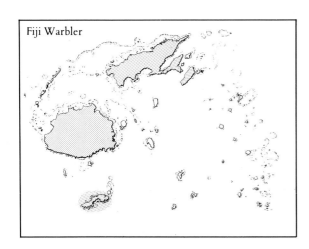

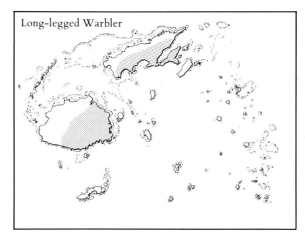

53. LONG-LEGGED WARBLER

Fiji: Manu kalo.

Trichocichla rufa
Reichenow, 1890

Identification	Plate 8. 17 cm. The entire bird is rufous except the chin and throat which are white and the belly which is white washed with rufous. The crown is darker with a conspicuous white eye stripe which extends to the nape where it becomes buff. The tail and legs are both long, relative to the body.
Flight, Voice, Food, Breeding	No information. It is probably a very secretive ground or substage dweller in dense vegetation.
Habitat and Range	Endemic on the two largest islands of the Fiji group, Viti Levu and Vanua Levu, where it has only been recorded from mature forest.

The Long-legged Warbler is known only from a very few specimens and was once considered extinct. A new subspecies was discovered on Vanua Levu by F. Clunie and F. Kinsky in 1974, and there was an unconfirmed sighting from the Vunidawa region of Viti Levu in 1973. The reasons for its rarity are unknown.

Subspecies　*T.r. rufa*　— Viti Levu, Fiji.
T.r. clunei　— Vanua Levu, Fiji.

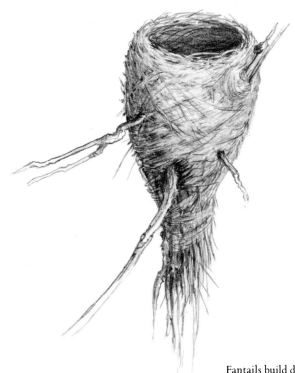

Fantails build distinctive nests with a long tapering tail.

54.　　SPOTTED FANTAIL

Rhipidura spilodera
Gray, 1870

Fiji: Manu sa, Sesi.

Identification　Plate 8. 16 cm. A small, restless bird with a distinctive long, white edged tail. The upperparts are a dark grey-brown, rather darker on the tail; the underparts are white, heavily streaked with brown and they merge into the tawny buff flanks. Two short white stripes on the head—one an eyebrow and the other just behind the ear—combine with the white throat to form a prominent facial pattern on the earth-brown plumage of the head. The beak is small, relatively broad and flanked by short bristles.

Flight　Restless with the white tipped tail, especially conspicuous.

Voice　A scolding "chur-chur" is the normal call; sometimes breaks into a brief burst of song which is a pleasant fluting twitter of four or five distinct syllables.

Food　Insectivorous. The Spotted Fantail generally forages in the substage or lower canopy, making brief aerial sallies after flying insects or else actively gleaning in the foliage.

Breeding　Fantails have a characteristic nest with a long tapering tail trailing beneath it, sometimes up to twenty centimetres long. The compact cup is constructed of fine grass, vine tendrils, or shredded bark fibres, lined with fine soft material and sometimes bound with cobwebs. A commonly used nesting material is the soft scales from the growing point of Tree Ferns *Cyathea* sp. Most nests are built fairly low down in the branches of young trees. The eggs, normally two, are whitish with light brown blotches concentrated on the broader end.

Habitat and Range	Confined to four of the larger islands of Fiji and a few of their off-shore islets. The Spotted Fantail is a bird of the forest or well-wooded areas.
Remarks and Allied Species	To those familiar with Australasian Fantails the identification of the three fantails in the Fiji region will pose no problem. Their restless nature and engaging curiosity make them the most conspicuous of the small forest birds. Rarely does one have to search for fantails since their inquisitiveness generally brings them to any strangers in the forest. Sidling along a branch, briefly fanning its tail or dropping its wings, a Spotted Fantail will harangue an observer with its scolding call, often following him for a short distance to emphasise the message. Spotted Fantails frequently join the mixed bands of insectivorous birds which are characteristic of the region's forests.
Subspecies	The Spotted Fantail is found in three subspecies in the Fiji archipelago: *R.s. layardi,* which is described above, is found on Viti Levu and Ovalau, *R.s. rufilateralis,* with its very rufous flanks, is restricted to Taveuni, and the rufous-backed *R.s. erythronota* is found on Vanua Levu and its offshore islands.

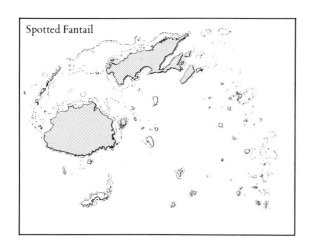
Spotted Fantail

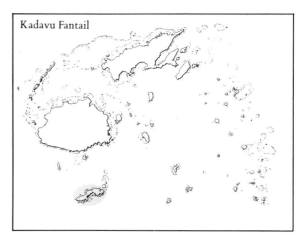
Kadavu Fantail

55. KADAVU FANTAIL

Rhipidura personata
Ramsay, 1876

Identification	Plate 8. 15 cm. The conspicuous facial and breast patterns readily distinguishes this typical fantail. The dark earth-brown head, neck and cheeks contrast with the two separate white eye marks and the white throat. The latter is bordered by a black band which separates it from the remaining creamy buff underparts. The back and wings are dark brown, the long tail black tipped with white.
Flight, Voice, Food, Breeding	In all respects, appears to be similar to the Spotted Fantail.
Habitat and Range	Confined to the island of Kadavu in Fiji.
Remarks and Allied Species	A common bird in the Kadavu forest.

Fantails often use the soft scales on emerging Tree Fern leaves for lining their nests.

110

56. SAMOAN FANTAIL

Rhipidura nebulosa
Peale, 1848

Samoa: SE'U.

Identification	Plate 8. 16 cm. An entirely sooty-grey fantail with similar facial stripes to the Spotted Fantail, white undertail coverts and white tips to the tail feathers.
Flight, Voice, Food, Breeding	Similar to the Spotted Fantail.
Habitat and Range	Endemic on the two Samoan islands of Savai'i and Upolu, where it is common in forested areas, but may also be frequently encountered in young secondary growth or village gardens.
Remarks and Allied Species	A common bird, the Samoan Fantail displays all the behavioural characteristics described for the Spotted Fantail.
Subspecies	*R.n. nebulosa* from Upolu is darker than *R.n. altera,* which is found on Savai'i.

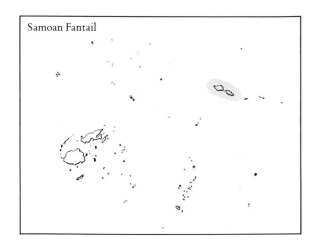

Samoan Fantail

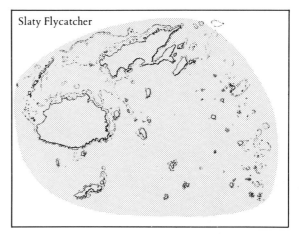

Slaty Flycatcher

57. SLATY FLYCATCHER
(Cinereous Flycatcher)

Mayrornis lessoni
(Gray, 1846)

Fiji: Sasaire.

Identification	Plate 8. 13 cm. A delicate, slate-grey flycatcher, darker above with a conspicuous white eye ring and a black tail with white tips, especially marked on the lateral tail feathers.
Flight	Generally fast and direct.
Voice	A harsh scolding chatter "tsic-tsic-tsic-tsic", with an intermittent "churr". Occasionally breaking into a high-pitched descending whistle.
Food	An insectivorous bird, the Slaty Flycatcher is an active gleaner in the subcanopy, occasionally dropping to ground level or ascending to the canopy. Aerial pursuits of flying insects are sometimes undertaken. The Slaty Flycatcher occasionally adds a small quantity of fruit to its diet.
Breeding	Slaty Flycatchers generally build their nest fairly low down but in a wide variety of locations from forest regrowth to thick reeds. Fine fibres or thin grass stems are usually used to bind leaf detritus or moss into a compact cup-shaped nest. Normally the nests are draped with spiders' webs and cocoons. Two creamy-white eggs, with a distinct band of dark lilac blotches around the broader end, form the usual clutch.
Habitat and Range	Endemic in the region, the Slaty Flycatcher is widespread in the Fiji archipelago, but is absent from Tonga and Samoa. It is a bird of the subcanopy in forest, but is also commonly encountered in well-wooded parks or gardens. On some of the smaller islands in its range, it is much more frequently found in open areas and in villages themselves.

Remarks and *Allied Species*	A common bird which attracts attention with its harsh call. It often joins the mixed flocks of forest birds, but engages in none of the charming antics of the fantail, although it does sometimes fan its tail.
Subspecies	Two races are recognised: *M.l. lessoni* found throughout Fiji except the Lau group, where *M.l. orientalis* occurs. The difference between the two races is slight and not discernible in the field.

58. VERSICOLOUR FLYCATCHER
(Mayr's Flycatcher)

Mayrornis versicolor
Mayr, 1933

Identification	Plate 8. 12 cm. The upperparts are dark slate-grey with a rufous wash on the tail, the latter being tipped with buff. The underparts are dull pinkish-cinnamon, paler on the throat.
Flight, Voice, *Food, Breeding*	Not recorded.
Habitat and *Range*	Confined to the small island of Ogea Levu, in the Lau group, Fiji.
Remarks and *Allied Species*	The closely related Slaty Flycatcher is a slightly larger, more robust bird, with a conspicuous white eye ring, and without the pinkish underparts of the Versicolour Flycatcher. The two species co-exist on the island of Ogea Levu and there is slight evidence that the two species may inter-breed.
	Nothing has been recorded on the habits of the Versicolour Flycatcher. It is probable that they are similar to those of the Slaty Flycatcher, but since the two species co-exist on the same island one would expect some differences.

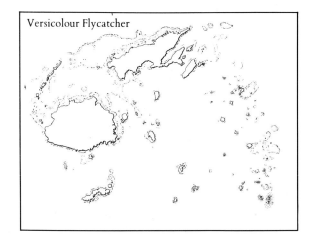

Versicolour Flycatcher

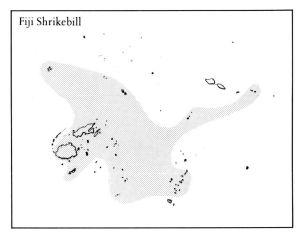

Fiji Shrikebill

59. FIJI SHRIKEBILL

Fiji: Kokosi.
Rotuma: Fa'aire.
Tonga: FUIVA.

Clytorhynchus vitiensis
(Hartlaub, 1866)

Identification	Plate 9. 19 cm. A featureless bird, with a dull olive-brown plumage, rather darker on the back and with a greyish tinge to the belly. The outer tail feathers sometimes have buff tips. The bill is black with light edges, long and wedge-shaped. The sexes do not differ and immature birds are similar.
Flight	Undulating.

<table>
<tr><td>*Voice*</td><td>The Fiji Shrikebill has a variety of whistled songs. It also harshly scolds human intruders or when involved in territorial disputes, often fanning its tail in the process.</td></tr>
</table>

Voice The Fiji Shrikebill has a variety of whistled songs. It also harshly scolds human intruders or when involved in territorial disputes, often fanning its tail in the process.

Food Insects and probably a little fruit. Fiji Shrikebills have a characteristic foraging method and are normally encountered as they noisily investigate dead vegetation, probing into curled leaves, pulling tangled vine tendrils apart and tearing off loose bark. Dislodged insects are pursued and caught as they fly off. Fiji Shrikebills may be found feeding at any height, but usually close to the larger tree limbs. They frequently join the wandering bands of insectivorous birds.

Breeding The nest of the Fiji Shrikebill is lightly built with rootlets, fine plant stems and especially vine tendrils, it is deeply cupped and generally lined with fine fibres. The nest is normally found between two and three metres off the ground in fairly thick foliage. Two eggs constitute the normal clutch; they have a white ground colour with variable red-brown or black speckling, especially around the broader end.

Habitat and Range The Fiji Shrikebill is a widespread endemic in the region, but has a curious discontinuous distribution. It is essentially a forest bird, but readily frequents any well wooded areas or mature scrub.

Remarks and Allied Species The Fiji Shrikebill is a common bird throughout its range. Its featureless plumage makes it readily confusable with the Wattled Honeyeater, but the latter's distinctive voice and behaviour make identification relatively easy. More difficulty is experienced in distinguishing it from the female Black-faced Shrikebill, a much rarer bird. The latter is larger with a heavier bill but these characteristics are not apparent in the field and without the confirming presence of a male Black-faced Shrikebill they are distinguishable only with experience.

Subspecies Of all the region's birds, the Fiji Shrikebill has caused more taxonomic problems than any other. There are several reasons for this, arising from the great individual variation in both size and plumage. This is nowhere more apparent than in the Fiji archipelago and as E. Mayr, the foremost taxonomist of the area, has stated, "it is somewhat a matter of opinion to which subspecies the population of some of the islands should be referred".[142] Bearing this in mind, it is not surprising that the majority of the twelve subspecies are not distinguishable in the field.

C.v. vitiensis	— Viti Levu, Lomaiviti group, Fiji.
C.v. compressirostris	— Kadavu group, Fiji.
C.v. buensis	— Vanua Levu, Kio, Fiji.
C.v. layardi	— Taveuni, Fiji.
C.v. pontifex	— Qamea, Rabi, Fiji.
C.v. vatuana	— Tuvuca, Yacata, Vatuvara, Fiji.
C.v. nesiotes	— Southern Lau group, Fiji.
C.v. heinei	— Ha'apai group, Tonga.
C.v. keppeli	— Niuatoputapu, Tafahi, Tonga.
C.v. fortunae	— Alofi, Futuna.
C.v. wiglesworthi	— Rotuma.
C.v. powelli	— Manua group, Samoa.

60.   BLACK-FACED SHRIKEBILL

Fiji: Kiro.

Clytorhynchus nigrogularis nigrogularis
(Layard, 1875)

Identification Plate 9. 21 cm. The mature male with his black head and throat that contrasts strongly with the grey-white ear coverts, is unmistakable. The remaining plumage is a uniform grey-brown, individuals varying from ashy-grey to a warm brown. Females are more consistently brownish and lack the head pattern. Immature males are similar to females. The bill is heavy, black with horn edgings and tip.

Flight Deliberate with quick wingbeats, slightly undulating.

Voice	The male has been recorded as delivering a harsh chuckling sound, but the song is a descending, wavering whistle, strongly delivered and drawn out.
Food	Insectivorous, feeding in a similar manner to the Fiji Shrikebill, but possibly more often above mid-height in the forest.
Breeding	No records.
Habitat and Range	The Black-faced Shrikebill is only found in mature forest and not in the more open wooded areas where the Fiji Shrikebill sometimes occurs. It is confined to the five largest islands in Fiji (excluding Gau).
Remarks and Allied Species	Despite the larger size and heavier bill of the female Black-faced Shrikebill, she is not readily distinguishable from Fiji Shrikebills in the field. Black-faced Shrikebills are not common, but they have a patchy distribution and as a result may be locally plentiful. Although they have similar feeding methods to the Fiji Shrikebill, they are less active, shyer and more easily overlooked.
Subspecies	Whilst the Fiji Shrikebill is a widespread endemic in the region, the Black-faced Shrikebill has a restricted distribution but is not endemic. A subspecies *C.n. santaecrucis* is found in the Santa Cruz Islands, and a closely related species *C. hamlini* is restricted to Rennell Island.

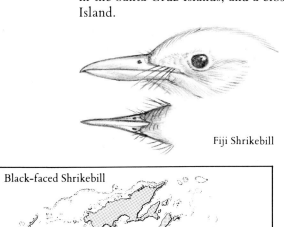

Fiji Shrikebill

Black-faced Shrikebill

Vanikoro Broadbill

Blue-crested Broadbill

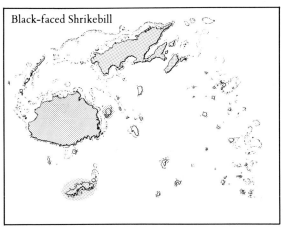

Black-faced Shrikebill

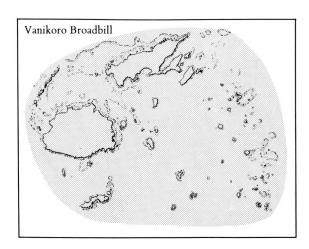

Vanikoro Broadbill

The delicate, well-camouflaged nest of the Vanikoro Broadbill is easily overlooked.

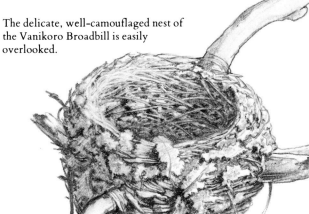

114

61. VANIKORO BROADBILL

Myiagra vanikorensis
(Quoy & Gaimard, 1830)

Fiji: SIASIA, Sigadruloa.

Identification Plate 9. 13 cm. The Vanikoro Broadbill is an attractive bird. The male has a gunmetal blue head and throat, a dark blue-grey back and rich rufous orange underparts, paler on the abdomen. The female is more conservative and lacks the glossy head and throat; the blue-grey upperparts extend up over the crown, and the throat and chin are whitish. Both sexes have blackish wings and tail. Immature birds are similar to females but have a grey bill instead of the adult's black bill.

Flight Direct, generally leisurely and slightly undulating as the wings are briefly closed.

Voice Both sexes deliver a whistling "tzweet-tzweet", usually repeated twice but sometimes three or four times. Intermittently a harsh "tsic-tsic" may be given.

Food Insectivorous. The Vanikoro Broadbill is an active "leaf-snatching" flycatcher which specialises in taking insects from the underside of leaves on short aerial sallies, and frequently hovering for this purpose. In forest it is a canopy species but in open woodland and gardens it feeds at all heights.

Breeding The nest of the Vanikoro Broadbill is a small inconspicuous cup, beautifully constructed of fine fibres, grass stems or rootlets, then decorated with pieces of lichen, moss or leaf debris and bound with spiders' webs. It is normally lined with cattle or horse-hair, and often built fairly high off the ground on smaller terminal limbs of large trees. One or two white eggs, speckled grey-brown with black blotches especially in a band around the maximum breadth, form the normal clutch.

Habitat and Range The Vanikoro Broadbill is one of a few indigenous birds which has fully adapted to man-modified habitats and can be seen in any habitat from montane forest to mangroves. It is widespread throughout the Fiji archipelago, but is absent from Tonga and is replaced in Samoa by a close relative.

Remarks and Allied Species Unlikely to be confused with any other bird, except perhaps the Blue-crested Broadbill (see the following species), the Vanikoro Broadbill is a very common bird in Fiji. Equally at home in gardens or in the mountain forest, its persistent call and active nature readily attract attention. Unconcerned by human presence, it often forages under the eaves of houses, in verandahs or open garages. When predatory birds appear, the Vanikoro Broadbill is generally the first to harass them and will continue persistently.

Subspecies The Vanikoro Broadbill is another bird from the Fiji region which has a close relative in the Santa Cruz Islands and nowhere else. In this case the nominate subspecies *M.v. vanikorensis* is found only on the island of Vanikoro, where it was first collected and hence obtained its name. Four subspecies are recognised in the region: the described form from central, northern and north-western Fiji—*M.v. rufiventris*. The much darker and more richly coloured *M.v. kandavensis* is found in the Kadavu group, Beqa and Vatulele. *M.v. dorsalis* from the Northern Lau group and the Moala group, and *M.v. townsendi* from the Southern Lau group, are both larger and darker subspecies.

62. BLUE-CRESTED BROADBILL

Myiagra azureocapilla
Layard, 1875

Fiji: Batidamu.

Identification Plate 9. 13 cm. The male is one of Fiji's most distinctive birds, with slate blue upperparts, and an azure crest and cheek patches overlaying an otherwise blackish head. The chin and throat are chestnut orange strongly contrasting with the remaining white underparts. The tail may or may not be tipped with white. The female has a slate-blue head, rufous-grey upperparts, and similar but duller underparts to the male. The flight and tail feathers are black with a blue suffusion in males and brownish in females. Both sexes have a conspicuous orange-coloured bill with prominent rictal bristles, flanking the mouth. Immature birds are similar to females but duller with a dark beak.

Flight Similar to the Vanikoro Broadbill, but sustained flight is rarely observed.

Voice	A monotonous but not unmelodious "tsling-tsling-tsling". A hoarse "weer" whistle has also been recorded. The male delivers an attractive whistling song with his crest raised.
Food	Similar food and feeding behaviour to the Vanikoro Broadbill, but it is more generally seen below the canopy.
Breeding	The clutch is a single egg, laid in a delicate cup-shaped nest, typically built low down in a forest shrub.
Habitat and Range	A forest dweller which, unlike the Vanikoro Broadbill, is not found outside mature forest. It is endemic on the three largest islands of the Fiji group (there is also an unconfirmed report of this species from Kadavu). The Blue-crested Broadbill is principally a subcanopy and mid-stage feeder.
Remarks and Allied Species	The female Blue-crested Broadbill may be confused with the female Vanikoro Broadbill, but its chestnut throat and white abdomen are distinctive. The Blue-crested Broadbill is a regular member of the wandering bands of insectivorous birds which frequent Fiji's forests, and is generally encountered in pairs or parents and a single young. It is not as common as the Vanikoro Broadbill, although quite regularly observed in suitable habitat. First collected in 1875 in Taveuni by Lieutenant Liardet, a disenchanted naval officer who became a planter, it was described by Edgar Layard.
Subspecies	The distinctive crest of the Blue-crested Broadbill is sufficient to separate this broadbill into its own subgenus—Lophomyiagra. Three subspecies are recognised: *M.a. azureocapilla* is found in Taveuni, *M.a. whitneyi* is restricted to Viti Levu and *M.a. castaneigularis* is confined to Vanua Levu. The Taveuni and Vanua Levu races have white tips to the tail, not always present on the Viti Levu birds.

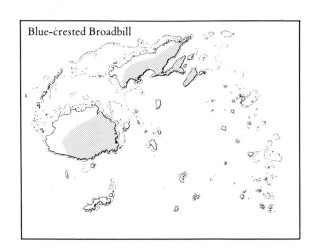

Blue-crested Broadbill

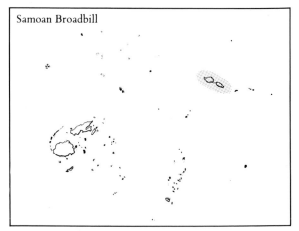

Samoan Broadbill

63.   SAMOAN BROADBILL
(White-bellied Flycatcher)

Myiagra albiventris
(Peale, 1848)

Samoa: TŌLAI FATU.

Identification	Plate 9. 13 cm. The male has a glossy gunmetal blue head and nape, a dark back and rump with a subdued green lustre. The flight feathers and tail are black. The chin and throat is an intense orange and the remaining underparts are white. The female is similar but with a greyer back and a paler chin. Immature birds are similar but duller.
Voice	A fluid "tsweet-tsweet" or "twee-twee".
Food	An insectivorous species with the same "leaf-snatching" behaviour as the Fijian broadbills.
Breeding	Not recorded.

The Samoan Broadbill is endemic on the islands of Upolu and Savai'i in Samoa. Although essentially a forest bird, it is regularly encountered in more open areas and on the forest edge, but does not penetrate suburban or agricultural habitats.

Remarks and Allied Species
Very little is known about the ecology of the Samoan Broadbill, a state of affairs which applies to all Samoa's endemic birds. An uncommon bird.

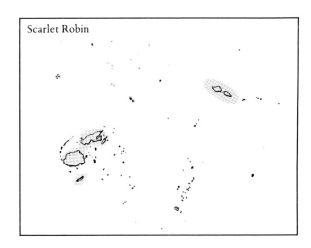

Scarlet Robin

64. **SCARLET ROBIN** *Petroica multicolor*
(Gmelin, 1879)

Fiji: Dri qala.
Samoa: TŌLAI ULA, Tōlai, Tōlai fatu, Tagi tagi.

Identification
Plate 8. 10 cm. The small size, upright posture and rather large head with a short sharp bill are diagnostic even without the distinctive plumage. The male has black upperparts, head and throat with a white forehead and wing patch. The breast is a bright cherry red, paler on the abdomen. Superficially, females are similar but they have dull brown upperparts and only pale pink underparts with a whitish central region. Immature birds are similar to females but still duller.

Flight
Rarely sustained, the flight is buoyant and usually consists of short aerial sallies. The white wing patch is conspicuous.

Voice
A plaintive, yet carrying "plink" frequently repeated, is the normal call. The male has a melodious song consisting of a rapid trill of run-together whistles, with the first two syllables generally extended.

Food
Scarlet Robins obtain most of their food on darting aerial pursuits of flying insects, but they also descend to the ground or acrobatically pick insects from tree trunks or branches.

Breeding
Nests are usually built in the crotch of a fork, straddling a branch or in a tree hollow. They are small and cup-shaped, generally constructed of fine plant fibres or rootlets; moss, lichen or Tree Fern scales are delicately interwoven on the outside and are sometimes bound with cobwebs. Soft fibres or the occasional feather are used as lining. Beautifully camouflaged, they can be easily overlooked. Two or three eggs form the normal clutch; the eggs have a white base, and have black or grey speckles and blotches, more intense around the broader end.

Habitat and Range
A bird which is generally encountered in the substage of mature forest or in forest clearings. Frequently it may be found in more open wooded areas, secondary shrub and occasionally on the periphery of agricultural land. It is restricted to Savai'i and Upolu in Samoa and to the four largest islands of the Fiji archipelago.

Remarks and Allied Species	A charming bird, the Scarlet Robin is one of the commoner species in Fiji's forests. This, together with its inquisitive disposition, make it a relatively easy bird to observe. Scarlet Robins are normally seen in pairs and are strongly territorial when nesting. Larger birds are not tolerated near the nest and even human observers are made perfectly well aware that they are not welcome — the male darting about flicking his wings and snapping the bill.
Subspecies	In the Fiji region four subspecies of the Scarlet Robin are recognised, none of which have distinguishing features that are apparent in the field. *P.m. pusilla* is found on the Samoan islands of Upolu and Savai'i; of the Fijian birds — *P.m. kleinschmidti* is found on Viti Levu and Vanua Levu, *P.m. taveunensis* is confined to Taveuni and in Kadavu *P.m. becki* occurs.

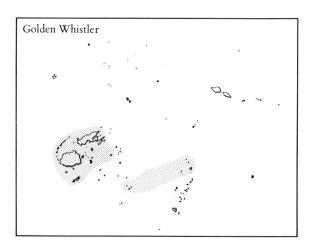

Golden Whistler

65.	GOLDEN WHISTLER	*Pachycephala pectoralis*
	(Golden Thickhead)	(Latham, 1801)

Fiji: KETEDROMO, Kedidromo, Bobokavisa (Bua), Didibesau, Kula oso, Ai sou.
Tonga: HENGEHENGA, HENGA.

Identification	Plate 9. 20 cm. The male is an unmistakable bird with deep lemon-yellow underparts contrasting strongly with the dark olive-green upperparts, and black head and nape. Two conspicuous yellow spots lie above and to the side of the beak, and a suffused black "necklace" is sometimes visible on the throat. The flight feathers and tail are olive-black, the latter with olive tips. The sombre female has dark olive-brown upperparts and cinnamon-grey underparts streaked with brown. Immature birds are similar to females but the wings and tail are rather more rufous.
Flight	Rapid wingbeats on a quick and direct flight.
Voice	The song is a short melody of fluted whistles, but there is individual variation in addition to very pronounced geographical variation in the song. Females often utter a subdued chattering.
Food	Although primarily insectivorous the Golden Whistler also feeds on fruit. Insects are caught in a variety of ways including aerial sallies after flying insects, leaf snatching, gleaning and occasionally probing into crevices. Stick Insects are a favourite food. Golden Whistlers are frequent attendants of wandering bands of insectivorous birds.
Breeding	The comparatively large nest is generally constructed of small twigs, rootlets or vine tendrils, rather coarse and not usually lined. The outside is commonly decorated with leaf detritus, occasionally leafy liverworts, and is sometimes draped with spiders' webs. In Fiji the normal clutch is a single pale blue egg with irregular black blotches concentrated at the obtuse end. In Tonga, two eggs is apparently the normal clutch.[31]

Habitat and Range   The Golden Whistler is essentially a bird of mature forest, where it may be encountered foraging at any level. It may also be seen in areas of immature secondary growth near forest. In the region the Golden Whistler is widespread in the Fiji archipelago; in Tonga it is restricted to the Vava'u group.

Remarks and Allied Species   No other bird of the region displays such marked geographical variation of the plumage, except perhaps the Island Thrush. Although races are essentially restricted to separate islands, zones of hybridisation are found. The Golden Whistler is common in Fiji's forests. However, except when foraging it tends to be inactive and, despite its penetrating calls, it is often difficult to find. It has the annoying habit of ceasing to sing just as location is imminent.

Subspecies   The Tongan race *P.p. melanops* is sometimes accorded full specific rank (as *P. jacquinoti*), but it is more suitably considered as a rather divergent subspecies.[87] The males differ considerably as a result of hybridisation between two waves of colonisation. The "northern group" is characterised by having a yellow throat, yellow loral spots on the forehead above the beak, whilst the black "necklace" is absent or incomplete. The "southern group" has a white chin and throat, no loral spots and a strong black necklace. The subspecies listed below are in themselves somewhat variable and show evidence of hybridisation between different subspecies. Whilst the males differ considerably, differences between females are generally not recognisable in the field. Males only are described below.

Northern Group:

P.p. graeffi — Viti Levu, Yasawa group, Fiji. Described above.

P.p. aurantiiventris — Vanua Levu, Fiji. Throat dark orange, only traces of a black necklace and conspicuous yellow loral spots.

P.p. torquata — Taveuni, Koro, Fiji. A narrow black necklace, loral spots may or may not be present.

P.p. bella — Vatu Vara (Northern Lau group), Fiji. Throat dark yellow, broad black necklace and loral spots present.

Southern Group:

P.p. kandavensis — Kadavu, Beqa, Fiji. Crown and sides of head black separated from dark olive upperparts by a narrow yellow hind collar. Chin and throat white, bordered by a strong black necklace. Rest of underparts yellow.

P.p. vitiensis — Gau, Fiji. Richer yellow underparts, broader black necklace.

P.p. lauana — Southern Lau group, Fiji. Similar to *P.p. vitiensis* but darker above.

P.p. melanops — Vava'u group, Tonga. The largest of all the subspecies. The male has a completely black head, chin and throat with deep yellow underparts and narrow hind collar. The wings and tail are dark brownish black. The female is olive brown above with a buffy white throat and chin and pale yellow underparts.

P.p. aurantiiventris   *P.p. torquata*

P.p. kandavensis   *P.p. vitiensis*   *P.p. melanops*

66.   SAMOAN WHISTLER

Samoa: VASAVASA, Latulatu.

Pachycephala flavifrons
(Peale, 1848)

Identification	Plate 9. 17 cm. The male has dull black upperparts and lemon-yellow underparts. The chin and throat are generally dull black with strong yellow mottling and the forehead yellow or white. Individuals vary in having the throat mottled white rather than yellow. The female has a plumage very similar in appearance to that of the male, it is duller, without the mark on the forehead and with a pale grey throat.
Flight, Voice, Food	Similar to the Golden Whistler.
Breeding	Not recorded.
Habitat and Range	Endemic on the islands of Upolu and Savai'i in Samoa, the Samoan Whistler appears to have a wider habitat tolerance than its Fijian counterpart. It is frequently observed away from mature forest in areas of secondary bush and village gardens.
Remarks and Allied Species	Although widely distributed on Upolu and Savai'i, the Samoan Whistler is not a common bird. It is considered an aberrant geographical representative of the Golden Whistler, and is especially interesting because of the female's similarity to the male. In all other races or close relatives of the Golden Whistler, the plumage of the females is very different to those of the males.

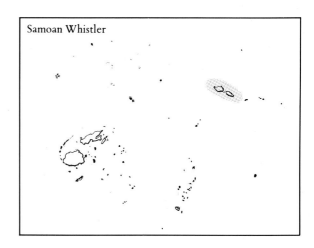

Samoan Whistler

67.   POLYNESIAN TRILLER

Fiji: SEASEA, Katebale, Sigiviu.
Rotuma: Jea.
Samoa: MITI, MITISINA, Mititai.
Tonga: SIKIVIU, KETĒKETE, Gikivia, Singiviu.
Niue: HEAHEA.

Lalage maculosa
(Peale, 1848)

Identification	Plate 10. 15 cm. At a glance, the Polynesian Triller is a robust medium-sized black and white bird. Adults have brownish-black upperparts with a white shoulder patch and eyebrow, the latter contrasting with a black eye stripe. The underparts and cheeks are pale buffy-grey with pronounced black barring. The tail is dark with a white tip.
Flight	Direct with quick rather fluttering wingbeats; the wings are broad and rounded.
Voice	A rasping "tsi-tsi-tsi" run together is the normal and frequently uttered call; a sustained whistling trill is the advertising song.
Food	Insects, especially caterpillars, and fruit.

Breeding	The nest is a compact cup-shaped structure consisting of interwoven fine-grass stems, rootlets or other fibres, and is generally placed in the crotch of a lateral fork, often high in a tree. One or two olive-green eggs with brown blotches—especially on the rounder end—constitute the normal clutch.
Habitat and Range	The Polynesian Triller is as much at home in montane forest as it is hopping across a suburban lawn, although it is probably most common in immature secondary habitats. It is a widespread species found on most islands of the region. (It is absent from American Samoa.) Elsewhere it is found only in the New Hebrides and the Santa Cruz Islands.
Remarks and Allied Species	Unlikely to be confused with any other species except in Samoa where it may be found alongside the Samoan Triller (see the following species). The Polynesian Triller is a pleasant, cheerful bird being common in most areas and conspicuous because of its un-retiring habits and incessant calling.
Subspecies	Twelve races of the Polynesian Triller are found in the region, more than any other species except the Fiji Shrikebill which also has twelve. The races are confined to separate islands or island groups and their differences are not striking, depending in the main on the extent of brown in the plumage as a whole, the degree of black on the upperparts and white on the underparts.

L.m. pumila — Viti Levu, Fiji.
L.m. soror — Kadavu, Fiji.
L.m. mixta — Ovalau and the Yasawas, Fiji.
L.m. woodi — Vanua Levu, Taveuni and offshore islands, Fiji.
L.m. nesophila — Lau group, Fiji.
L.m. maculosa — Western Samoa.
L.m. keppeli — Niuatoputapu, Tafahi, Tonga (not found on Niuafo'ou).
L.m. vauana — Vava'u group, Tonga.
L.m. tabuensis — Ha'apai and Tongatapu group, Tonga.
L.m. rotumae — Rotuma.
L.m. whitmeei — Niue.
L.m. futunae — Uvea, Futuna.

Polynesian Triller

Caterpillars are a staple in the diet of the Polynesian Triller.

68.   SAMOAN TRILLER

Lalage sharpei
Rothschild, 1900

Identification	Plate 10. 12 cm. A rather featureless bird with grey-brown upperparts, and white underparts, which are lightly barred on the flanks. The cheeks are brown, contrasting with the white throat. The iris is conspicuously white and the bill orange-yellow.
Flight	Broad wings and conspicuous white tips on the tail feathers.
Voice	Only a short "tweet-tweet" has been recorded.
Food	Caterpillars and probably other insects.

Breeding   A single nest has been described which was cup-shaped and draped with moss and lichen. It was built about five metres off the ground at the end of an horizontal branch. The clutch consisted of a single egg.[59]

Habitat and Range   An endemic species found only on the islands of Upolu and Savai'i in Samoa. Very little is known about the Samoan Triller, but a recent observer found it not uncommon in forest and around the forest edge on Upolu.[59]

Remarks and Allied Species   The Samoan Triller is a smaller, more graceful bird than its close relative the Polynesian Triller, without the latter's conspicuous black and white appearance. The little that has been recorded on the Samoan Triller is remarkably contradictory and there is an urgent need for reliable information on its ecology in order to determine the requirements for its conservation.

Subspecies   *L.s. sharpei* is restricted to the island of Upolu, whilst *L.s. tenebrosa,* a rather darker bird, is found on Savai'i.

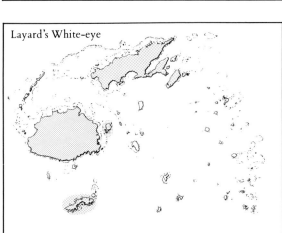

Samoan Triller

Layard's White-eye

White-eyes frequently feed on the fruit of *Lantana camara* and help in the spread of this unpleasant, exotic weed.

69.   LAYARD'S WHITE-EYE

Fiji: QIQI.

Zosterops explorator
Layard, 1875

Identification   Plate 10. 11 cm. A small yellowish-green bird with darker more olive upperparts and a conspicuous white eye ring. The tail and wing feathers are blackish olive. The small pointed bill is black.

Flight   Sustained flight is rapid and slightly undulating.

Voice   A high pitched "tzi-tzi"is the contact call.

Food   A mixed feeder which readily gleans insects in the canopy foliage, feeds also on fruit and berries at any height from the ground, and occasionally takes nectar.

Habitat and Range   An endemic bird found on Fiji's five largest islands (excluding Gau). It is normally a forest species which will be readily found in well-wooded areas or gallery forest and occasionally strays into agricultural land.

Remarks and Allied Species   Layard's White-eye is easily confused with the Grey-backed White-eye, with which it often associates. The Grey-backed White-eye is a more robust bird with a distinct grey belt around the body, but the latter is only visible at close quarters. It also has a slightly lower-pitched contact call. The ecological separation of the two species is not at all clear cut. Altitude is not involved and there is total habitat overlap. It is apparent that the Grey-backed White-eye is the generalised species, found in any habitat, whilst Layard's White-eye is restricted to forested or heavily-wooded areas. The latter is also the more insectivorous of the two.

Both birds are habitually gregarious forming loose trailing flocks of five to fifteen birds which keep in constant contact with each other with their thin high-pitched calls. Layard's White-eye is less frequently observed but is by no means uncommon and in some areas is the more common of the two.

Layard's White-eye was first collected in Kadavu by John Murray, a naturalist on the Challenger Expedition which visited Fiji in 1874. Edgar Layard, the Acting Consul at the time, recognised it as a new species. He was unable to make a full description before it was packed away and sent to Europe with the other expedition specimens. However, indicating its presence he called it *explorator* after the expedition, but the common name is Layard's own.

The nest of Layard's White-eye.

70.   GREY-BACKED WHITE-EYE

Zosterops lateralis flaviceps
Peale, 1848

Fiji: QIQI.

Identification   Plate 10. 11 cm. A small olive-green bird with a strong yellowish tinge on the breast, throat and undertail coverts. A distinct grey belt encircles the body, the tail and flight feathers are olive-brown. The white eye ring is prominent.

Flight   Rapid and direct, slightly undulating.

Voice   The contact call is a high pitched "tzwit-tzwit" and the song, which is infrequently heard, is a short medley of whistles.

Food   Similar to Layard's White-eye, but probably takes more fruit.

Breeding   A small compact nest with a slightly straggly appearance is slung between the vertical stems of a bush or small tree. Grass stems are normally used and the nest is often lined with hair. Between two and four, but usually three, turquoise blue eggs are laid.

Habitat and Range	The race found in the Fiji region is a representative of a wide ranging species found from Australia through to New Zealand, and in Tahiti where it is a successful exotic. It is widespread in the Fiji archipelago, although not present in the Lau group or elsewhere in the Fiji region. The Grey-backed White-eye has a wide habitat tolerance and may be found in any habitat, at any altitude. It is equally at home foraging in the forest canopy as in the substage or in low secondary scrub, agricultural fields or in gardens.
Remarks and Allied Species	A very common bird which may be confused with Layard's White-eye — under which the distinguishing features are described.

The Cape Gooseberry is an abundant weed of cultivation. It is a favourite food of the Grey-backed White-eye as well as the Red-vented Bulbul.

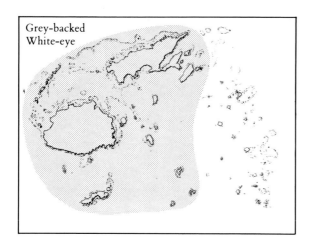

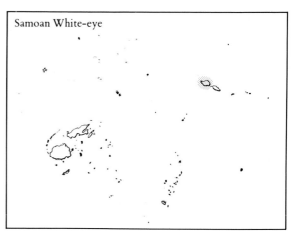

71.　SAMOAN WHITE-EYE

Zosterops samoensis
Murphy & Mathews, 1929

Identification	Plate 10. 11 cm. A small yellowish white-eye with olive-yellow upperparts which are paler on the rump. The underparts are white with a yellow suffusion, especially on the chin and throat; the flanks are greenish.
Flight, Voice, Food, Breeding	Nothing has been recorded on the ecology of the Samoan White-eye, but it is probably similar to those of the Fijian White-eyes.
Habitat and Range	The Samoan White-eye is endemic on the island of Savai'i in Samoa, where it is restricted to forested areas.
Remarks and Allied Species	The Samoan White-eye and the Versicolour Flycatcher of Fiji are the only birds from the region, to be discovered this century. The Whitney South Sea Expedition was responsible for first collecting both of them.

124

72. ORANGE-BREASTED HONEYEATER

Myzomela jugularis
Peale, 1848

Fiji: KERI KERI SAI, DRUI, MISI KULA (Lau group),
Drui delakula, Delakula, Drui delaturaga, Miti kula.

Identification   Plate 11. 9 cm. A tiny bird which appears black and white at first glance, with flashes of red. The male has black upperparts with a scarlet nape and crown, lower back and rump. The throat is black with a prominent scarlet chin and the remaining underparts are pale yellow, rather orange on the chest. The female is similar but duller with smaller red patches. Both sexes have the wing feathers edged with olive and the tail tipped white. The immature bird is still duller with no red on the upperparts. The relatively long, fine bill is black and slightly down-curved.

Flight   Swift and direct with rapid wingbeats.

Voice   A strident "chit-chit" frequently uttered, especially when groups have formed. The song is a demanding two or three syllable "tzwee-tzwee" or "tsu-tzwee-tzwee", repeated at intervals over monotonous lengths, and can be particularly aggravating.

Food   Nectar from a wide variety of flower types, at any height from the ground. They are particularly fond of the flowers of the introduced weed Blue Rat's Tail *Stachytarpheta* sp. The nectar is taken either by hovering in front of the flower and inserting the bill, or by perching on stems, and occasionally by stabbing the corolla near the nectaries. Spiders and insects form a significant proportion of the diet, and Orange-breasted Honeyeaters can frequently be seen gleaning for them around flowers or amongst the smaller branches of a tree.

Breeding   The nest is loosely constructed of grass stalks or fine rootlets, slung between vertical stems in a thickly foliaged shrub or small tree. Two pinkish-white eggs with red speckling form the normal clutch.

Habitat and Range   The Orange-breasted Honeyeater is one of the region's endemic birds; widespread throughout Fiji but absent from Tonga, and replaced by a closely related species in Samoa. (There are, however, old records of it being seen in Samoa.) It may be found in any habitat and is a cheerful visitor to many suburban gardens.

Remarks and Allied Species   A common bird, although never particularly abundant except when large numbers aggregate at a favourite flowering tree. At such times they are petulant, appearing to spend more time chasing their neighbours than actually feeding. Normally, they are solitary or are found in small groups, and are generally encountered in a state of feverish activity as they dart between flowering shrubs or trees. However, when the male takes up his singing post, usually high up in a tree and at any time of the day, he may be there for an hour or more endlessly repeating his demanding song.

    In the dryer western parts of Viti Levu, the Orange-breasted Honeyeater is not sedentary, but undertakes local movements, sometimes in small flocks. Frequently, one may not see one for many months before they suddenly reappear.

Orange-breasted
Honeyeater

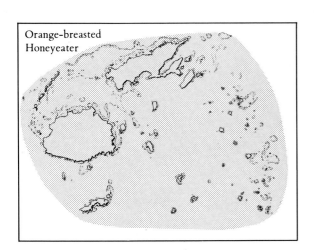

Orange-breasted Honeyeaters
can often be seen taking nectar
from the flowers of Blue Rats Tail.

73. **CARDINAL HONEYEATER** *Myzomela cardinalis*
(Black-bellied Honeysucker) (Gmelin, 1788)

Samoa: SEGA SEGAMAU'U, Segamau.

Identification Plate 11. 9 cm. The male is a striking bird, black with vivid scarlet upperparts, chin and throat. The back is slightly mottled with black. The female is a drab olive-grey with paler underparts and a scarlet rump and lower back. Immature birds are similar to the female but with the scarlet plumage further reduced.

Flight Fast and direct.

Voice When foraging a high-pitched "zeet" is frequently given.

Food Nectar and small insects.

Breeding The small cup-shaped nest is built on forked branches, generally constructed of grass stems. Three to five white eggs with a few red spots are laid.

Habitat and Range In the region confined to the three largest islands of Samoa and to Rotuma, the Cardinal Honeyeater displays a wide habitat tolerance, similar to the Orange-breasted Honeyeater in Fiji. Its range extends from Samoa westwards including the New Hebrides, the Loyalty Islands and the eastern Solomons, and north through much of Micronesia.

Remarks and Allied Species A common bird which frequently forms fairly large aggregations at favoured feeding sites.

Subspecies The Rotuman Honeyeater is sometimes accorded full specific status, but is best considered as a subspecies — *M.c. chermesina*.[116] It is restricted to the island of Rotuma and has more extensive scarlet markings on the underparts but lacks the scarlet head and nape of *M.c. nigriventris,* the race found in Samoa, (Plate 11).

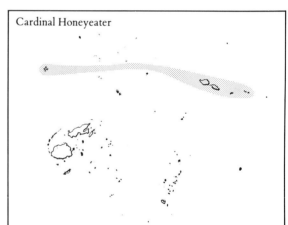

Cardinal Honeyeater

Flowers of the African Tulip Tree *Spathodea campanulata* are a rich nectar source.

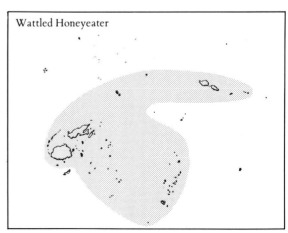

Wattled Honeyeater

74. WATTLED HONEYEATER

Foulehaio carunculata
(Gmelin, 1788)

Fiji: KIKAU, KAISAU (Vanua Levu), KAISEVAU (Lau group), Kikauliki, Sevai, Sovau, Kitou (Yasawa group), Vihilu (Vatulele Island), Uluvai.
Samoa: IAO, Jao, Mosomoso.
Tonga: FULEHEU, Fulehau, Foule haoi.

Identification Plate 11. 19 cm. A medium-sized, featureless bird with drab olive-green plumage. The underparts are rather paler and sometimes appear scaled. On some birds the yellow wattle below the eye is conspicuous. A fine, slightly down-curved bill.

Flight Direct with pronounced undulation.

Voice A wide variety of calls are given by this attractive songster. The majority are strong, chiming calls, the commonest being a two syllable "keekow", from which it derives its Fijian name, and with which it is usually the first bird to herald the approaching dawn. When foraging they often give an intermittent subdued chuckle. The bubbling alarm call is unmistakable and the surest indication that a predatory bird is in the vicinity.

Food Primarily nectar, but also a little fruit and a fair proportion of spiders and insects, especially when breeding. It also kills lizards and geckos which it may sometimes eat.

Breeding A fragile nest composed of fine grass stalks, *Casuarina* needles or rootlets and commonly draped with spiders' webs is strung between the forked stems of a bush or tree. One, occasionally two, pinkish eggs lightly speckled with red spots is the normal clutch.

Habitat and Range One of the most widely distributed birds of the region, in which it is endemic, the Wattled Honeyeater may be found in any habitat from montane forest to the seaward edge of mangroves; it is one of the most common birds of suburban gardens. It is found throughout the region, including some of the smallest islets, except Kadavu (although there is one record from Kadavu).

Remarks and Allied Species One of the region's most characteristic species, it is difficult not to hear or observe the Wattled Honeyeater. Its drab plumage bears a superficial resemblance to that of the Fiji Shrikebill but its down-curved bill, and distinctive feeding behaviour and voice soon distinguish it.

Many species of honeyeater are aggressive birds and the Wattled Honeyeater is no exception. It fearlessly drives off larger Mynahs or Spotted Turtle-doves as well as any smaller species from the vicinity of the nest. Occasionally some of the smaller birds are caught and mercilessly battered. Favoured sources of nectar are jealously guarded, especially, but not always successfully, from the attention of Red-vented Bulbuls. These two species are constant adversaries.

Subspecies Three races are recognised in the region, the nominate *F.c. carunculata* has a wide range through Tonga, the Lau group of Fiji, north to Samoa and including Uvea and Futuna. *F.c. procerior* is restricted to Viti Levu, the Yasawas, Ovalau, Beqa and Vatulele, whilst *F.c. taviunensis* is found in Vanua Levu, Taveuni and their offshore islands.

75. KADAVU HONEYEATER

Xanthotis provocator
(Layard, 1875)

Identification Plate 11. 19 cm. A featureless bird with drab olive-grey plumage which is heavily streaked on the back and underparts. The pointed black bill is long and slightly down-curved. Surrounding the eye is a conspicuous rosette of bare skin. The female has similar plumage to the male but is considerably smaller.

Flight Strongly undulating.

Voice A variety of mellow whistling calls similar to the Wattled Honeyeater.

Food Nectar, spiders and insects.

Breeding   The nest is similar to that of the Wattled Honeyeater, a rather fragile structure constructed of fine grass stems or rootlets and lined with softer material. A single egg is the normal clutch. Its colour is pale salmon, spotted with dark red and bearing indistinct purplish blotches in a ring around the obtuse end.

Habitat and Range   Endemic on the island of Kadavu, Fiji, where it may be found in all habitats.

Remarks and Allied Species   A common bird which is the ecological counterpart of the Wattled Honeyeater on the island of Kadavu. It is another bird which was first collected by the naturalists of the Challenger Expedition during its visit to Kadavu in 1874. It is probable that this bird may be suitably placed in the genus *Foulehaio* together with the Wattled Honeyeater.

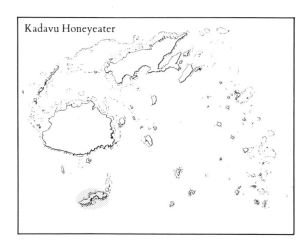

Kadavu Honeyeater

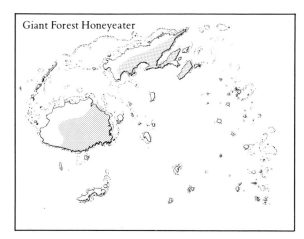

Giant Forest Honeyeater

76.   GIANT FOREST HONEYEATER

Fiji: KIKAULEVU, MANULEVU, SOVAULEVU, Ero.

Gymnomyza viridis
(Layard, 1875)

Identification   Plate 11. 27 cm. A large honeyeater with typically slender, slightly down-curved bill and drab plumage. The entire bird is olive-green.

Flight   Strongly undulating, usually close to the treetops.

Voice   A loud ringing "keekow", which is often run together in a series. Frequently one bird initiates the call, and it is taken up by another or by several others, resulting in a loud and characteristic cacophany reverberating through the forest. The call is often delivered several hours before dawn.

Food   Nectar, also insects and soft fruit.

Breeding   Not recorded.

Habitat and Range   The Giant Forest Honeyeater is endemic on the three largest islands of the Fiji group. It is restricted to large contiguous areas of mature forest where it feeds primarily in the canopy, although it may be observed at lower levels.

Remarks and Allied Species   Few visitors will leave the forests of Viti Levu, Vanua Levu, or Taveuni, without hearing the resonant carol of the Giant Forest Honeyeaters. To many, however, it will be the nearest they get to actually observing the birds, for they are timid and hurriedly depart at the slightest suspicion of something strange.

Subspecies   *G.v. viridis* from Taveuni and Vanua Levu has a yellow bill and feet and is slightly darker than the Viti Levu race — *G.v. brunneirostris* — which has an olive bill and feet (the juveniles, however, have a yellow bill).

77.   MAO

Gymnomyza samoensis
(Hombron & Jacquinot, 1814)

Samoa: MA'U MA'U.

Identification   Plate 11. 28 cm. A large, very dark looking honeyeater — uniformly olive-black with a brown suffusion, except for an olive stripe beneath the eye. The slender down-curved bill and feet are black.

Voice   The Mao is recorded as being a noisy bird with a "loud wailing call", or "a series of low, hoarse, nasal mewing notes at times rising in pitch and developing into loud upslurred clear yelps, that fall back again". The bouts of calling lasting a minute.[182]

Flight, Food, Breeding   Not recorded.

Habitat and Range   An endemic species on Savai'i, Upolu and Tutuila of Samoa, where it is found in mature forest, although it is recorded as also visiting coconut trees near the coast.

Remarks and Allied Species   The Mao is a rare bird and — as with the Giant Forest Honeyeater in Fiji — more commonly heard than seen.

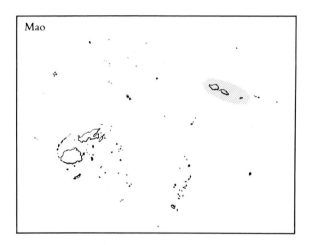

Mao

78.   RED-HEADED PARROTFINCH

Erythrura cyaneovirens
(Peale, 1848)

Fiji: KULA LAILAI, TURAGA (Macuata), REGU TEQU, Qiqi, Sici, Kiki, Micimici kula, Midimidi kula, Siti.
Samoa: MANU AI PA'U LA'AU, Sega segamau'u.

Identification   Plate 10. 10 cm. A small, vivid green finch with a striking scarlet rump and tail, and a crimson head. The chin is blackish and the throat has a blue suffusion, two features which are subject to considerable individual and seasonal variation in intensity. They are generally reduced in females, which also have lighter flanks. Immature birds are similar to adults but the colour of the head is variable; some individuals have a distinctly blue crown whilst others show traces of red. Adults have grey-black bills; those of the young are yellowish-horn with a dark tip, very young birds have a pair of turquoise beads on either side of the yellow gape.

Flight   Fast with rapid wingbeats, sustained flight is undulating. The Red-headed Parrotfinch has a delightful courtship flight which takes place above tree level with the pair following one another on a strongly oscillating path, one ascending whilst the other descends. Sometimes they oscillate out of phase around a fixed point. At all times the flight is accompanied by their high-pitched calls.

Voice   The flight call is a high-pitched "peep"; the song, usually delivered from high up in a tree, is a persistent double note similar to, but not as demanding or as loud as that of the Orange-breasted Honeyeater.

Food	Primarily a graminivorous bird which specialises in seeds at the "milk-stage", a favoured food is Guinea Grass *Panicum maximum*. Rather surprisingly the Red-headed Parrotfinch is also strongly insectivorous and is commonly seen displaying remarkable agility as it searches and probes for insects under loose bark or in the crevices of large tree trunks. On occasions it also feeds on nectar and small berries.
Breeding	The domed nest with a side entrance is constructed mainly with fresh grass blades and placed at any height from the ground in thick foliage. Four off-white, rather spherical eggs form the normal clutch.
Habitat and Range	The Red-headed Parrotfinch is restricted to the four largest islands of the Fiji group and curiously to the Yasawa group as well. In Samoa it is found on Savai'i and Upolu. It has a wide habitat tolerance and may be found anywhere from montane forest to suburban gardens.
Remarks and Allied Species	A charming, perky little bird which, when not breeding, is usually encountered in small flocks. It has adapted well to man-modified habitats and not only because Carpet Grass *Axonopus compresus*, the seeds of which are a favoured food, is the most common lawn grass; in some areas it is, unfortunately, a menace to rice growers.
Subspecies	Recently a new subspecies of the Red-headed Parrotfinch was described from Savai'i, Samoa,[65] and the Fijian birds have been afforded full specific rank.[245] However, in the absence of a large series of new material (needed because the Red-headed Parrotfinch displays great variation, not only individually but also as a result of seasonal wear), it is preferable to retain the more conservative classification of E. Mayr.[138] The latter recognises two races in the region, *E.c. cyaneovirens* from Samoa and *E.c. pealii* from Fiji.

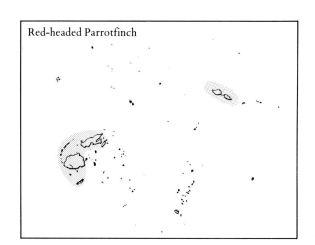

Red-headed Parrotfinch

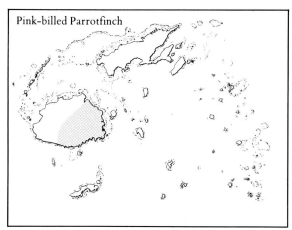

Pink-billed Parrotfinch

79.   PINK-BILLED PARROTFINCH

Erythrura kleinschmidti
(Finsch, 1878)

Identification	Plate 10. 11 cm. A slightly larger, more robust bird than the Red-headed Parrotfinch, with a black face, a bluish crown and nape and red rump. The remaining plumage is olive green. The glossy pink bill is conspicuously large. Immature birds are similar to adults, with orange-buff bills tipped with black.
Voice	A high pitched "chee-chee" and a clicking sound have been reported.
Food	The Pink-billed Parrotfinch is strongly insectivorous and feeds in a manner reminiscent of the shrikebills. Actively moving up and down tree trunks and vines, using its heavy bill as a lever to probe likely caches and to crush dead twigs and stems. It also feeds on flower buds and fruit, but is not a specialised fig-eater (c.f.[245]). Pink-billed Parrotfinches frequently join the bands of insectivorous birds.

Breeding   The only nest recorded was domed and similar to those of the Red-headed Parrotfinch, an untidy globular structure composed of dead leaves, small twigs, lichens and bamboo leaves. The entrance was at one side.

Habitat and Range   The Pink-billed Parrotfinch is endemic on Viti Levu, Fiji. It is generally restricted to mature forest, not necessarily at high elevations. However, it has also been found to be common in one area of secondary forest-scrub, and it nested unsuccessfully in this location.

Remarks and Allied Species   A rare bird which is possibly locally common. The reasons for its scarcity are not known, and are apparently not new, as only a few specimens have ever been collected and until recently nothing recorded on its ecology.[43]

  The specific name of the Pink-billed Parrotfinch commemorates Theodore Kleinschmidt, a German naturalist-ethnologist who spent five years in Fiji from 1873. Initially a merchant, he was for the last three years of his sojourn in the islands a full time collector for the Godeffroy Museum in Hamburg, and travelled widely in the archipelago. He made an important contribution to Fijian ornithology, including the discovery of both subspecies of the Silktail. Unfortunately he was unable to collate and publish his material before his untimely death in a native squabble in the Solomon Islands, in 1881.

Guinea grass.

Red-headed Parrotfinch (adult).   Pink-billed Parrotfinch (adult).

Red-headed Parrotfinch (juvenile).   Pink-billed Parrotfinch (juvenile).

80.   RED AVADAVAT
(Strawberry Finch)

Amandava amandava
(Linnaeus, 1758)

Fiji: Qili yago.

Identification   Plate 10. 10 cm. In breeding plumage, the male is uniformly dark crimson, faintly mottled with ashy brown and with a black abdominal patch. Much of the body is finely spangled with white. The flight and tail feathers are blackish-brown. The non-breeding plumage of the male is similar to that of the female, with brown upperparts and fawn underparts, which are paler on the throat. The stout, conical bill is red.

Flight   Fast with rapid wingbeats.

Voice   High-pitched chirps (usually uttered in flight). The male appears to have two songs, one a double chirrup followed by a short three or four note warble, and the other is a long drawn out double note. They are usually delivered from the top of a defoliated branch, or from a reed tip.

Food   Graminivorous, especially partial to the seeds of Jungle Rice *Echinochloa colonum* but very rarely taking cultivated varieties.

Breeding	The substantial oval nest with the entrance at one side is built with fresh grass and is usually well concealed, low down in thick reeds or in cane-fields. The cavity is lined with finer material or feathers. Four or more pure white eggs are laid.
Habitat and Range	A bird of open country, agricultural land and gardens, but also found at the forest edge, or in substantial clearings. An exotic bird naturalised on Viti Levu and Vanua Levu, Fiji.
Remarks and Allied Species	The Red Avadavat was introduced soon after the turn of the century to Suva, and subsequently to Vanua Levu. It is a native of India, Burma, Thailand and Cochin China, but has been introduced to many parts of the world as it is an amenable and popular cage bird. It is common and usually seen in small groups; on occasions—especially on flight to the communal roost—large flocks are formed. The subspecies is probably *A.a. flavidiventris*.

Jungle Rice.

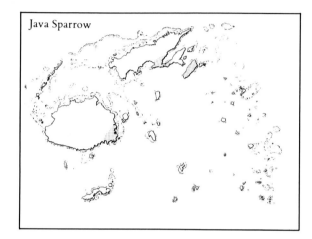

Java Sparrow

81. JAVA SPARROW
(Rice Sparrow)

Padda oryzivora
(Linnaeus, 1758)

Identification	Plate 10. 14 cm. A rather large finch, with light grey plumage and contrasting black head with white cheek patches. The belly is vinaceous pink and the undertail coverts white; the rump and tail feathers are black. The large conical bill is pink. Immature birds have dull grey upperparts with brownish-grey cheeks and underparts, and a black bill.
Voice	A weak "plink-plink" is frequently rendered.
Food	A graminivorous bird which can be a serious pest of rice paddies.
Breeding	A substantial rather untidy nest is built in the eaves of buildings; three to six white eggs are normally laid.
Habitat and Range	An introduced bird which is restricted to south-east Viti Levu, the Savusavu area of Vanua Levu and several pockets in Taveuni, Fiji. It is found only in agricultural and suburban habitats.
Remarks and Allied Species	The Java Sparrow was first collected in Fiji by the artist-naturalist William Belcher, in 1925. Within its restricted range it is a common bird, but for some reason has been unable to spread further. Of similar size, but very different appearance to the Java Sparrow, is the House Sparrow *Passer domesticus*. The adult male House Sparrow has a dark grey crown, a rufous nape and a black throat which contrasts strongly with the pale cheeks. The remaining underparts are buff and the upperparts dull brown with dark streaking. The female and juvenile are dull brown above with dark streaking on the mantle and shoulder, and buff-white below. The House Sparrow has been recorded once in Suva, Fiji, almost certainly arriving on a cargo ship.

PART FOUR
The Sea Birds

82. WANDERING ALBATROSS

Diomedea exulans
Linnaeus, 1758

Tonga: KĀTAFA (any albatross).

Identification   Plate 12. 75-125 cm. Enormous size, completely white head and back; white underwing with black wing tips and thin black rear border, and a massive pink bill, distinguish adults of this species from all other albatrosses except the Royal Albatross *D. epomorphora* and Short-tailed Albatross *D. albatrus.* Immature Wandering Albatrosses are uniformly dark brown with a white face and during the slow progression to maturity (up to ten years) they become whiter. The white underwing with black wing tips and thin black rear border is found in birds of all ages.

Flight   In a fair wind the effortless gliding on stiff, outstretched wings, interrupted only briefly by short periods of awkward flapping, is diagnostic of all albatrosses.

Voice   Generally silent at sea, but a variety of hoarse croaks can be heard when squabbling over food.

Food   Predominantly squid; also a scavenger, it will readily feed on galley waste.

Habitat and Range   Oceanic, circumpolar principally between 25° south and 65° south. It is rare in the tropics.

Remarks and Allied Species   Adult Wandering and Royal Albatrosses are difficult to distinguish in the field. At close quarters the black edging to the upper mandibles of the Royal Albatross, lacking in the Wandering Albatross, is sometimes discernible. Immature Royal Albatrosses are similar to adults, unlike immature Wandering Albatrosses which are dark. The smaller Black-browed Albatross *Diomedea melanophris,* has also been recorded in the region. It has a yellow bill, and a pure white head and body with slate-grey mantle, and dark upperwings and tail. A dusky eyebrow which can be seen only at close range gives it a perpetual frown. The underwing is white with a thick black leading edge and a thinner black trailing edge. Immature birds are more likely to be seen in the region.

83. SOUTHERN GIANT PETREL

Macronectes giganteus
(Gmelin, 1789)

Identification   Plate 12. 50-75 cm. Almost the size of an albatross, this large petrel can be distinguished from them by its heavier build and shorter wingspan. The plumage is highly variable but two phases occur. Individuals range from almost pure white through mottled birds to blackish-brown. Immatures of the brown phase are a rich glossy brown with a pale bill, the white-phase birds are white when immature. The massive horn-coloured bill of adults with the two nostrils enclosed in a long tube is diagnostic, and the prominence with which it shows up against the dark plumage is a useful characteristic for identification.

Flight   Fluent in a fair wind, the Giant Petrel becomes noticeably ponderous on calm days when it has to flap more frequently.

Voice   Not vocal, but a variety of throaty croaks have been recorded.

Food   The only petrel to feed on land, this species will come ashore to feed on carrion. At sea, it is a surface feeder, but can dive well. Cephalopods and fish are important food items, but birds are also taken.

Habitat and Range   Circumpolar in the southern seas, the adults are generally sedentary in the vicinity of breeding sites. Immatures range widely and a few straggle into the tropics.

Remarks and Allied Species   In the field this species can only be distinguished with difficulty from the Northern Giant Petrel *Macronectes halli.* They differ principally in breeding habits. Southern Giant Petrels have been recorded twice in the Fiji region, once at Ha'apai, Tonga, and a banded immature was picked up in Suva Harbour, Fiji. It had been ringed as a nestling seven months previously on Macquarie Island. *M. halli* has been recorded from eastern Polynesia.

84. CAPE PETREL
(Cape Pigeon, Pintado Petrel)

Daption capense
(Linnaeus, 1758)

Identification Plate 13. 44 cm. A distinctive black and white petrel, unlikely to be confused with any other species. The head and neck are black, the mantle back and wings are white dappled with black. The tail is white with a broad black sub-terminal band. The underparts are wholly white.

Flight A characteristic stiff-winged flight, resembling a heavy gadfly petrel.

Voice Pugnacious and very noisy when feeding in flocks.

Food Inveterate scavengers, they also include fish, squid and crustacea in their diet.

Habitat and Range A pelagic species that breeds on Antarctic and sub-Antarctic islands; stragglers are not infrequently seen in the southern waters of the region.

85. PHOENIX PETREL
Tonga: LAFU (petrels).

Pterodroma alba
(Gmelin, 1789)

Identification Plate 13. 38 cm. A medium-sized gadfly petrel with dark brown upperparts and breast. Belly and undertail are white. A small white patch on the throat, combined with the white belly, gives prominence to the brown chest. This, together with the dark-brown underwings are characteristic field marks.

Flight A graceful flight of high-banking arcs, and loose, deep wingbeats.

Voice Silent at sea, but whilst breeding they utter a wide variety of wails, moans and quick, high-pitched calls .

Food Mainly squid but also fish and crustaceans.

Habitat and Range A predominantly Southern Hemisphere species, it has been recorded as breeding on many island groups of the South Pacific, including Tonga. Stragglers range north to the Hawaiian Islands and south to the Kermadec Isles.

Remarks and Allied Species At sea, the Phoenix Petrel can only be safely distinguished from the uncommon Tahiti Petrel *P. rostrata,* at close range by its lighter build, paler plumage and variable white throat. Confusion might also arise with the White-necked Petrel *P. externa cervicalis,* and the Juan Fernandez Petrel *P.e. externa,* both of which have been recorded in the region. These gadfly petrels are larger with relatively long wings, and a short tail. The upperparts are grey and bear an indistinct dark "M" across the wings and mantle. Both species have distinct black caps, and white underparts including the underwing. The White-necked Petrel can be distinguished by its broad white nape.

86. BLACK-WINGED PETREL
Tonga: LAFU (petrels).

Pterodroma nigripennis
(Rothschild, 1893)

Identification Plate 13. 33 cm. A small gadfly petrel with a short wedge-shaped tail. The upperparts are grey with an indistinct dark "M" across the wings and back. Forehead, underparts and undertail coverts are white. The underwings are white with a dark rear edge and a broad black patch from carpel joint to axillaries. Bill short, stout and black.

Flight A rather fast, erratic flight, generally staying close to the water. Periods of fast deep wingbeats are interspaced with gliding arcs. Wings are noticeably bent at the carpal joint.

Voice A shrill "tee-tee-tee" uttered both at sea and near the breeding ground.

Food Mainly squid.

Habitat and Range	A pelagic, tropical and subtropical species, it breeds on several island groups in the extreme South-west Pacific and on the mainland of east Australia. It migrates annually to the North-central Pacific, at which time it probably regularly passes through the Fiji region. It has, however, been recorded with certainty only once—from Tonga.
Remarks and Allied Species	This is one of several petrels (others include the Mottled Petrel *P. inexpecta,* Tahiti Petrel *P. rostrata,* and the Kermadec Petrel *P. neglecta*) which are probably regular passage migrants or stragglers in the Fiji region, but do not breed here. The Black-winged Petrel, Mottled Petrel and Tahiti Petrel have been recorded.

87. HERALD PETREL
(Trindade Petrel)

Pterodroma arminjoniana heraldica
(Salvin, 1888)

Tonga: LAFU (petrels).

Identification	Plate 13. 35 cm. A medium-sized gadfly petrel found in two colour phases with graded intermediates. The light phase has grey-brown upperparts and white underparts. The forehead and lores are finely vermiculated, with a white patch on either side of the base of the beak. Throat and chin are white but the breast and flanks of some individuals are lightly scaled with grey. The legs are pale, and the feet have black on the webs and toes. The dark phase is a uniform dark grey-brown with legs and feet black. The underwing pattern of both phases has a distinctive white stripe with a pale area at the base of the primaries, contrasting with a dark background, especially the black trailing edge.
Flight	Less hurried and erratic than the flight of the Black-winged Petrel, usually close to the surface with loose deep wingbeats.
Voice	A variety of coos and moans from birds on the breeding grounds and an often repeated "squeaky sibilant" note has also been reported.
Habitat and Range	This is a pelagic, pantropical species breeding on many island groups of the South Pacific, including Tonga. Other races breed in the Indian Ocean (Mauritius) and in the Atlantic (Trindade).
Remarks and Allied Species	This petrel is a recent coloniser of Fakave Island in Tonga, where about one hundred pairs presently breed. It probably also breeds on many other islands in the region. The normal breeding season is from December to February, but nestlings have also been recorded in July. When breeding these birds show little fear of man and are remarkably docile.

88. WHITE-WINGED PETREL
(Collared Petrel)

Pterodroma leucoptera brevipes
(Peale, 1848)

Fiji: LAGIO (Kadavu group).
Tonga: LAFU (petrels).

Identification	Plate 13. 30 cm. A small gadfly petrel with grey upperparts and an indistinct dark "M" across the wings and lower back. The underparts are white with grey on the breast, darker individuals have grey on the abdomen as well. The underwing is white with a dark trailing edge and sooty leading edge. The bill and feet are black.
Flight	Typical of gadfly petrels—steeply banked arcs and rapid wingbeats. Wings slightly bent at the wrist.
Voice	Not recorded.
Food	Squid feature prominently in the diet.
Habitat and Range	A pelagic non-migratory petrel which breeds in Fiji and the New Hebrides. It has been recorded from the Phoenix Islands and it probably disperses into the central Pacific. It is commonly seen in Fiji waters.

Remarks and Allied Species	This petrel would be difficult to distinguish at sea from other "white-winged" petrels, which might be encountered in the region's waters as vagrants. These include Gould's Petrel *P.l. leucoptera*, Stejneger's Petrel *P. longirostris*, Pycroft's Petrel *P. pycrofti* and Cook's Petrel *P. cookii*.

89. MacGILLIVRAY'S PETREL

Pterodroma macgillivrayi
(Gray, 1859)

Identification	(Not illustrated.) 28 cm. A slightly larger, heavier bird than Bulwers Petrel with a stouter bill and no buff wing bars.
Flight, Voice, Food	Not known.
Habitat and Range	Known only from Gau, Fiji.
Remarks and Allied Species	This species is known only from a single fledgling collected in October 1855. It was collected by T. M. Rayner, the Medical Officer of HMS *Herald,* which did a considerable amount of survey work in Fiji in 1855-56, and named after John MacGillivray who was the *Herald's* naturalist.

90. BULWERS PETREL

Bulweria bulwerii
(Jardine & Selby, 1828)

Identification	Plate 13. 30 cm. A small dark-brown petrel with buff-coloured bars running diagonally across the upper wing surface. It can be distinguished from dark storm-petrels by its longer wedge-shaped tail, and different flight.
Flight	More akin to a typical petrel than a storm-petrel—fast and erratic, close to the sea surface with occasional loose, fluttery wingbeats and long glides.
Voice	Not recorded.
Food	Feeds mainly at night, and recorded food includes planktonic animals and fish.
Habitat and Range	A widespread subtropical, pelagic species: in the South Pacific it breeds in the Marquesas and Phoenix Islands. It has been recorded as a vagrant in Fiji waters.

91. WHITE-THROATED STORM-PETREL
(Sooty, Striped or Samoan Petrel)

Nesofregetta albigularis
(Finsch, 1877)

Identification	Plate 13. 25 cm. Sooty black upperparts contrast with a white rump. Underparts are variable. Light birds have pale underparts with a brown breast band, dark birds are totally sooty-black.
Flight	A very erratic flight, dancing and jumping over the waves with rapid fluttering wingbeats.
Voice	Silent, except for soft notes at breeding colonies.
Food	Small planktonic animals including squid.

Its recorded range has strong affinities with the South Equatorial Current. The White-throated Storm-petrel breeds in the Line and Phoenix Islands in the Central Pacific and Samoa, Fiji, the New Hebrides and the Marquesas in the South and South-west Pacific. It generally nests under overhanging grass or in rock screes or crevices. A single egg is laid. The type specimen was a female collected from Kadavu, Fiji, by Theodore Kleinschmidt.

92. BLACK-BELLIED STORM-PETREL

Fregetta tropica
(Gould, 1844)

Identification Plate 13. 20 cm. A small storm-petrel with sooty-black upperparts, throat and breast, and white rump. Chin is vermiculated with white. The belly and flanks are white with a central black stripe of varying width. In some individuals this is entirely absent, but at sea it is difficult to observe even if present.

Flight Light and erratic, often fluttering along the surface with legs dangling.

Voice A repeated shrill, piping whistle has been recorded near the breeding ground.

Food Not recorded, but sometimes follows ships.

Habitat and Range A pelagic species with a wide range in the southern oceans, principally in temperate and polar regions. It is a straggler in tropical waters and has been recorded from Samoa.

Remarks and Allied Species Probably indistinguishable at sea from the White-bellied Storm-petrel *F. grallaria,* which is likely to occur in the region.

93. WEDGE-TAILED SHEARWATER

Fiji: VAVABIAU.
Tonga: LAFU, MANU'ULI (Niuafo'ou, 'Eua, Tofua).
Niue: KALANGI.

Puffinus pacificus
(Gmelin, 1789)

Identification Plate 13. 44 cm. A large, heavily built shearwater. Upperparts are a uniform grey-brown, darker on the wings and tail. Underparts are variable. The dark phase, found predominantly in the southern Pacific, has all-dark underparts, which are whitish-grey in the pale phase. Legs are variable but generally flesh-coloured. The long wedge-shaped tail is diagnostic.

Flight A distinctive shearwater flight, lighter and more graceful than most species. Long wheeling glides, low over the water with wings slightly bent, are interspaced with a few shallow wingbeats.

Voice Silent at sea, but very vocal at night on the breeding grounds where a great variety of wails, groans and screams are uttered.

Food Fish and squid, usually procured on the surface by flying close to the water and with wings held back as if to hover, its head and neck are plunged down into the water. It rarely follows ships.

Habitat and Range This widespread and common species has a wide breeding range in the tropical and sub-tropical Pacific and Indian Oceans. Its marine range is only slightly larger than its breeding range, but it may be seen far out to sea. A common sea bird in the region, it is known to breed in each of the island groups.

Remarks and Allied Species Breeding is colonial and takes place during the summer. Tunnels, one or two metres long with a terminal chamber, are normally excavated, although some birds breed on the surface. A single white egg is laid. Rafts of several hundred individuals are sometimes formed near the breeding islands.

Like the Herald Petrel, the Wedge-tailed Shearwater can be decoyed into land by wailing sounds or music and on some Tongan islands they are captured for food in this manner.

The uncommon Buller's Shearwater *P. bulleri* is similar to the Wedge-tailed Shearwater, but the latter lacks the grey back with a dark "M" marking and black cap of Buller's Shearwater.

94. SHORT-TAILED SHEARWATER
(Slender-billed Shearwater)

Puffinus tenuirostris
(Temminck, 1835)

Identification Plate 13. 42 cm. A dark, sooty-brown shearwater with a short fan-shaped tail. The underwing coverts are greyish and the legs and feet are dark.

Flight Fast and direct.

Voice Usually silent at sea.

Food Fish, squid and crustaceans. Whilst on migration through the region it does not generally feed.

Habitat and Range Short-tailed Shearwaters breed only in Australia. In late April or May (at the end of the breeding season), they undertake a rapid trans-equatorial migration to their wintering grounds in the North Pacific. The return journey commences in August or September.

Remarks and Allied Species On a few occasions, spectacular concentrations of Short-tailed Shearwaters have been observed on passage through the region, during their southward migration in September through to November. As yet no northward migrants have been recorded.

The Short-tailed Shearwater may be distinguished from the Wedge-tailed Shearwater by the very different flight, the different shape of the tail and the former's dark legs and feet.

The Sooty Shearwater *P. griseus* which has been recorded in the region, is very similar to the Short-tailed Shearwater; it may be distinguished by its silvery-white underwing linings, and larger tail.

95. AUDUBON'S SHEARWATER
Tonga: TEIKO.

Puffinus lherminieri
Murphy, 1927

Identification Plate 13. 30 cm. A small shearwater, much smaller than the Wedge-tailed Shearwater, with blackish upperparts and dark undertail coverts, white underparts. The black head, and white chin and throat, produce a distinctive capped appearance.

Flight Generally level and direct with frequent glides. These shearwaters often give sweeping displays near the breeding grounds.

Voice A high-pitched bubbling squeal is the normal vocalisation, often accompanying display flights. Unlike the Wedge-tailed Shearwater it is generally silent on the ground.

Food Small planktonic animals. Flying-fish and squid.

Habitat and Range Audubon's Shearwater is a widespread species in the Pacific and breeds on many island groups including all three archipelagos of the Fiji region. It can be found far from land, but probably does not disperse widely from the breeding grounds. Audubon's Shearwater is a colonial breeder, sometimes in association with the Wedge-tailed Shearwater. It lays a single egg in similar situations. The breeding season is probably extended.

96.   RED-TAILED TROPICBIRD   *Phaethon rubricaudus*
                                                Boddaert, 1783

Fiji: LAWEDUA, Manu ni liwa.
Samoa: TAVA'E ULA, TAVA'E TOTO.
Tonga: TAVAKE TOTO, Tavaki.
Niue: TUAKI.

Identification Plate 12. 45 cm A large, heavily-built white bird, with thin red tail streamers which may be up to 30 cm long. A black stripe runs from the base of the bright red bill through the eye, black markings on the wing. Breeding adults often have a radiant pink flush. The immature has a strongly barred black and white back and lacks the red tail streamers.

Flight A direct flight with rapid shallow wingbeats interspaced with short glides. Aerial displays are commonly given near the breeding ground.

Voice Harsh grating sounds recorded near the breeding ground.

Food Fish and squid, generally taken far out to sea. Plunging, often from a considerable height, is the normal feeding method.

Breeding Red-tailed Tropicbirds nest solitarily or in loose colonies. No nest is constructed and the single, occasionally two, blotched, buff-coloured egg is laid generally on a rock ledge, in tree hollows or sometimes in the open. The nesting site is defended fiercely by sitting birds.

Habitat and Range A wide ranging pelagic species, generally seen singly or in small groups. Breeds throughout the tropical and subtropical Pacific and Indian Oceans.

Remarks and Allied Species A larger and more heavily built bird than the following species. The red tail streamers have long been prized in the region for ornamental head-dresses.

97.   WHITE-TAILED TROPICBIRD   *Phaethon lepturus*
       (Bosunbird)   Daudin, 1802

Fiji: LAWEDUA, Manu ni liwa.
Samoa: TAVA'E.
Tonga: TAVAKE, Tavaki.
Niue: TUAKI.

Identification Plate 12. 40 cm (excluding streamers which may be up to 30 cm). A smaller more delicate bird than the preceding species. The long white tail streamers are conspicuous and it has more black on the back than the Red-tailed Tropicbird. The bill is yellow or orange.

Flight Similar to the preceding species but with more graceful rowing wingbeats. Stiff-winged courtship flights are commonly given over the breeding grounds with small groups wheeling and cavorting over potential nest sites.

Voice Chattering screech in flight. Harsh screams when handled or disturbed at the nest.

Food Food and feeding method are the same as for the Red-tailed Tropicbird, but this species more commonly follows ships.

Breeding As for the Red-tailed Tropicbird, but more regularly nests inland and in trees.

<table>
<tr><td>Habitat and Range</td><td>A wide ranging species found in tropical or subtropical seas around the world. It is rare in the Eastern Pacific but breeds on most of the island groups elsewhere in the Pacific, including Fiji, Tonga and Samoa. It is strongly pelagic and disperses widely from its breeding grounds.</td></tr>
<tr><td>Remarks and Allied Species</td><td>Common in the region, these beautiful sea birds are regularly encountered both out to sea and in coastal waters, and commonly well inland on the smaller islands. This is a commoner species than the Red-tailed Tropicbird. Its tail streamers are also prized for ornamental purposes, and used as articles of trade in some parts of the region.</td></tr>
</table>

98.   MASKED BOOBY

(Blue-faced, White Booby)

Sula dactylatra
Lesson, 1831

Fiji: GUTULEI (Lau group), TORŌ and TARŌ (Kadavu group), Droi.
Tonga: NGUTULEI.

<table>
<tr><td>Identification</td><td>Plate 12. 85 cm. The largest booby, body conspicuously white with a diagnostic black tail. This, together with the black primaries and tips to the secondaries, is conspicuous in flight. The bill of the male is yellow, duller in the female, and its base and the facial skin are black. Both sexes have a bright yellow eye. These features, set off by the white head plumage, produce the striking masked appearance. Immature birds have a dark brown head and neck, and grey-brown back with a distinct white patch. Like adults they have a dark black-brown tail.</td></tr>
<tr><td>Flight</td><td>Typical booby; fast and deliberate with powerful wingbeats interspaced with short glides.</td></tr>
<tr><td>Voice</td><td>Differs between the sexes, the male is higher-pitched — akin to a whistle — whilst the female's is low-pitched, more trumpet like.</td></tr>
<tr><td>Food</td><td>Predominantly fish, caught by diving from the air. Does not usually feed inshore.</td></tr>
<tr><td>Breeding</td><td>A colonial breeder, this species lays its eggs in a slight depression in the ground, sometimes with a few sticks pulled together. Occasionally it nests on cliffs but always close to the sea. Two bluish-white eggs are laid, but only a single chick survives.</td></tr>
<tr><td>Habitat and Range</td><td>A widespread species in the tropical and subtropical Pacific and Indian Oceans. It breeds on many island groups of the Pacific including Fiji and Samoa, but has not been recorded as breeding in Tonga.</td></tr>
<tr><td>Remarks and Allied Species</td><td>In flight the Masked Booby can be distinguished from white-phased individuals of the Red-Footed Booby by its heavier body and black, not white, tail. The immature can be distinguished from the Brown Booby because the breast of the immature Masked Booby is white, only the neck is dark. Immature Brown Boobies have a dark breast and neck.</td></tr>
</table>

99.   BROWN BOOBY

Sula leucogaster
(Boddaert, 1783)

Fiji: GUTULEI (Lau group), TORŌ and TARŌ (Kadavu group), Droi, Ga ni wai.
Tonga: NGUTULEI.

<table>
<tr><td>Identification</td><td>Plate 12. 75 cm. The combination of chocolate-brown plumage with white lower breast and belly is characteristic. It has less white on the underwing than the Masked Booby. The bill is greyish-yellow and the feet yellowish. Immatures are dull brown with the lower breast and belly light brown or buff, but the division is distinct.</td></tr>
<tr><td>Flight</td><td>As for the Masked Booby, but lighter and more agile.</td></tr>
<tr><td>Voice</td><td>Males have a high-pitched wheeze and females a harsh crackle.</td></tr>
<tr><td>Food</td><td>Fish and squid caught by diving to the surface; often feeds inshore as well as in deep water.</td></tr>
</table>

Breeding   A colonial breeder, on open ground or amongst vegetation. The nest site is generally a shallow depression with a few leaves as a lining; sometimes a more substantial nest is constructed. Two, sometimes three, greenish-white eggs, covered in a chalky substance are laid. One chick usually survives. Breeding colonies are noisy with continuous squabbles and bickering between neighbouring birds.

Habitat and Range   A similar overall range to the Masked Booby. It is less pelagic than the other two boobies found in the region, and has been recorded as breeding in each of the three island groups.

Remarks and Allied Species   This is a common booby in the region and frequently encountered because of its coastal affinities.

100.   RED-FOOTED BOOBY   *Sula sula*
(Linnaeus, 1766)

Fiji: GUTULEI (Lau group), TORŌ and TARŌ (Kadavu group), Droi, Ga ni wai.
Tonga: NGUTULEI, TAISENI (Niuatoputapu and Tafahi Islands).

Identification   Plate 12. 70 cm. The smallest of the three boobies, it is a lighter and more delicate species which is found in two colour phases with a range of intermediates. The light phase is predominantly white with a golden wash on the head and neck and black on the wings. The dark phase is a uniform dark-brown with a white belly and tail, the latter being conspicuous in flight and diagnostic. The legs and feet are coral red, and the bill blue-grey. The immature is all brown with a conspicuous darker brown breast band. Bill and feet are dark.

Flight   Typical of boobies but more delicate.

Voice   No difference between the sexes. Noisy clattering sounds have been recorded whilst feeding and on the breeding grounds.

Food   Fish, caught by diving to the surface; regularly sits on the sea and plunges its head into the water. Sometimes catches flying fish between the waves.

Breeding   A colonial breeder. Frail nests are built low down in a bush or tree. A single chalky-white egg is laid.

Habitat and Range   Similar overall range to the Masked Booby. It breeds or visits nearly every tropical island group in the Pacific including all three in the Fiji region.

Remarks and Allied Species   A common species and, like the Brown Booby, prefers coastal waters. It is generally encountered in groups of up to a hundred birds; the Brown Booby, on the other hand, is less gregarious and generally seen singly or in pairs.

101. GREAT FRIGATEBIRD

Fregata minor
(Gmelin, 1789)

Fiji: KASAGA, MANU NI CAGI, Yalewa qilaqila.
Samoa: 'ATAFA.
Tonga: HELEKOSI, LOFA.
Niue: KOTA, MANU FOLAU.

Identification   (Not illustrated.) 100 cm. The male Great Frigatebird is all black, with lighter wing coverts. A green sheen is sometimes discernible on the head and back. The female is black with a white breast and throat. Immatures are dark brown above with lighter wing coverts. The underparts, head and neck are white tinged with rust, especially on the breast. In breeding condition the male has a red throat pouch which is inflated during courtship.

Flight   Similar to the Lesser Frigatebird.

Voice   A variety of rattling croaks.

Breeding   As for the Lesser Frigatebird.

Habitat and Range   Similar to the Lesser Frigatebird, although far less common in the Fiji region.

Remarks and Allied Species   Distinguishing features of the two frigatebirds are given under the Lesser Frigatebird. The anomalous specific name of the Great Frigatebird—*minor*—is a relic of the days when it was called the Lesser Pelican. Both frigatebirds are sometimes called Man-of-War birds, or Hurricane birds, the former due to their piratical activities, and the latter because their appearance is supposed to forewarn of bad weather at sea.

102. LESSER FRIGATEBIRD

Fregata ariel
(Gray, 1845)

Fiji: KASAGA, MANU NI CAGI, Yalewa qilaqila.
Samoa: 'ATAFA.
Tonga: HELEKOSI, LOFA.

Identification   Plate 12. 80 cm. The silhouette of frigatebirds is unmistakable with long pointed wings and a long deeply forked tail. The male Lesser Frigatebird is all black except for two white abdominal patches, and sometimes an indistinct purplish sheen can be detected. In breeding condition, males have a red throat pouch which is inflated during courtship. The female generally has a white breast and belly, and black throat. A smaller bird than the Great Frigatebird but this is not a good field feature, except in mixed flocks and when combined with other characteristics.

Flight   Both frigatebirds are adept gliders, often soaring for long periods on motionless, bent wings, resorting to a low deep flapping only when forced to do so. Such flight gives no indication of the great dexterity and speed with which frigatebirds can pursue other sea birds, or catch disgorged food in mid-air or from the sea's surface.

Voice   A deep rattling "kukukuk".

Food   Efficient pirates, frigatebirds commonly harass other sea birds, forcing them to disgorge or drop food, which is then deftly caught in the air. Food items are also taken off the sea surface, but frigatebirds do not land on the water as their plumage lacks waterproofing properties and their long wings would preclude take-off. Occasionally frigatebirds turn predatory and take nestlings or injured birds.

Breeding   A colonial breeder on offshore islands, often in association with boobies. They make an untidy platform of twigs in a bush or a tree. A single white egg is laid. The breeding cycle takes longer than a year, so that successful breeders can only nest every other year.

Habitat and Range   A widespread species found in tropical seas of the Pacific, Indian and West Atlantic Oceans. It breeds or visits nearly every island group in the Pacific and breeds in all three island groups of the Fiji region.

Remarks and Allied Species   The Lesser and Great Frigatebirds are difficult to distinguish, although the Lesser is a smaller bird this is rarely apparent in the field and females of both species are distinctly larger than males. Whereas all adults have a black head, immatures have a pale buff head. The male Great Frigatebird lacks the two white abdominal patches of the Lesser Frigatebird. Females of both species have a variable amount of white on the underside and, although the Lesser generally has a dark throat, they can only be distinguished by experienced observers. The Lesser is the more common of the two frigatebirds in the region.

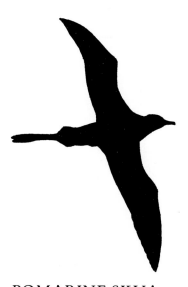

103.   **POMARINE SKUA**   *Stercorarius pomarinus*
(Temminck, 1815)

Identification   Plate 12. 55 cm. A large, robust, dark-looking bird. The upperparts are dark brown, generally with a lighter collar. The underparts are variable, usually white with a brown chest band. Adults have the central tail feathers projecting beyond the otherwise fan-shaped tail and their rounded tips are twisted. Immature birds lack the tail streamers and are heavily mottled.

Flight   Ponderous wingbeats are interspersed with brief periods of gliding. A white wing bar at the base of the primary feathers is conspicuous in flight. The normal flight belies the great manouverability with which they pursue other sea birds.

<table>
<tr><td>*Food and Range*</td><td>Essentially a scavenger, the Pomarine Skua is a straggler to subtropical waters. It breeds on Antarctic and sub-Antarctic islands.</td></tr>
<tr><td>*Remarks and Allied Species*</td><td>The similar Arctic Skua *S. parasiticus* is a smaller and more delicate species with a similar plumage. The distinguishing features are the two central tail feathers which are not blunt and twisted but taper to a fine point. Both species are uncommon visitors to the region.</td></tr>
</table>

104. COMMON TERN

Sterna hirundo
Linnaeus, 1758

<table>
<tr><td>*Identification*</td><td>Plate 14. 35 cm. A small, slim tern. In non-breeding plumage adults are white with a grey mantle. The forehead is white merging into a streaked black nape, the bill is black and legs reddish brown. Birds in full breeding plumage are unlikely to be seen in the region. They have a distinct black cap and the bill is red with a black tip (although the eastern race *S.h. longipennis* has a wholly black bill in nuptial plumage). The tail is deeply forked and does not project beyond the tips of the folded wing. Immatures are similar to non-breeding adults, but have a dark patch on the carpal joint.</td></tr>
<tr><td>*Flight*</td><td>Distinctive buoyant flight with deep deliberate wingbeats. Hovers frequently.</td></tr>
<tr><td>*Voice*</td><td>A harsh "kee-yah" and a "kik-kik-kik" contact note used by birds whilst fishing.</td></tr>
<tr><td>*Food*</td><td>Fish, caught by diving from up to ten metres with wings folded or partly closed. It often submerges totally before flying off in a flurry of sea water.</td></tr>
<tr><td>*Habitat and Range*</td><td>Only seen in the region as a passage migrant from the Northern Hemisphere where it breeds in temperate areas. It generally frequents inshore or coastal waters, it has been recorded from Fiji but is not common.</td></tr>
<tr><td>*Remarks and Allied Species*</td><td>The Roseate Tern *S. dougallii*, is similar but is pure white, and at rest the streamers of the deeply forked tail project beyond the folded wings. This species has been recorded from Tonga.</td></tr>
</table>

105. SOOTY TERN
(Wideawake Tern)

Sterna fuscata
Linnaeus, 1766

Tonga: TALATĀ, TALATAHI (Ha'apai group).

<table>
<tr><td>*Identification*</td><td>Plate 14. 43 cm. A distinctive tern with contrasting black upperparts and white underparts with a long deeply-forked tail. The white forehead, extending to just above the eye and the black loral stripe running to the base of the beak are diagnostic features. Immatures are dark with pale speckling on the back and have a lighter belly.</td></tr>
<tr><td>*Flight*</td><td>Light and buoyant with slow deliberate wingbeats. As with most terns the body appears to move up and down on each wingbeat.</td></tr>
<tr><td>*Voice*</td><td>The name Wideawake is derived from its three syllable rasping call.</td></tr>
</table>

Food	Small fish and planktonic animals, taken by diving to the surface. Sooty Terns are highly gregarious, sometimes feeding in immense flocks following schools of predatory fish such as Bonito.
Breeding	A highly colonial breeder. Breeding is heralded by the arrival of enormous chattering flocks soaring over the breeding grounds. One, or occasionally two, off-white eggs blotched with purple or chocolate are laid in a scrape in the ground.
Habitat and Range	The Sooty Tern is a common pantropical or subtropical species. In the Pacific it has been recorded as breeding in nearly every island group including Fiji, Tonga and Samoa.
Remarks and Allied Species	Probably the most common sea bird in the Pacific, the Sooty Tern is renowned for its immense breeding colonies and gregarious feeding behaviour. It is a pelagic species and outside the breeding season is not often found near land. It rarely if ever lands on the water and may sleep on the wing. It may be confused with the Bridled Tern.

106. BRIDLED TERN
(Brown-winged Tern)

Sterna anaethetus
Scopoli, 1786

Identification	Plate 14. 40 cm. Overall appearance is similar to the Sooty Tern, it differs in its paler brown-grey wings and mantle, and clouded grey underparts. The diagnostic difference is the white forehead which extends backwards to well beyond the eye. The immature has mottled upperparts and is pale below.
Flight	More buoyant than that of the Sooty Tern with more rapid wingbeats.
Voice	A distinctive yapping or laughing call.
Food	Small fish and squid normally caught by plunging to the surface. They are sometimes to be seen sitting on the water.
Breeding	A colonial nester on islands or cliffs. It has similar pre-breeding displays to the Sooty Tern, but in smaller numbers. Nests are rarely placed in the open, usually being under the protection of a ledge or shrub. A single, blotched off-white egg is laid.
Habitat and Range	A vagrant in the region, the Bridled Tern breeds on the Pacific coasts of Central and South America, the Philippines, Formosa, Australia, the Solomons and the Bismarks.
Remarks and Allied Species	Difficult to distinguish from the Sooty and Grey-backed Terns, especially when immature.

107. GREY-BACKED TERN
(Spectacled Tern)

Sterna lunata
Peale, 1848

Identification	Plate 14. 35 cm. The grey mantle, tail and wings distinguish this species from the Sooty and Bridled Terns which have darker upperparts. The head pattern is similar to that of the Bridled Tern. Immature birds have pale underparts and mottled grey-brown upperparts. They are not readily distinguished from immature Bridled Terns.
Flight	As for Bridled Tern.
Voice	Not recorded.
Food	Takes small fish and squid by diving to the surface.
Habitat and Range	This species has been erroneously recorded as breeding in Fiji, but is apparently only a straggler in the Western Pacific, being most common in the Central Pacific.
Remarks and Allied Species	This species is considered the ecological counterpart of the Bridled Tern and overall they have distinct ranges. Fiji is close to the boundary and both species have been recorded.

| 108. | BLACK-NAPED TERN | *Sterna sumatrana* Raffles, 1822 |

108. BLACK-NAPED TERN *Sterna sumatrana* Raffles, 1822

Fiji: I CO, Dre.
Samoa: FUA'Ō, Gogouli.

Identification Plate 14. 35 cm. General appearance is a small white tern with a deeply forked tail and black nape. The upperparts are grey and underparts white or pale grey. The bill and legs are black. Immatures are similar to adults but the black crescent on the nape is mottled and they lack the long outer tail feathers.

Flight Delicate and graceful but with strong wingbeats.

Voice A noisy species with varied short, sharp calls, e.g., a rapid "tsee-chee-chi-chip". Alarm call is a "chit-chit-chit-ver".

Food A surface feeder rather than an aerial diver, it commonly hovers above the water when taking food.

Breeding A colonial nester either on bare ground or on cliff ledges. One or two white eggs blotched with rust or dark grey are laid in a depression or in an insubstantial nest.

Habitat and Range A coastal species, this tern is not found far from land. Its range stretches through the tropical Indian Ocean to the Western Pacific. It breeds in Fiji and Tonga, but has only been recorded as a vagrant in Samoa.

109. CRESTED TERN *Sterna bergii* Lichtenstein, 1823

Fiji: I CO, Dre.
Samoa: TALA, Tola.

Identification Plate 14. 46 cm. A large, white-looking tern, with light grey upperparts, deeply forked tail, white forehead and a partially erectile black crest. The latter is regularly visible in resting birds. When not breeding the black cap is streaked with white. Immatures are mottled brown on the back. The bill is heavy and bright yellow-horn in both adults and immature birds.

Flight Heavy, with strong deliberate wingbeats.

Voice A variety of short, harsh disyllabic calls.

Food Crested Terns fish singly or in small groups over shallow coastal waters or lagoons, diving to the surface to capture small fish.

Breeding A colonial breeder, on a rocky substrate, cliffs or on sand. One or two, pale buff-coloured eggs blotched with black and brown are laid in a depression with no nesting material.

Habitat and Range A tern showing strong coastal affinities, it is rarely found far from land. Its range includes the Indian Ocean and the West, South and Central Pacific. It breeds in Fiji and probably Tonga, but as yet is only recorded as a vagrant in Samoa.

Remarks and Allied Species A widespread and common species, but never in large numbers. It is one of the characteristic species of Polynesian coastal waters.

110. GREY NODDY
(Blue-grey Noddy, Grey Ternlet)

Procelsterna cerulea (Bennett, 1840)

Samoa: Laia.

Identification Plate 14. 28 cm. A distinctive, small grey tern with a shallow forked tail and a conspicuous black eye. The entire body is pale grey, darker on the wings and tail. The bill and feet are black. The immature bird is darker, slate-grey with dark primaries.

Flight Buoyant and erratic with rapid wingbeats.

Voice	A purring "cror-r-r-r" has been recorded from birds on land, and a noisy alarm scream when on the wing.
Food	A delicate feeder on planktonic animals and fish, picking food off the surface and sometimes paddling on the water.
Breeding	Nests on cliff ledges or rock crevices. A single speckled egg is laid.
Habitat and Range	A sedentary, coastal species, the Grey Noddy breeds throughout its range in tropical and temperate waters of the Pacific. It is absent from much of the Western Pacific but has been recorded as breeding in Tonga and Samoa and may well breed in Fiji.

111. COMMON NODDY
(Brown Noddy)

Anous stolidus
(Linnaeus, 1758)

Fiji: I CO LOALOA, GOGO (Lau group and Taveuni Island).
Samoa: FUA'O.
Tonga: NGONGO, NGONGOFALA (Ha'apai group).
Niue: NGONGO.

Identification	Plate 14. 38 cm. A dark brown tern-like bird with long pointed wings and a wedge-shaped tail often bearing a central notch. The forehead and crown are greyish-white.
Flight	Direct with steady wingbeats, sometimes soars.
Voice	Deep guttural calls.
Food	Fish and squid usually caught whilst hovering over the surface and plunging a short distance to seize prey. Occasionally dives from a height.
Breeding	Generally nests in trees, often in coconut palms, constructing a bulky nest of dry vegetable matter, but may nest on the ground or in rock crevices. A single buff-coloured egg with dark blotches is laid. It has an extended breeding season in the region.
Habitat and Range	An offshore and pelagic species with a wide range in tropical and subtropical seas, extending into temperate areas. It is a common species and breeds in all three island groups of the region.
Remarks and Allied Species	Together with the closely related Black Noddy, this noddy is a common and characteristic sea bird of the region. They are frequently encountered in coastal waters and farther offshore, often in large fishing groups following schools of Bonito.

112. BLACK NODDY
(White-capped Noddy)

Anous tenuirostris minutus
(Boie, 1844)

Fiji: I CO LOALOA, GOGO (Lau group and Taveuni Island).
Tonga: NGONGO.

Identification	Plate 14. 33 cm. A smaller species than the Common Noddy, but in flight they are not safely distinguishable. The beak is slightly longer and more delicate, and the feet and legs are yellowish brown.
Flight	More erratic with faster wingbeats than the Common Noddy.
Voice	Similar to the Common Noddy, but higher pitched.
Food	Fish and squid picked from the surface, or obtained by shallow dives.
Breeding	A colonial breeder, constructing a substantial nest of dried twigs and other material, commonly in *Pandanus* or *Casuarina* trees. A single buff-coloured egg with brown spots is laid.
Habitat and Range	Coastal and offshore waters in the Pacific, Indian and western Atlantic Oceans. Breeds in all three archipelagos of the Fiji region.

113. **WHITE TERN**
(Fairy Tern)

Gygis alba candida
Gmelin, 1789

Fiji: Droe.
Samoa: MANUSINA.
Tonga: 'Ekiaki, Tala (Niuafo'ou Island).
Niue: TAKETAKE.

Identification Plate 14. 25 cm. A delicate pure white tern, unlikely to be confused with any other species. The slender beak is black with a blue base and slightly upturned. The black eye is prominent. The tail has a shallow fork. In flight, the wings appear translucent from below. The immature bird has a mottled mantle and the black eye ring of adults is absent, being replaced by a black spot behind the eye.

Flight Characteristic delicate, ethereal flight, fluttering erratically on its way.

Voice A variety of noises recorded, including a twanging and often repeated quack, a purring "crorr-r-r-rr" and a thin whistling note.

Food Small fish and squid, also crustaceans and planktonic animals. Dives to the surface on occasions, or picks food from the water.

Breeding Usually breeds in loose colonies; the single heavily streaked light green egg is laid on a bare branch or rock with no nesting material.

Habitat and Range The White Tern is commonly seen in coastal waters or over land when breeding. It has a wide circum-equatorial range and has been recorded as breeding in Fiji, Tonga and Samoa.

Remarks and Allied Species A very common and characteristic species in the region. During the breeding season, the White Tern is frequently seen inland, although never very far from the coast, and the cavorting courtship flights performed by two or three birds are conspicuous.

The Little Tern *Sterna albifrons,* which has been recorded as a rare vagrant in the region, may be confused with the White Tern on account of their similarly small size, but in all other characteristics it is distinct. In non-breeding plumage it is pale grey above and white below, with a black cap streaked with white, and white forehead. Immature birds have a mottled brownish-black mantle.

114. **LESSER GOLDEN PLOVER**
(Pacific Golden Plover)

Pluvialis dominica fulva
(Gmelin, 1789)

Fiji: DILODILO, DILIO, Dili-dilio.
Rotuma: Juli.
Samoa: TULĪ.
Tonga: KIU (any migratory wader).
Niue: KIU.

Identification Plate 15. 23 cm. This migrant may be found either in full breeding dress, in non-breeding plumage or in intermediate plumage. The non-breeding plumage (most birds November to February) is nondescript; strongly mottled brown and grey above, with diffused pale underparts. The white stripe above the eye is conspicuous. As breeding plumage is assumed, a golden tinge appears on the upperparts, and black feathers on the breast and belly. In full breeding plumage the breast, belly, throat and undertail are black and separated by a white stripe from the upperparts, which are richly spangled with gold.

Flight Fast and direct with strong regular wingbeats.

Voice A two or three syllable whistle, with emphasis on the last note. Usually given singly or twice, either at rest or on rising.

Food Insects, crustaceans and worms. The typical feeding method is to run a few paces, stop and search and then repeat the process.

Habitat and Range	Found in any coastal situation or as commonly on short grass expanses near the coast. Frequently follows rivers inland and can often be seen in rice fields. A migrant, the subspecies *P.d. fulva* breeds in North America and Siberia, dispersing widely in the Pacific in the northern winter.
Remarks and Allied Species	A very common summer visitor to the region. Most birds arrive in September and leave in April; some individuals over winter, usually on the coast. Its non-breeding status has long been realised by all natives of the region, and in Fiji a well known proverb intimates that something may be "as hard to find as the egg of the Golden Plover".

115. MONGOLIAN PLOVER
(Mongolian Dotterel)

Charadrius mongolus
Pallas, 1776

Identification	Plate 15. 19 cm. Individuals in all states of plumage may be encountered. The eclipse plumage is generally grey above and white below, with a conspicuous white forehead and throat with a grey eye stripe. The Mongolian Plover assumes an unmistakable breeding plumage with a broad chestnut band on the breast extending around to the nape. A black eye stripe runs through to the bill and a black line separates the white forehead and rufous crown. Chin and throat are white.
Voice	A clear "trick" and soft "ticket", also a penetrating "drrit" and short "triks" have been recorded. Noted as generally silent in Fiji.
Habitat and Range	Tidal mud and sand flats; in the region it is only recorded with certainty from Fiji. A summer visitor from eastern Asia.
Remarks and Allied Species	Probably a regular visitor in small numbers, difficulties in identification have led it to be considered as rare. Some individuals remain throughout the year, and whenever present may be found in mixed wader flocks. In eclipse plumage this species is difficult to distinguish from other small and medium-sized waders which may be present. Only with great care may it be separated from the Double-Banded Plover. The Mongolian Plover has a whiter face, grey rather than rufous upperparts and white underparts with grey banding faintly visible at the sides of the lower breast. The Large Sand Plover *C. leschenaultii,* the Oriental Plover *C. veredus,* the Ringed Plover *C. hiaticula,* and the Semi-palmated Plover *C. semipalmatus,* are all species which might occur in the Fiji region and would be difficult to distinguish from this species and from the Double-banded Plover. As yet they have not been recorded.

116. DOUBLE-BANDED PLOVER
(Banded Plover or Dotterel)

Charadrius bicinctus
Jardine & Selby, 1827

Identification	Plate 15. 18 cm. In breeding plumage (which may be seen on a few birds) this plover is unmistakable because of the two bands on its chest. A narrow black band on the upper breast is separated by white from a broader chestnut band on the lower breast; the remainder of the underparts are white. In non-breeding plumage the upperparts are brownish grey and the underparts white. The legs are olive green.
Voice	An incisive "chip-chip".

Habitat and Range	Mud and sandflats. In New Zealand it also frequents short-cropped pastures near the sea. The Double-banded Plover breeds in New Zealand and disperses mainly to southern and eastern Australia in the non-breeding season.
Remarks and Allied Species	Probably a regular visitor in small numbers, throughout the region, but has to date only been recorded from Fiji, between the months of May and August.

117.	**WHIMBREL**	*Numenius phaeopus variegatus* (Scopoli, 1786)

Identification	(Not illustrated.) 40 cm. A large, heavily built bird with a distinctly down-curved bill. The upperparts are vermiculated dark and light brownish-grey, paler below with brown streaked breast, belly whitish. A pale eye stripe and median stripe on the crown. The Asiatic subspecies *N.p. variegatus,* can be distinguished by its pale rump (although this is a variable feature) from the American subspecies *N.p. hudsonicus,* which always has a uniform brown rump.
Voice	A distinctive rippling "ti-ti-ti-ti-ti", usually five to seven syllables.
Food	Worms and crustacea taken by thrusting its bill deep into the substrate, and from under stones and litter.
Habitat and Range	Sandbanks and tidal mudflats, occasionally on open reefs and beaches. A summer visitor from the Northern Hemisphere.
Remarks and Allied Species	A regular migrant, but never in large numbers, both subspecies have been recorded in the region, but the Asiatic race predominates. Some individuals remain over winter. The Whimbrel may be confused with either of the curlews found in the region — see the two succeeding species.

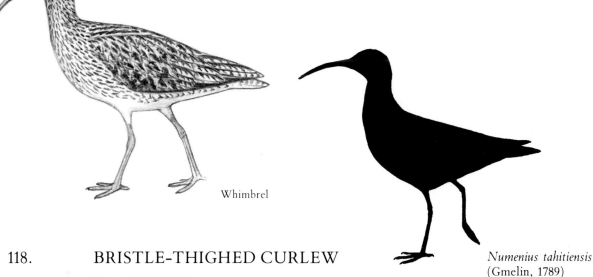

Whimbrel

118.	**BRISTLE-THIGHED CURLEW**	*Numenius tahitiensis* (Gmelin, 1789)
	Niue: MOTUKU	

Identification	Plate 1. 44 cm. Similar in general appearance to the Whimbrel, including the head pattern, but larger with upper tail coverts uniform buffy-white, tail tawny with black bars. Long down-curved bill and bluish-grey legs.
Flight	Steady and direct.
Voice	A mellow whistling "pi-ow", "oui-oui-he" or "aweu-wit".
Habitat and Range	Tidal flats, beaches and occasionally on short grass near the coast. A summer migrant which breeds in Alaska and spends the northern winters mainly in the Central and Eastern Pacific. The Fiji region is at the edge of its winter range, but it has been regularly recorded from each of the island groups within the region.

A regular summer migrant in small numbers. It can be distinguished from both sub-species of the Whimbrel by its larger size, barred tail and distinctive call. It is much smaller than the Eastern Curlew which lacks the conspicuous pattern on the head.

119. **EASTERN CURLEW**
(Long-billed Curlew)

Numenius madagascariensis
(Linnaeus, 1766)

Identification Plate 1. 60 cm. The largest wader, it is easily recognised by its size, long down-curved bill (19 cm) and distinctive call. Upperparts streaked brown and buff, similar underparts but paler. No white rump, tail and tail coverts barred. Legs bluish grey.

Flight Rather ponderous and heavy wingbeats.

Voice A ringing, tuneful "ker-lee".

Food Worms, crustacea and other marine organisms.

Habitat and Range A migrant, breeding in Siberia and wintering mainly in South-east Asia and northern Australasia. It has been recorded from Fiji and Samoa.

Remarks and Allied Species A regular summer visitor to the region, but probably only in very small numbers. The specific name *madagascariensis* is misleading, since the range of this species does not reach Madagascar. The anomaly stems from a geographical error when first described; the correct location was Macassar in Celebes.

120. **EASTERN BAR-TAILED GODWIT**
Tonga: KIU FOA'UNGA, Kiu.

Limosa lapponica baueri
Naumann, 1836

Identification Plate 1. 40 cm. Large size with a long, slightly up-turned bill distinguishes this species from other waders. Upperparts are mottled grey and brown, the rump and tail barred white and brown. Underparts are pale grey, which in males become bright rufous-red in the breeding plumage; females assume only a rufous tinge — they are slightly larger than males, with a distinctly longer bill.

Flight Direct and fast. No wing bar is displayed. Often flies in orderly lines or in chevrons.

Voice A double, fluted "tiu-tiu", rather harsh and usually repeated.

Habitat and Range All tidal areas, commonly feeding in tidal pools, rocky beaches or on fringing reefs. An Arctic migrant breeding in Siberia and wintering throughout South-east Asia, Australasia and the South-western Pacific.

A common summer visitor throughout the region and unlike many waders readily approachable. Only small numbers have been recorded in Tonga and Samoa, but large flocks have been seen in Fiji. A gregarious species often mixing with other waders. Some birds remain throughout the year and birds in breeding plumage are to be seen before departure in March and April.

121.   **WANDERING TATTLER**   *Heteroscelus incanus*
                                       (Gmelin, 1789)

Fiji: DOLI, Dolidoli.
Rotuma: Juli.
Tonga: KIU, Kiu lega lega.
Niue: KIU TAHI.

Identification   Plate 15. 28 cm. A rather nondescript, medium-sized wader. Dark grey above, the underparts are pale grey in winter but often finely barred. In breeding plumage, the underparts have strong narrow barring; there is a distinct white stripe leading from above the eye to the bill, and a dark eye stripe beneath this. The bill is long and dark; the legs yellowish green.

Flight   Fast and direct.

Voice   A strident "tulee, tu-lee-lei", often rapidly repeated, especially when disturbed.

Food   Aquatic animals from a wide variety of situations.

Habitat and Range   A very common visitor which favours rocky pools or fringing reefs. It frequently follows rivers inland, and may be seen sixty kilometres or more from the coast of Viti Levu, Fiji. The Wandering Tattler breeds in northern America and disperses through the Pacific in the northern winter. It is a characteristic wader throughout Polynesia.

Remarks and Allied Species   Probably the most common and certainly the most widespread shore bird of the region. During the summer months, solitary birds or pairs are a common sight on all coasts and up the larger rivers. Many individuals remain throughout the year, usually on the coast. After landing the tail is often gently bobbed up and down, as is the head when alerted.

The Wandering Tattler is similar to the Grey-tailed Tattler *H. brevipes,* but the latter is slightly smaller and less robust, with a darker plumage and distinct call — a high pitched double whistle. At close quarters, or in the hand, the nasal groove of the Wandering Tattler can be seen to extend to two-thirds of the length of the bill, whilst it only reaches half way in the Grey-tailed Tattler. The latter has been recorded from Fiji and is probably a regular visitor in small numbers.

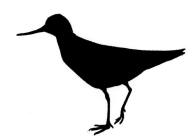

122.   **TEREK SANDPIPER**   *Xenus cinereus*
                                     (Güldenstaedt, 1774)

Identification   Plate 15. 23 cm. A medium-sized wader, with a long, distinctly up-turned bill and orange-yellow legs. Upperparts brownish-grey, underparts white.

Flight   Quick with rapid wingbeats. A noticeable white bar on the trailing edge of the wing.

Voice   A melodious trill, variously described as "tee-tee-tee", "weeta-wetta-weet" or "hir-irir".

<table>
<tr><td>*Habitat and Range*</td><td>Sandbanks and tidal mudflats. The Terek Sandpiper has a wide breeding range in northern Europe and Asia. Non-breeding birds disperse widely to winter in Africa, southern Eurasia and Australasia. A single recent record exists from Fiji.</td></tr>
<tr><td>*Remarks and Allied Species*</td><td>The distinct up-turned bill and yellow legs are conspicuous field characters. It is a noticeably active bird and frequently bobs its tail. Although only recorded once it is probably an irregular straggler in the region.</td></tr>
</table>

123. RUDDY TURNSTONE

Tonga: Kiu.

Arenaria interpres
(Linnaeus, 1758)

Identification	Plate 15. 23 cm. A distinctive medium-sized wader with a short neck, a heavy body, sharply pointed black bill and bright orange legs. In non-breeding plumage, the upperparts are variable — dark with black and red-brown mottling. White below with a brown breast band. Chin always white. Breeding plumage is a conspicuous harlequin pattern of black, white and rufous.
Flight	In flight, it shows a distinctive double white wing bar and a white rump and tail with two broad sub-terminal black bars. Flocks often rise and fly in unison.
Voice	A twittering trill on taking flight and a sharp hard "tuk-a-tuk".
Food	Crustaceans and other marine organisms. Insects when on land. An energetic feeder turning stones and foreshore debris.
Habitat and Range	Fringing reefs, rocky beaches, breakwaters and sometimes mudflats. Occasionally, seen inland on open ground. A circumpolar breeder in the Northern Hemisphere, non-breeding birds disperse throughout the Southern Hemisphere.
Remarks and Allied Species	A common migrant found throughout the region, but not in very large numbers; often associating with Lesser Golden Plovers. Some individuals overwinter. Birds with traces of breeding plumage are frequently encountered.

124. SANDERLING

Calidris alba
(Pallas, 1764)

Identification	Plate 15. 20 cm. A small, plump, sandpiper with noticeably short legs. In non-breeding plumage, white with a pale grey mantle, pale mottled wings, a dark tail and often a dark carpal patch. In breeding plumage head and upperparts bright chestnut. Stout black bill, and black legs with no hind toe.
Flight	Characteristic black carpal joint and wing tips separated by a broad white stripe.
Voice	Sharp "quit", often repeated.
Food	Feeds energetically on sandy beaches near the tide line. Often aptly described as behaving like a clockwork toy.
Habitat and Range	Strongly favours sandy beaches or sandbanks. Breeds in the Arctic and non-breeding birds disperse around the world.
Remarks and Allied Species	A distinctive species unlikely to be confused with any other. Although only recorded from Fiji, it is probably a regular visitor in small numbers throughout the region.

125. RED-NECKED STINT
(Little Stint)

Calidris ruficollis
(Pallas, 1776)

Identification Plate 15. 15 cm. A diminutive grey and white wader. Non-breeding plumage is grey above, with mottling on the wings and back; underparts are white with a grey neck patch. Birds in partial breeding plumage have rusty red feathers on the neck or head. Bill and legs are black.

Flight Fast, with a pale wing bar noticeable.

Voice Liquid "twick, twick".

Habitat and Range Generally frequents tidal mudflats or sandbanks. The Red-necked Stint breeds in Siberia and is a common migrant to Australia. There are two recent records from Fiji.

Remarks and Allied Species Probably an irregular and uncommon visitor to the region, it is smaller than the Sanderling with a narrower wing bar, different feeding behaviour and a distinctive call.

126. SHARP-TAILED SANDPIPER
(Siberian Pectoral Sandpiper)

Calidris acuminata
(Horsfield, 1821)

Identification Plate 15. 21 cm. A medium-sized rufous-grey wader, with pale underparts. Upperparts streaked or scalloped and the breast mottled grey or buff. The pointed tail is dark with white sides. Breeding birds have heavily spotted underparts and more rufous upperparts. Bill black and slightly down-curved, legs yellowish.

Voice Recorded as a rather silent species. A sharp "whit-whit" and soft "pleeps" have been recorded.

Habitat and Range Tidal mudflats and sandbanks. Breeds in Siberia and sometimes migrates to Australasia and the West Pacific. Only once recorded in the region, from Fiji. The Sharp-tailed Sandpiper closely resembles the Pectoral Sandpiper *C. melanotos,* but the latter has a more densely spotted and streaked breast, contrasting strongly with the white belly and abdomen. Its distinctive call—a sharp "kreek"—is a diagnostic character.

127. KNOT
(Eastern Red Knot)

Calidris canutus
(Linnaeus, 1758)

Identification Plate 15. 25 cm. A rather featureless medium-sized wader, stocky with a short black bill. Non-breeding plumage is grey with dark mottling above, paler below with white belly. Breeding birds have rich rufous underparts. Legs greenish.

Flight In flight an indistinct pale grey rump and narrow white wing bar are noticeable.

Voice Described as a throaty "knut-knut" or a double whistle.

Habitat and Range	Tidal mudflats, sandbanks and occasionally inland. Non-breeding birds disperse through South-east Asia and Australasia. Probably a regular migrant passing through the region in small numbers, although a flock of about twenty birds has been reported.
Remarks and Allied Species	As yet the Great Knot *C. tenuirostris,* has not been recorded in the region. It is a larger bird (29 cm) with dark, more mottled upperparts, a longer bill and whiter rump and wing bar. In breeding plumage the underparts are not rufous but heavily spotted.

128.   AUSTRALIAN PELICAN

Pelecanus conspicillatus
Temminck, 1824

Identification	(Not illustrated.) 150 cm. Wingspan 250 cm. An unmistakable waterbird with a long bill and large throat pouch. A predominantly white pelican, with black flight feathers, a broad black "V" on the rump and a black tail. The nape bears a short greyish crest. The bare ring around the eye, throat pouch and bill are flesh coloured, the bill sometimes having bluish sides. The legs and feet are slate-blue. Young birds are similar to adults but the black plumage is replaced by brown.
Flight	Pelicans fly with their head retracted and with deep, heavy wingbeats interspersed with long glides. They often soar to great heights.
Voice	Low pitched "pep-pep-purr" and a high pitched "peep-pee-pee" have been recorded in Australia.
Food	Pelicans feed on fish, caught by plunging their head down whilst paddling on the surface. The Australian Pelican has occasionally been recorded as diving for fish whilst flying.
Breeding	The Australian Pelican is a colonial nester in bushes over water or on isolated islands, either on inland lagoons or in coastal areas.
Habitat and Range	The Australian Pelican may be found either in shallow marine habitats or on inland waters. It is resident in Australia and Tasmania but is a vagrant as far afield as Indonesia, New Guinea, New Zealand and it was recently recorded for the first time in Fiji.

The Australian Pelican is a rare vagrant which was recently recorded in the region for the first time.

PART FIVE
Appendices

GLOSSARY

Aberrant. Divergent, exceptional.

Anecdote. Story containing some factual information, not scientifically reported.

Aquatic. Associated with water.

Avifauna. Birds.

Binomial. Consisting of the generic and specific names, (for example — *Butorides striatus*).

Carpal. The wrist joint.

Cere. A soft, swollen area on the maxilla (cf). The nostrils are placed within or at the edge of this structure. Found commonly in the hawks, parrots and owls.

Clutch. The number of eggs laid by a female during one breeding attempt

Commensal. Living in close association with, but not parasitic upon, another animal or organism.

Cosmopolitan. Found in most parts of the world.

Cryptic. Adapted for concealment.

Diagnostic. Features which are important for identification of a particular bird.

Diminuendo. Gradual decrease of sound.

Dimorphic. Having two distinct forms of the same species.

Echolocation. The ability to navigate by emitting high-frequency sounds and then picking up their echo from surrounding objects.

Ecology. The study of living things, in relation to their surroundings.

Endemic. Indigenous; naturally occurring with a restricted distribution. Not introduced or found elsewhere.

Estuary. The area subject to tidal influence at the mouth of a river.

Evolution. The process by which new forms or species develop.

Fiji region. Term introduced for convenience in this book. With the exception of Tuvalu, the Union and Phoenix Islands, it is identical to the Central Polynesian District of the Polynesian Subregion which is a zoogeographical region distinguished by zoologists. The Fiji region consists of the Fiji, Samoa and Tonga archipelagos, Niue, Uvea, Futuna, Alofi and Rotuma.

Frugivore, (Frugivorous). Fruit-eating.

Gape. The mouth opening, (specifically the angle formed by the borders of the jaw).

Graminivorous. Grain-eating.

Hybrid. The progeny of unlike parents.

Indigenous. A native of, or belonging naturally to, an island or area.

Insectivore, (Insectivorous). Insect-eating.

Iridescent. Shiny colouring which may change depending on the angle from which it is viewed.

Lores. The area between eyes and the bill.

Maxilla. Upper mandible of the beak.

Melanistic. A dark form, owing to increased amounts of black pigment.

Migrant. A bird which travels regularly (usually seasonally) from one place to another.

Montane. Higher elevations and the tops of mountains.

Moult. Renewal of plumage, by dropping the old feathers and growing new ones.

Niche. All facets of the environment to which a species is adapted.

Nomadic. Wandering.

Ochraceous. A yellowish-brown.

Olivaceous. A dull green, brownish or grey green.

Omnivorous. Having a varied diet and not confining it to one class of food.

Papillae. Small projections on the tongue.

Pelagic. Of the open sea.

Phase. A specific form or morph.

Precocious. Advanced development for its age.

Raptor. A bird of prey.

Raucous. Harsh, hoarse or rough sounds.

Resident. Remains throughout the year in one area.

Rictal. Of the gape.

Rufous. Reddish-brown.

Seaboard. At the edge of the sea — reefs, mudflats, beaches etc.

Sedentary. Remains in one area, non-migratory.

Silhouette. The outline against a light background.

Skin. A term used when referring to a stuffed bird, generally prepared for study purposes.

Speculum. A metallic or brightly coloured wing patch which contrasts with surrounding wing colouration. Found mainly on ducks.

Subspecies. A local population of a species, which inhabits a part of the range of the species. It differs taxonomically from other populations of the same species.

Substage. A level within a forest; it extends from the ground level to middle height.

Suffusion. Spread lightly or indistinctly.

Taxonomy. The theory and practice of classifying organisms.

Terrestrial. Living on land.

Trinomial. Consisting of the subspecific name in addition to the generic and specific names (for example — *Butorides striatus diminutus*, cf. binomial).

Ubiquitous. Present everywhere.

Undulate. Rising and falling.

Vagrant. A wanderer.

Ventriloquism. Sounds whose source is either difficult to locate or appears to come from an erroneous direction.

Vermiculated. With fine "worm-like" markings.

Vernacular. (names) specific to a country or region.

Vertebrate. Any animal with a backbone.

Vinaceous. A reddish-pink.

Wattle. A naked, fleshy (usually wrinkled and highly coloured) flap or area of skin on the head.

Wing bars. A strip(s) of different colour seen on the extended wing.

Zoogeography. The distribution of animals.

Terminology of the Parts of a Bird

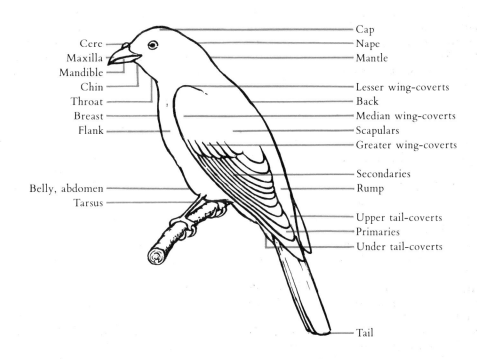

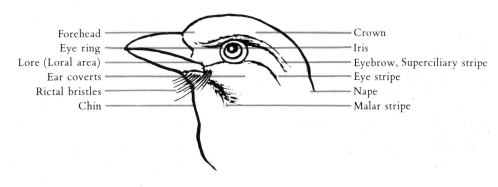

BIBLIOGRAPHY

1. Amadon, D. 1942a. Birds collected during the Whitney South Sea Expedition, 1L. Notes on some non-passerine genera, 1. *Am. Mus. Novit.* 1175: 1-11.

2. Amadon, D. 1942b. Birds collected during the Whitney South Sea Expedition, L. Notes on some non-passerine genera, 2. *Am. Mus. Novit.* 1176: 1-21.

3. Amadon, D. 1943. Birds collected during the Whitney South Sea Expedition, LII. Notes on some non-passerine genera, 3. *Am. Mus. Novit.* 1237: 1-22.

4. Anon. 1876. Kleine Muttheilungen aus dem Museum Godeffroy. VII Erneute Exploration der Viti-Inseln. *J. Mus. Godeffroy* 5(12):162-175.

5. Anon. 1940. List of Fijian birds. *Trans. Fiji Soc.* 2(1): 39-45.

6. Armstrong, J. S. 1932. *Hand-list to the Birds of Samoa.* John Bale, Sons and Danielson Ltd, London. 91 pp.

7. Ashmole, M. J. 1963. *Guide to the Birds of Samoa.* Pacific Scientific Information Centre, Bernice P. Bishop Museum, Honolulu, Hawaii. 21 pp (cyclostyled).

8. Bahr, P. H. 1911-1912. Notes on some Fijian birds in captivity. *Avicult. Mag.*, 3rd Ser., Vol. III(2): 49-56.

9. Bahr, P. H. 1912. On a journey to the Fiji islands, with notes on the present status of their avifauna. *Ibis* 1912: 283-314.

10. Baker, J. R., Marshall, A. J. and Harrisson, T. H. 1940. The seasons in a tropical rainforest (New Hebrides). Part 5. Birds (*Pachycephala*). *J. Proc. Linn. Soc. Lond. Zool.* 41: 50-70.

11. Baker, R. H. 1951. The avifauna of Micronesia, its origin, evolution and distribution. *Univ. Kansas Publ. Mus. Nat. Hist.* 3: 1-359.

12. Ball, S. C. 1933. Jungle fowls from Pacific islands. *Bull. Bernice P. Bishop Mus.* 108: 1-121.

13. Beaglehole, J. C. 1965-74. *The Journals of Captain James Cook on his voyage of discovery.* 4 vols. and charts. Hakluyt Soc., London.

14. Beckon, B. and R. 1978. Fiji Scarlet Robin eating worms on the ground. (Short note.) *Notornis* 25: 154-156.

15. Belcher, W. J. 1929. Fragmentary notes on bird life in the Fiji's. *Condor* 31: 19-20.

16. Belcher, W. J. and Sibson, R. B. 1972. *Birds of Fiji in Colour.* Collins.

17. Bennett, G. 1862. Letter addressed to the Secretary. *Proc. Zool. Soc. Lond.* 1862: 247.

18. Bennett, G. 1864. Notes on the *Didunculus strigirostris* or tooth-billed pigeon. *Proc. Zool. Soc. Lond.* 1864: 139-143.

19. Berlioz, J. 1929. Les Caractères de la Faune Avienne de Polynésie. *Rev. d'Hist. Nat.* X(9-10): 1-19.

20. Blackburn, A. 1971. Some notes on Fijian birds. *Notornis* 18(3): 147-174.

21. Blackman, T. M. 1944. *Birds of the Central Pacific Ocean.* Tongg Publ. Co., Honolulu. 70 pp.

22. Bogert, C. 1937. Birds collected during the Whitney South Sea Expedition XXXIV. The distribution and the migration of the long-tailed cuckoo (*Urodynamis taitensis,* Sparrmann). *Am. Mus. Novit.* 933: 1-12.

23. Bregulla, H. 1976. *Birds of the New Hebrides.* New Hebrides Cult. Centre, Vila.

24. Brewster, A. B. *Document 24, Fiji Museum Coll.*

25. Brown, B. and Child, P. 1975. Notes on a field trip to Fiji. *Notornis* 22(1): 10-22.

26. Burton, P. J. K. 1974. Jaw and tongue features in Psittaciformes and other orders, with special reference to the anatomy of the tooth-billed pigeon (*Didunculus strigirostris*). *Proc. Zool. Soc. Lond.* 174: 255-276.

27. Cain, A. J. 1954a. Subdivisions of the genus *Ptilinopus* (Aves, Columbae). *Bull. Br. Mus. Nat. Hist. Zool.* 2: 267-284.

28. Cain, A. J. 1954b. Affinities of the fruit pigeon *Ptilinopus perousii,* Peale. *Ibis* 96: 104-110.

29. Cain, A. J. and Galbraith, I. C. 1956. Field notes on birds of the eastern Solomon Islands. *Ibis* 98: 100-134; 262-295.

30. Capell, A. 1973. *A new Fijian Dictionary* (4th Edition) Govt. Printer, Suva, Fiji.

31. Carlson, E. 1974. *Avifauna of Tonga.* Unpubl. mss.

32. Carrick, R. and Walker, C. 1958. Report on the European Starling *Sturnus vulgaris* at Ono-i-Lau. *Trans. Fiji Soc.* 1951-54, 5, No. 3: 51-58.

33. Cassin, J. 1858. *United States Exploring Expedition during the years 1838-42, under the command of Charles Wilkes USN.* Atlas, Mammalogy, Ornithology. C. Sherman, Philadelphia (53 pl.).

34. Cassin, J. *United States Exploring Expedition during the years 1838-42, under the command of Charles Wilkes USN.* Vol. VIIIB, Mammalogy, Ornithology. C. Sherman, Philadelphia. 466 pp.

35. Cheshire, N. 1974. Sighting of Buller's Shearwaters in Fijian and Tongan waters. *Notornis* 21, 2: 182.

36. Cheshire, N., Jenkins, J. and Nesfield, P. 1979. Distribution of the Cape Pigeon in the Tasman Sea and South-west Pacific. *Notornis* 26: 37-46.

37. Child, P. 1979. Some bird observations from Western Samoa. *Notornis* 26: 171-179.

38. Clapp, R. C. and Sibley, F. C. 1966. Notes on the birds of Tutuila, American Samoa. *Notornis* 13: 157-164.

39. Clunie, F. 1972a. *Fijian Birds of Prey.* Fiji Times & Herald, Suva. pp 14.

40. Clunie, F. 1972b. A contribution to the natural history of the Fiji Peregrine. *Notornis* 19(4): 302-321.

41. Clunie, F. 1972c. Short notes on Fijian birds. *Notornis* 19(4): 335-336.

42. Clunie, F. 1973a. Fan-tailed Cuckoo parasitises Fiji Warbler. *Notornis* 20: 168.

43. Clunie, F. 1973b. Pink-billed Parrotfinches near Nailagosakelo Creek, Southern Viti Levu. *Notornis* 20: 202-209.

44. Clunie, F. 1973c. Nest helpers at a White-breasted Woodswallow nest. *Notornis* 20: 378-380.

45. Clunie, F. 1974. A Fiji Black-faced Shrikebill anting with a millipede. *Notornis* 21: 80-81.

46. Clunie, F. 1976a. A Fiji Peregrine (*Falco peregrinus*) in an urban-marine environment. *Notornis* 23: 8-28.

47. Clunie, F. 1976b. The behaviour and nesting of Fiji White-breasted Woodswallows. *Notornis* 23: 61-75.

48. Clunie, F. 1976c. Jungle Mynah anting with a millipede. *Notornis* 23: 77.

49. Clunie, F. 1976d. Long-tailed Fruit Bats as Peregrine prey. *Notornis* 23: 245.

50. Clunie, F. 1978. Fiji White-throated Pigeon nesting in an epiphyte fern. (Short note.) *Notornis* 25: 217.

51. Clunie, F. 1979. Australian Pelicans in Fiji. (Short note.) *Notornis* 26: 22.

52. Clunie, F. 1979. Red-headed Parrotfinch copulation. (Short note.) *Notornis* 26: 62.

53. Clunie, F. 1980. Two more Giant Petrel records from Fiji. (Short note.) *Notornis* 27: 95.

54. Clunie, F. and Perks, I. 1972. Notes on the Pink-billed Parrotfinch of Fiji. *Notornis* 19: 335-336.

55. Clunie, F., Kinsky, F. C. and Jenkins, J. A. 1978. New bird records from the Fiji Archipelago. *Notornis:* 25: 118-127.

56. Cottrell, G. W. 1967. A problem species: *Lamprolia victoriae. Emu* 66: 253-266.

57. Davidson, M. E. M. 1931. On the breeding of *Puffinus chlororhynchus* in the Tonga Group. *Condor* 32: 217-218.

58. Dhondt, A. 1976a. Bird notes from the Kingdom of Tonga. *Notornis* 23(1): 4-7.

59. Dhondt, A. 1976b. Bird observations in Western Samoa. *Notornis* 23(1): 29-43.

60. Dhondt, A. 1977. Notes on the breeding and postnuptial moult of the Red-vented Bulbul *Pycnonotus cafer bengalensis* in Western Samoa. *Condor.* 79: 257-260.

61. Diamond, J. M. 1972. Further examples of dual singing by southwest pacific birds. *Auk* 89: 180-183.

62. Diamond, J. M. and Marshall, A. G. 1976. Origin of the New Hebridean Avifauna. *Emu* 76: 187-200.

63. Diamond, J. M. 1977. Niche shifts in New Hebridean birds. *Emu* 77: 61-72.

64. Dorst, J. 1950. Considerations biogéographiques sur l'avifaune des îles Fidji. *C. R. Som. Séances Soc. Biogéogr.* 236: 120-125.

65. du Pont, J. E. 1972. Notes from Western Samoa, including the description of a new parrotfinch (*Erythrura*). *Wilson Bull.* 84: 375-376.

66. du Pont, J. E. 1976. *South Pacific Birds.* Del. Mus. Nat. Hist., Monograph No. 3. pp 218.

67. Dunmire, W. W. 1960. Some 1960 bird observations in Samoa and Fiji. *Elepaio* 20: 76-78.

68. Field, L. B. 1938. Mynah Birds. *Fiji Agric. J.* 9(2): 19-22.

69. Finsch, O. 1872. Ornithology of the Samoan Islands, *J. fur. Orn.* 1872: 30-58.

70. Finsch, O. 1873. On *Lamprolia victoriae,* a most remarkable new Passerine Bird from the Feejee Islands. *Proc. Zool. Soc. Lond.* 1873: 733-735.

71. Finsch, O. 1875. Notes on the Fruit Pigeons of the Genus *Chrysoena. Proc. Zool. Soc. Lond.* 1875: 557.

72. Finsch, O. 1876a. Notes on some Fijian birds, including description of a new genus and species *Drymochaera badiceps. Proc. Zool. Soc. Lond.* 1876: 19-20.

73. Finsch, O. 1876b. Zur Ornithologie der Südsee-Inseln. Ueber neue und weniger gekannte Vögel von den Viti, Samoa und Carolinen-Inseln. *Jour. Mus. Godeffroy* 12: 1-42.

74. Finsch, O. 1877a. On a new species of Petrel from the Feejee Islands. *Proc. Zool. Soc. Lond.* 1877: 722.

75. Finsch, O. 1877b. Reports on the collection of birds made during the voyage of HMS *Challenger.* No. IV. On the birds of Tongatabu, the Fiji Islands, Api (New Hebrides), and Tahiti. *Proc. Zool. Soc. Lond.* 1877: 723-742.

76. Finsch, O. 1877c. On a collection of birds from Eua, Friendly Islands. *Proc. Zool. Soc. Lond.* 1877: 770-777.

77. Finsch, O. 1877d. On a collection of birds from Niuafou Island, in the Pacific. *Proc. Zool. Soc. Lond.* 1877: 782-787.

78. Finsch, O. 1878. On a new species of finch from the Fiji Islands; *Amblynura kleinschmidti. Proc. Zool. Soc. Lond.* 1878: 440.

79. Finsch, O. 1881. On the birds collected in Tongatabu, Fiji, New Hebrides, Tahiti. In *Challenger Exped. Zool.,* Vol. 2, pt. 2C, pp 34-58.

80. Finsch, O. and Hartlaub, G. 1867. *Ornithologie der Viti, Samoa und Tonga Inseln.* pp 1-290.

81. Finsch, O. and Hartlaub, G. 1869. On a small collection of birds from the Tonga Islands. *Proc. Zool. Soc. Lond.* 1869: 544-547.

82. Finsch, O. and Hartlaub, G. 1870. Ornithologie der Tonga Inseln. *J. f. Orn.* 18: 119-140.

83. Forbes, W. 1878. On a small collection from the Samoan Islands and the Island of Rotumah, Central Pacific. *Proc. Zool. Soc. Lond.* 1878: 351.

84. Friedländer, B. 1899. Uber die Nestlöcher des *Megapodius pritchardii* auf der Insel Niaufou. *Orn Monatsb.* 7: 37.

85. Fry, F. X. 1966. Birds observed on various Polynesian Islands aboard the research ship *Te Vega. Elepaio* 27: 3-5, 16-19.

86. Gadow, H. 1898. List of the birds of the Island of Rotumah. *Ibis* 1898: 42-46.

87. Galbraith, I. J. 1956. Variation, relationships and evolution in the *Pachycephala pectoralis* super-species (Aves: Muscicapidae). *Bull. Brit. Mus. Nat. Hist. Zool.* 4: 131-222.

88. Goodman, R. A. 1969. "Manu Papalagi" of Western Samoa. *Elepaio* 30: 9.

89. Goodwin, D. 1960. Taxonomy of the genus *Ducula. Ibis* 102: 526-535.

90. Goodwin, D. 1970. *Pigeons and Doves of the World.* BMNH, London.

91. Gorman, M. 1972. Origin of the avifauna of urban and suburban Suva, Fiji. *Fiji Agric. J.* 34: 35-38.

92. Gorman, M. 1975. Habitats of the land-birds of Viti Levu, Fiji Islands. *Ibis* 117: 152-161.

93. Gorman, M. 1979. The avifauna of the exotic pinewoods of Viti Levu, Fiji Islands. *Bull. B.O.C.* 99: 9-12.

94. Gould, J. 1871. Description of a new species of Fruit Pigeon from the Fiji Islands. *Proc. Zool. Soc. Lond.* 1871: 642-643.

95. Gräffe, E. 1870. Die Vogelwelt der Tonga Inseln. *J. f. Orn.* 18: 401-420.

96. Gray, G. R. 1859. Catalogue of the birds of the tropical islands of the Pacific Ocean in the collection of the British Museum.

97. Gray, G. R. 1864. On a new species of megapode. *Proc. Zool. Soc. Lond.* 1864: 41.

98. Green, R. H. 1965. Bird observations in Western Samoa. *Elepaio* 26: 19-21.

99. Hartlaub, G. 1854. Zur Ornithologie Oceanie. *J. f. Orn.* 2: 160-171.

100. Hartlaub, G. 1864. Provisional list of a collection of birds in the Feejee Islands. *Ibis* 1864: 232.

101. Hartlaub, G. 1866. On five new species of birds from the Feejee Islands. *Ibis* 1866: 171.

102. Hartlaub, G. 1879. On a new species of Barn Owl from the Island of Viti-Levu. *Proc. Zool. Soc. Lond.* 1879: 295.

103. Hartlaub G. & Finsch, O. 1871. On a collection of birds from Savai'i and Rarotonga islands in the Pacific. *Proc. Zool. Soc. Lond.* 1871: 21-32.

104. Heather, B. 1977. The Vanua Levu Silktail *Lamprolia victoriae kleinschmidti.* A preliminary look at its status and habits. *Notornis* 24: 94-128.

105. Hill, W. R. 1959. Occurrences of the European Starling in Fiji. *Trans. Fiji Soc.* 1951-54 5(1): 26-28.

106. Hinckley, A. D. 1962. Ecological notes on common birds in Fiji. *Elepaio* 23: 18-20; 24-27.

107. Holyoak, D. T. 1979. Notes on the birds of Viti Levu and Taveuni, Fiji. *Emu* 79: 7-18.

108. Holyoak, D. T. and Thibault J. C. 1978. Notes on the phylogeny, distribution and ecology of frugivorous pigeons in Polynesia. *Emu* 78: 201-206.

109. Jenkins, J. A. 1973. Seabird observations around the Kingdom of Tonga. *Notornis* 20: 113-119.

110. Jenkins, J. A. 1979. Observations on the Wedge-tailed Shearwater in the South-west Pacific. *Notornis* 26: 331-348.

111. Jenkins, J. A. 1980. Giant Petrel in Fijian waters. (Short note.) *Notornis* 27: 95.

112. Kaigler, C. G. 1973. Birding in Samoa. Elepaio 33: 96-98.

113. Keith, A. R. 1957. Bird observations in Fiji and Samoa, as furnished to E. H. Bryan, Jr. by A. R. Keith. *Elepaio* 18: 25-27.

114. King, W. B. 1967. *Seabirds of the Tropical Pacific Ocean.* Washington DC. Preliminary Smithsonian Identification Manual. 126 pp. illus. Smithsonian Institute, Washington DC.

115. Kinsky, F. C. 1975. A new subspecies of the Long-legged Warbler *Trichocichla rufa* Reichenow, from Vanua Levu, Fiji. *Bull. Brit. Orn. Club* 95(3): 98-101.

116. Koopman, K. 1957. Evolution in the genus *Myzomela* (Aves: Meliphagidae). *Auk* 74: 49-72.

117. Layard, E. L. 1875a. Description of a new species of *Trichoglossus* from Fiji. *Ann. Mag. Nat. Hist.* 1875, 16: 344.

118. Layard, E. L. 1875b. Ornithological Notes from Fiji, with descriptions of supposed new species of birds. *Proc. Zool. Soc. Lond.* 1875: 27-30; 149-151; 423-442.

119. Layard, E. L. 1875c. Description of a new Flycatcher belonging to the Genus *Myiagra* and notes on some other Fijian birds, *Ibis* 1875: 436-447.

120. Layard, E. L. 1876a. Description of a new Thrush, from Taveuni, one of the Fiji Islands. *Proc. Zool. Soc. Lond.* 1876: 420.

121. Layard, E. L. 1876b. Notes on the birds of the Navigators and Friendly Islands, with some additional ornithology of Fiji. *Proc. Zool. Soc. Lond.* 1876: 490-506.

122. Layard, E. L. 1876c. Notes on some little-known birds of the new Colony of the Fiji Islands. *Ibis* 1876: 137-157.

123. Layard, E. L. 1876d. Description of a new species of Flycatcher (*Myiagra*) from the Fijis, and some remarks on the distribution of the birds found in the islands. *Ibis* 1876: 387-394.

124. Layard, E. L. 1878. Letter to the editor. *Ibis* (4) 2: 198-199.

125. Layard, E. L. 1881. Letter to the editor of the Ibis. *Ibis* 1881: 170.

126. Legge, W. V. 1904. The zoogeographical observations of the Ornis of the various sub-regions of the "Australian region" with the geographical distribution of the principal genera therein. *Rep. Aust. Ass. Adv. Sci.* X: 217-285.

127. Lovegrove, T. G. 1978. Seabird observations between New Zealand and Fiji. *Notornis* 25: 291-298.

128. Lowe, 1924-25. Note on *Puffinus pacificus whitneyi. Bull. Brit. Orn. Club.* 45: 106.

129. Lysaght, A. M. 1953. A rail from Tonga, *Rallus phillipensis ecaudata.* Miller, 1783. *Bull. Brit. Orn. Club* 73: 74-75.

130. Lysaght, A. M. 1956. A note on the Polynesian black or sooty rail. *Bull. Brit. Orn. Club* 76: 97-98.

131. McHugh, L. J. 1950. Fiji birds (Introductory Notes). *Trans. Fiji Soc.* 4(3): 68-69.

132. Martin, A. H. 1938. The birds of Fiji. *Trans. Fiji Soc. Sci. & Ind.* 1: 4-7.

133. Mason Mitchell. 1909. *Birds of Samoa.* Malua.

134. Mathews, G. M. 1927. *Systema Avium Australasianarum,* part I, pp 1-426.

135. Mathews, G. M. 1930. *Systema Avium Australasianarum,* part II, pp 427-1048.

136. Mathews, G. M. 1936. A note on the black Fiji petrel. *Ibis.* VI, 1936: 309.

137. Mayr, E. 1931a. Birds collected during the Whitney South Sea Expedition, XII. Notes on *Halcyon chloris* and some of its subspecies. *Am. Mus. Novit.* 469: 1-10.

138. Mayr, E. 1931b. Birds collected during the Whitney South Sea Expedition, XV. The parrot-finches (genus *Erythrura). Am. Mus. Novit.* 489: 1-10.

139. Mayr, E. 1931c. Birds collected during the Whitney South Sea Expedition, XVI. Notes on fantails of the genus *Rhipidura. Am. Mus. Novit.* 502: 1-21.

140. Mayr, E. 1932a. Birds collected during the Whitney South Sea Expedition, XVIII. Notes on *Meliphagidae* from Polynesia and the Solomon Islands. *Am. Mus. Novit.* 516: 1-30.

141. Mayr, E. 1932b. Birds collected during the Whitney South Sea Expedition, XXI. Notes on thickheads (*Pachycephala*) from Polynesia. *Am. Mus. Novit.* 531: 1-23.

142. Mayr, E. 1933a. Birds collected during the Whitney South Sea Expedition, XXIV. Notes on Polynesian flycatchers and a revision of the genus *Clytorhynchus* Elliot. *Am. Mus. Novit.* 628: 1-21.

143. Mayr, E. 1933b. Birds collected during the Whitney South Sea Expedition, XXV. Notes on the genera *Myiagra* and *Mayrornis. Am. Mus. Novit.* 651: 1-20.

144. Mayr, E. 1934a. Birds collected during the Whitney South Sea Expedition, XXVIII. Notes on some birds from New Britain, Bismark Archipelago. *Am. Mus. Novit.* 709: 1-15.

145. Mayr, E. 1934b. Birds collected during the Whitney South Sea Expedition, XXIX. Notes on the genus *Petroica. Am. Mus. Novit.* 714: 1-19.

146. Mayr, E. 1935. Birds collected during the Whitney South Sea Expedition, XXX. Descriptions of twenty-five new species and subspecies. *Ams. Mus. Novit.* 820: 1-6.

147. Mayr, E. 1936. Birds collected during the Whitney South Sea Expedition, XXXI. Descriptions of twenty-five new species and subspecies. *Am. Mus. Novit.* 828: 1-19.

148. Mayr, E. 1941a. Borders and subdivision of the Polynesian region as based on our knowledge of the distribution of birds. *Proc. VIth Pac. Sci. Congr.* IV: 191-195.

149. Mayr, E. 1941b. The origin and the history of the bird fauna of Polynesia. *Proc. VIth Pac. Sci. Congr.* IV: 197-216.

150. Mayr, E. 1941c. Birds collected during the Whitney South Sea Expedition, XLVII. Notes on the genera *Halcyon, Turdus,* and *Eurostopodus. Am. Mus. Novit.* 1152: 1-7.

151. Mayr, E. 1942. Birds collected during the Whitney South Sea Expedition, XLVIII. Notes on the Polynesian species of *Aplonis. Am. Mus. Novit.* 1166: 1-6.

152. Mayr, E. 1944. Birds collected during the Whitney South Sea Expedition, LIV. Notes on some genera from the South-west Pacific. *Am. Mus. Novit.* 1269: 1-8.

153. Mayr, E. 1945. *Birds of the Southwest Pacific.* Macmillan, New York. 316 pp.

154. Mayr, E. 1945. Bird conservation problems in the Southwest Pacific. *Audubon Mag.* 47: 29-282.

155. Mayr, E. 1949. Artbildung und Variation in der *Halcyon-chloris*-Gruppe. In E. Mayr and E. Schüz (eds.), *Ornithologie als biologische Wissenschaft,* pp 55-60. Universitätsverlag, Heidelberg.

156. Mayr, E. and Ripley, D. 1941. Birds collected during the Whitney South Sea Expedition, XLIV. Notes on the genus *Lalage* Boie. *Am. Mus. Novit.* 1116: 1-18.

157. Mees, G. F. 1969. A systematic review of the Indo-Australian Zosteropidae (Part III). *Zool. Verh. Leiden.* (102).

158. Mees, G. F. 1977. Enige gegevens over de Uitgestorven Ral *Pareudiastes pacificus.* Hartlaub & Finsch. *Zool. Meded. Leiden.* 50: 230-242.

159. Mercer, R. 1964. Shore birds of Fiji and their migration habits. *Trans. Fiji Soc.* 10: 35-38.

160. Mercer, R. 1966. *A Field Guide to Fiji Birds.* Fiji Museum Special Publications No. 1. Government Press, Suva. 40 pp.

161. Miles, J. A. 1964. Notes on the status of certain birds in Fiji. *Emu* 63(5): 422.

162. Morgan, B. and Morgan, J. 1965. Some notes on birds of the Fiji Islands. *Notornis* 12(3): 158-168.

163. Murphy, R. C. 1924a. Birds collected during the Whitney South Sea Expedition, I. *Am. Mus. Novit.* 115: 1-11.

164. Murphy, R. C. 1924b. Birds collected during the Whitney South Sea Expedition, II. *Am. Mus. Novit.* 124: 1-13.

165. Murphy, R. C. 1924c. Birds collected during the Whitney South Sea Expedition, III. *Am. Mus. Novit.* 149: 1-2.

166. Murphy, R. C. 1928. Birds collected during the Whitney South Sea Expedition, IV. *Am. Mus. Novit.* 322: 1-5.

167. Murphy, R. C. 1929. Birds collected during the Whitney South Sea Expedition, X. *Am. Mus. Novit.* 370: 1-17.

168. Murphy, R. C. 1936. *Oceanic Birds of South America.*

169. Murphy, R. C. 1951. The populations of the wedge-tailed shearwater *Puffinus pacificus*. *Am. Mus. Novit.* 1512: 1-21.

170. Murphy, R. C. and Mathews, G. M. 1928. Birds collected during the Whitney South Sea Expedition, V. *Am. Mus. Novit.* 337: 1-18.

171. Murphy, R. C. and Mathews, G. M. 1929a. Birds collected during the Whitney South Sea Expedition, VI. *Am. Mus. Novit.* 350: 1-21.

172. Murphy, R. C. and Mathews G. M. 1929b. Birds collected during the Whitney South Sea Expedition, VII. *Am. Mus. Novit.* 356: 1-14.

173. Nehrkorn, A. 1879. Mittheilungen über Nester Eier des Museums Godeffroy zu Hamburg. *J. f. Orn.* 27: 393-410.

174. Newman, T. H. 1910. Nesting of the White-throated Pigeon. *Avicult. Mag.*, 3rd Ser., Vol. 1: 158-164; 193-195.

175. Newman, T. H. 1912. The White-throated Pigeon. *Avicult. Mag.*, 3rd Ser., Vol. IV: 110-115.

176. Nicoll, M. J. 1904. Ornithological Journal of a voyage round the world in the *Valhalla*. *Ibis* 1904, Vol. IV, 8th Series: 62.

177. Oates, E. W. and Reis, S. G. 1905. *Catalogue of the collection of birds eggs in the British Museum (Natural History)*, 4. Brit, Mus. Nat. Hist., London.

178. Olson, S. L. 1973. A classification of the Rallidae. *Wilson Bull.* 85: 381-416.

179. Olson, S. L. 1974. The South Pacific gallinules of the genus *Pareudiastes. Wilson Bull.* 87: 1-5.

180. Olsen, S. L. 1980. *Lamprolia* as part of a South Pacific radiation of Monarchine flycatchers. *Notornis* 27: 7-10.

181. Orenstein, R. I. and Bruce, M. D. 1976. Comments on the nesting and plumage of the Orange Dove *Ptilinopus victor. Bull. Brit. Orn. Club* 96: 2-4.

182. Orenstein, R. I. 1979. Notes on the Ma'o *Gymnomyza samoensis* a rare samoan honeyeater. *Notornis* 26: 181-184.

183. Parham, B. E. 1955. Birds as pests in Fiji. *Agric. J. of Fiji* 25: 9-14.

184. Parker, S. 1967. Some eggs from the New Hebrides, South-west Pacific. *Bull. Brit. Orn. Club* 87: 90-91.

185. Peale, T. R. 1848. *United States Exploring Expedition during the years 1838-1842, under the command of Charles Wilkes USN.* Vol. VIIIA, Mammalia & Ornithology. C. Sherman, Philadelphia. 338 pp.

186. Pernetta, J. C. & Watling, D. 1978. The Introduced and Native Terrestrial Vertebrates of Fiji. *Pacific Sci.* 32: 223-244.

187. Porter, S. 1935. Notes on the birds of Fiji. *Avicult. Mag.* 13: 90-104; 126-139; 164-171.

188. Ramsay, E. P. 1864. On the *Didunculus strigirostris* or tooth-billed pigeon from Upolo. *Ibis* 1864: 98-100.

189. Ramsay, E. P. 1875-76a. Characters of a new genus and species of Passerine Bird from the Fiji Islands, proposed to be called *Vitia. Proc. Linn, Soc., NSW.* 1: 41-42.

190. Ramsay, E. P. 1875-76b. Description of a new species of Blackbird (*Merula*) and Flycatcher (*Rhypidura*). *Proc. Linn. Soc., NSW.* 1: 43-44.

191. Ramsay, E. P. 1875-76c. Description of a new species of *Pachycephala* from Fiji, in the collection of William Macleay Esq. FLS. *Proc. Linn. Soc., NSW.* 1: 65-66.

192. Ramsay, E. P. 1875-76d. Remarks on a collection of birds lately received from Fiji, with a list of all species at present known to inhabit the Fiji Islands. *Proc. Linn. Soc., NSW.* 1: 69-80.

193. Ramsay, E. P. 1875-76e. Description of a new species of the genus *Lamprolia* Finsch, from Fiji; *Lamprolia klinesmithi*, sp. nov. *Proc. Linn. Soc., NSW.* 1: 68-69.

194. Ramsay, E. P. 1878. Notes on some birds from Savage Island, Tutuila, etc. in the collection of the Rev. Mr Whitmee, FRGS etc. *Proc. Linn. Soc., NSW.* 2: 139.

195. Ramsay, E. P. 1883. Description of the eggs of five species of Fijian birds. *Ibis* 1883: 108.

196. Reichenow, A. 1890. Vorlänfiges über eine neue Gattung und Art von den Fidschi-Inseln. *J. f. Orn.* 38: 489.

197. Reichenow, A. 1891. Uber eine Vogelsammlung von den Fidschi-Inseln. *J. f. Orn.* 39: 126-130.

198. Ripley, D. and Birckhead, H. 1942. Birds collected during the Whitney South Sea Expedition, LI. On the fruit pigeons of the *Ptilinopus purpuratus* group. *Am. Mus. Novit.* 1192: 1-14.

199. Rowley, G. D. 1876-78. On the birds of the Fiji Islands. In G. D. Rowley (ed.), *Ornithological Miscellany*, 3 vols. Trübner, London. Vol. I, pp 259-262; Vol. II, pp 23-39, 393-396.

200. Sachet, M. H. 1954. A summary of information on Rose Atoll. *Atoll Res. Bul.* 29: 1-25.

201. Salvadori, T. 1877. Notes on two birds from the Fiji Islands. *Ibis* 1877: 142.

202. Salvin, O. 1879. On some birds transmitted from the Samoan Islands by the Rev. T. Powell. *Proc. Zool. Soc. London.* 1979. 128.

203. Sclater, P. L. 1876. Exhibition of, and remarks upon, a series of skins of the Parrots of the Fiji Islands, obtained by Mr E. L. Layard. *Proc. Zool. Soc. Lond.* 1876: 307-308.

204. Sclater, P. L. 1880. On the birds collected in Tongatabu, the Fiji Islands, Api (New Hebrides), and Tahiti. By Dr O. Finsch. CMZS…with notes and additions by P. L. Sclater, FRS. *Challenger Exped. Zool.* 8: 34-58.

205. Seebohm, H. 1891. On the Fijian species of the genus *Pachycephala. Ibis* 1891: 93-99.

206. Shorthouse, J. F. 1967. Notes on the sea birds of Vatu-i-ra Island, Fiji. Sept. 1966. *Sea Swallow* 19: 35-38.

207. Sibley, F. C. & Clapp, R. B. 1967. Distribution and dispersal of Central Pacific Lesser Frigate-birds, *Fregata ariel Ibis.* 109: 328-337.

208. Sibson, R. B. 1965. A note on wandering tattlers in Fiji. *Notornis* 12: 248-250.

209. Smart, J. B. 1971. Notes on the occurrence of waders in Fiji. *Notornis* 18: 267-279.

210. Stair, J. B. 1897. On the Red Bird of Samoa. *Proc. NZ Instit.* 1897: 293-298.

211. Stickney, E. H. 1943. Birds collected during the Whitney South Sea Expedition, LIII. Northern shore birds in the Pacific. *Am. Mus. Novit.* 1248: 1-9.

212. Stoner, D. 1924. Ornithological and entomological experiences in Fiji. *U. of Iowa Studies In Nat. Hist.* 10(5): 121-141.

213. Tarburton, M. K. 1978. Some recent observations on seabirds breeding in Fiji. *Notornis* 25: 303-316.

214. Todd, D. M. 1978. Preliminary study of Pritchard's Megapode, *Megapodius pritchardii.* 37 pp. Unpublished report.

215. Townsend, C. H. & Wetmore, A. 1919. *Bull. Mus. Comp. Zool.* LXIII. No.4.

216. Turbott, E. G. 1956. Bulbuls in Auckland. *Notornis* 6(7): 185-192.

217. Ward, A. E. 1924. Aves vitienses. *Trans. Fiji Soc. Sci. & Ind.* 1923: 7-13.

218. Ward, A. E. 1940. Birds of Fiji. *Trans. Fiji Soc. Sci. & Ind.* 1 (1939-40): 23-26.

219. Watling, D. 1975. Observations on the ecological separation of two introduced congeneric Mynahs *(Acridotheres)* in Fiji. *Notornis* 22: 37-53.

220. Watling, D. 1977. The ecology of the Red-vented Bulbul in Fiji. Ph.D. Thesis, University of Cambridge.

221. Watling, D. 1978. Observations on the naturalized distribution of the Red-vented Bulbul in the Pacific, with special reference to the Fiji Islands. *Notornis* 25: 109-117.

222. Watling, D. 1978. A Myna matter. *Notornis* 25: 117.

223. Watling, D. 1978. A collection of Fijian and Tongan landbirds. *Bull. Brit. Orn. Club.* 98(3): 95-98.

224. Watling, D. 1979. The Bulbul gets a clean Bill. *New Scientist* 81: 963-965.

225. Watling, D. (In press.) A collection of bird and bat ectoparasites from Viti Levu, Fiji. *Fiji Agric. J.*

226. Watson, J. M. 1960a. Some aspects of wildlife in Fiji with special reference to its conservation. *Trans. Fiji Soc.* 8: 54-64.

227. Watson, J. M. 1960b. Notes on the wildlife in Fiji and its conservation. *Agric. J.* 30: 67-70.

228. Wattel, J. 1973. *Geographical differentiation in the genus Accipiter.* Nuttal Orn. Club, Cambridge.

229. Weir, D. 1973. Status and habits of *Megapodius pritchardii. Wilson Bull.* 85: 79-82.

230. Whitmee, S. J. 1874. Letter to P. L. Sclater on birds of Samoa. *Proc. Zool. Soc. Lond.* 1874: 183-186.

231. Whitmee, S. J. 1874b. Letter. *Proc. Zool. Soc. Lond.* 1874: 605-606.

232. Whitmee, S. J. 1875. List of Samoan birds, with notes on their habits. *Ibis* 1875: 436-447.

233. Whitmee, S. J. 1876. List of Samoan birds, with notes on their habits. *Ibis* 1876: 504-506.

234. Wiglesworth, L. W. 1892. Aves Polynesiae. A catalogue of the Birds of the Polynesian Sub-region. *Abh. d. Bericht des konig. zool.-eth Mus. Dresden,* No. 6.

235. Wodizicki, K. 1971. The birds of Niue Island, South Pacific: an annotated check list. *Notornis* 18: 291-304.

236. Wood, C. A. 1923a. The Fijian crimson-breasted parrot. *Emu* 23: 118-123.

237. Wood, C. A. 1923b. *Ornithological notes of a voyage to Fiji, Australia, New Zealand, etc.* Typescript at Brit. Mus. (Nat. Hist.), London.

CHECKLIST OF BIRDS
RECORDED IN THE FIJI REGION

Diomedeidae — Albatrosses
Wandering Albatross *Diomedea exulans* . . . .
Black-browed Albatross *Diomedea melanophris* . . . .
Royal Albatross *Diomedea epomorphora* . . . .

Procellariidae — Petrels and Shearwaters
Southern Giant Petrel *Macronectes giganteus* . . . .
Cape Petrel *Daption capense* . . . .
Phoenix Petrel *Pterodroma alba* . . . .
Black-winged Petrel *Pterodroma nigripennis* . . . .
Herald Petrel *Pterodroma arminjoniana* . . . .
White-winged Petrel *Pterodroma leucoptera* . . . .
MacGillivrays Petrel *Pterodroma macgillivrayi* . . . .
Tahiti Petrel *Pterodroma rostrata* . . . .
White-necked Petrel *Pterodroma externa* . . . .
Mottled Petrel *Pterodroma inexpectata* . . . .
Bulwers Petrel *Bulweria bulwerii* . . . .
Wedge-tailed Shearwater *Puffinus pacificus* . . . .
Short-tailed Shearwater *Puffinus tenuirostris* . . . .
Audubon's Shearwater *Puffinus lherminieri* . . . .
Buller's Shearwater *Puffinus bulleri* . . . .
Sooty Shearwater *Puffinus griseus* . . . .

Hydrobatidae — Storm-petrels
White-throated Storm-petrel *Nesofregetta albigularis* . . .
Black-bellied Storm-petrel *Fregetta tropica* . . . .

Phaethontidae — Tropicbirds
Red-tailed Tropicbird *Phaethon rubricaudus* . . . .
White-tailed Tropicbird *Phaethon lepturus* . . . .

Pelecanidae — Pelicans
Australian Pelican *Pelecanus conspicillatus* . . . .

Sulidae — Boobies
Masked Booby *Sula dactylatra* . . . .
Brown Booby *Sula leucogaster* . . . .
Red-footed Booby *Sula sula* . . . .

Fregatidae — Frigatebirds
Great Frigatebird *Fregata minor* . . . .
Lesser Frigatebird *Fregata ariel* . . . .

Ardeidae — Herons
Reef Heron *Egretta sacra* . . . .
White-faced Heron *Ardea novaehollandiae* . . . .
Mangrove Heron *Butorides striatus* . . . .

Threskiornithidae — Ibises
Glossy Ibis *Plegadis falcinellus* . . . .

Anatidae — Ducks
Pacific Black Duck *Anas superciliosa* . . . .
Wandering Whistling-duck *Dendrocygna arcuata* . . . .

Accipitridae — Hawks
Fiji Goshawk *Accipiter rufitorques* . . . .
Swamp Harrier *Circus approximans* . . . .

Falconidae — Falcons
Peregrine Falcon *Falco peregrinus* . . . .

Megapodiidae — Megapodes
Niuafo'ou Megapode *Megapodius pritchardii* . . . .

Phasianidae — Pheasants
Jungle Fowl *Gallus gallus* . . . .
Swamp Quail *Synoicus ypsilophorus* . . . .

Rallidae — Rails
Barred-wing Rail *Nesoclopeus poecilopterus* . . . .
Banded Rail *Gallirallus philippensis* . . . .
White-browed Crake *Poliolimnas cinereus* . . . .
Spotless Crake *Porzana tabuensis* . . . .
Purple Swamphen *Porphyrio porphyrio* . . . .
Samoan Wood Rail *Pareudiastes pacificus* . . . .

Charadriidae — Plovers
Lesser Golden Plover *Pluvialis dominica* . . . .
Mongolian Plover *Charadrius mongolus* . . . .
Double-banded Plover *Charadrius bicinctus* . . . .

Scolopacidae — Sandpipers
Whimbrel *Numenius phaeopus* . . . .
Bristle-thighed Curlew *Numenius tahitiensis* . . . .
Eastern Curlew *Numenius madagascariensis* . . . .
Eastern Bar-tailed Godwit *Limosa lapponica* . . . .
Black-tailed Godwit* *Limosa limosa* . . . .
Grey-tailed Tattler *Heteroscelus brevipes* . . . .
Wandering Tattler *Heteroscelus incanus* . . . .
Terek Sandpiper *Xenus cinereus* . . . .
Ruddy Turnstone *Arenaria interpres* . . . .
Sanderling *Calidris alba* . . . .
Little Stint *Calidris ruficollis* . . . .
Sharp-tailed Sandpiper *Calidris acuminata* . . . .
Knot *Calidris canutus* . . . .

Stercorariidae — Skuas
Pomarine Skua *Stercorarius pomarinus* ....
Arctic Skua *Stercorarius parasiticus* ....

Laridae — Gulls and Terns
Common Tern *Sterna hirundo* ....
Sooty Tern *Sterna fuscata*...........................
Bridled Tern *Sterna anaethetus* ....
Roseate Tern *Sterna dougallii* ....
Little Tern *Sterna albifrons*........................
Grey-backed Tern *Sterna lunata* ....
Black-naped Tern *Sterna sumatrana* ....
Crested Tern *Sterna bergii* ....
Grey Noddy *Procelsterna cerulea*.....................
Common Noddy *Anous stolidus* ....
Black Noddy *Anous tenuirostris* ....
White Tern *Gygis alba*..............................

Columbidae — Pigeons and Doves
Feral Pigeon *Columba livia* ....
White-throated Pigeon *Columba vitiensis* ....
Spotted Turtle-dove *Streptopelia chinensis* ....
Friendly Ground-dove *Gallicolumba stairii* ....
Pacific Pigeon *Ducula pacifica* ....
Peale's Pigeon *Ducula latrans* ....
Tooth-billed Pigeon *Didunculus strigirostris*............
Many-coloured Fruit-dove *Ptilinopus perousii* ....
Crimson-crowned Fruit-dove *Ptilinopus porphyraceus* ..
Golden Dove *Ptilinopus luteovirens* ....
Orange Dove *Ptilinopus victor* ....
Whistling Dove *Ptilinopus layardi*....................

Psittacidae — Parrots
Collared Lory *Phigys solitarius*......................
Red-throated Lorikeet *Charmosyna amabilis* ....
Blue-crowned Lory *Vini australis* ....
Yellow-breasted Musk Parrot *Prosopeia personata* ......
Red-breasted Musk Parrot *Prosopeia tabuensis*.........

Cuculidae — Cuckoos
Fan-tailed Cuckoo *Cacomantis pyrrophanus* ....
Long-tailed Cuckoo *Eudynamis taitensis* ....

Tytonidae — Barn Owls
Barn Owl *Tyto alba*................................
Grass Owl *Tyto capensis*............................

Apodidae — Swifts
White-rumped Swiftlet *Collocalia spodiopygia* ....
Spine-tailed Swift *Chaetura caudacuta*................

Alcedinidae — Kingfishers
White-collared Kingfisher *Halcyon chloris* ....
Flat-billed Kingfisher *Halcyon recurvirostris* ....

Hirundinidae — Swallows
Pacific Swallow *Hirundo tahitica*.....................

Campephagidae — Cuckoo-shrikes
Polynesian Triller *Lalage maculosa* ....
Samoan Triller *Lalage sharpei*.......................

Pycnonotidae — Bulbuls
Red-vented Bulbul *Pycnonotus cafer* ....

Muscicapidae — Thrushes, Old World Warblers,
Old World Flycatchers
Island Thrush *Turdus poliocephalus* ....
Silktail *Lamprolia victoriae* ....
Fiji Warbler *Vitia ruficapilla* ....
Long-legged Warbler *Trichocichla rufa*................
Spotted Fantail *Rhipidura spilodera* ....
Kadavu Fantail *Rhipidura personata*...................
Samoan Fantail *Rhipidura nebulosa* ....
Slaty Flycatcher *Mayrornis lessoni* ....
Versicolour Flycatcher *Mayrornis versicolor* ....
Fiji Shrikebill *Clytorhynchus vitiensis* ....
Black-faced Shrikebill *Clytorhynchus nigrogularis* ....
Vanikoro Broadbill *Myiagra vanikorensis* ....
Blue-crested Broadbill *Myiagra azureocapilla*...........
Samoan Broadbill *Myiagra albiventris* ....
Scarlet Robin *Petroica multicolor* ....
Golden Whistler *Pachycephala pectoralis* ....
Samoan Whistler *Pachycephala flavifrons* ....

Zosteropidae — White-eyes
Layard's White-eye *Zosterops explorator* ....
Grey-backed White-eye *Zosterops lateralis*............
Samoan White-eye *Zosterops samoensis* ....

Meliphagidae — Honeyeaters
Orange-breasted Honeyeater *Myzomela jugularis* ......
Cardinal Honeyeater *Myzomela cardinalis* ....
Wattled Honeyeater *Foulehaio carunculata* ....
Kadavu Honeyeater *Xanthotis provocator* ....
Giant Forest Honeyeater *Gymnomyza viridis*...........
Mao *Gymnomyza samoensis*.........................

Ploceidae — Sparrows and Weavers
House Sparrow *Passer domesticus* ....

Estrildidae — Grass Finches, Waxbills and
Parrotfinches
Red-headed Parrotfinch *Erythrura cyaneovirens* ....
Pink-billed Parrotfinch *Erythrura kleinschmidti* ....
Red Avadavat *Amandava amandava* ....
Java Sparrow *Padda oryzivora* ....

Sturnidae — Starlings
European Starling *Sturnus vulgaris* ....
Polynesian Starling *Aplonis tabuensis* ....
Samoan Starling *Aplonis atrifusca*....................
Common Mynah *Acridotheres tristis* ....
Jungle Mynah *Acridotheres fuscus* ....

Artamidae — Woodswallows
White-breasted Woodswallow *Artamus leucorhynchus*..

Cracticidae — Magpies and Butcherbirds
Australian Magpie *Gymnorhina tibicen* ....

*Skinner N. J. & N. P. E. Langham, 1981 (in press)
Hudsonian Godwit in Fiji. *Notornis.*

167

INDEX OF SCIENTIFIC NAMES

All numbers refer to Species Numbers not to page numbers. Roman = birds which have an individual Species Account. Italic = bird species mentioned only in the Allied Species or Subspecies section.

INDEX OF ENGLISH NAMES

Bold numbers refer to colour plates. Other numbers refer to Species Numbers not to page numbers. Roman = birds which have an individual Species Account. Italic = bird species mentioned only in the Allied Species section.

INDEX OF LOCAL NAMES

Numbers refer to Species Numbers not to page numbers. All names use local orthography (see page 13). Key to letters in parentheses — F = Fiji, R = Rotuma, T = Tonga, S = Samoa, N = Niue.

Ai sou, 65(F)
'Aleva, 35(S)
Atafa, 101(S), 102 (S)

Batidamu, 62(F)
Belo, 1(F)
Bidi, 11(F), 12(F)
Bici, 12(F)
Bici vuka i lagi, 35(F)
Bisi, 12(F)
Bobokavisa, 65(F)
Borabora tana, 27(F)
Bulidamu, 27(F)
Bulubulu, 44(F)
Bune karawa, 26(F), 27(F), 28(F)
   soluve, 24(F)
Bunedamu, 27(F)
Bunedromo, 26(F), 27(F)
Buneko, 26(F)

Coqe, 22(F)

Delakula, 72(F)
Didibesau, 65(F)
Dili dilio, 114(F)
Dilio, 114(F)
Dilodilo, 114(F)
Doli, 121(F)
Dolidoli, 121(F)
Doti, 40(F)
Dre, 30(F), 108(F), 109(F)
Dree, 43(F)
Dri qala, 64(F)
Droe, 113(F)
Droi, 98(F), 99(F), 100(F)
Drui, 72(F)
Drui delakula, 72(F)
   delaturaga, 72(F)

'Ekiaki, 113(T)
Ero, 76(F)

Fa'aire, 59(R)
Fiaui, 18(S)
Foule haoi, 74(T)
Fua'o, 108(S), 111(S)
Fuia, 48(S)

Fiuva, 44,(T), 59(T)
Fulehau, 74(T)
Fuleheu, 74(T)

Ga, 3(F)
   damu, 4(F)
   loa, 3(F)
   ni vatu, 7 (F)
   ni veikau, 3 (F)
   ni viti, 3 (F)
   ni wai, 99(F), 100(F)
Galamakadrau, 43(F)
Gigi, 13(F)
Gogo, 111(F), 112(F)
Goguli, 108(S)
Gikivia, 67(T)
Gikota, 40(T)
Gila, 20(F)
Gutulei, 98(F), 99(F), 100(F)

Heahea, 67(N)
Hecala, 40(F)
Helekosi, 101(T), 102(T)
Henga, 31(T), 31(N), 65(T)
Hengehenga, 65(T)
Hikohikorere, 43(F)
Husila, 47(F, R)

Iao, 74(S)
I co, 108(F), 109(F)
   co loaloa, 111(F), 112(F)

Jao, 74(S)
Jea, 67(R)
Juli, 114(R), 121(R)

Ka, 32(F)
Ka damu, 33(F)
   kula, 33(F)
Kabalamodrau, 39(F)
Kabalata, 39(F)
Kabote, 32(F)
Kaisau, 74(F)
Kaisevau, 74(F)
Kaka, 32(F), 33(F, T)
Kakaba, 39(F)
Kakabe, 42(F)

Kakabace, 39(F)
Kakakula, 29(F)
Kalae, 15(T)
Kalangi, 93(N)
Kale, 15(R, N)
Kaleva, 35(T)
Kalevaleva, 35(T)
Kaliva, 35(T)
Kalue, 35(N)
Kanedromo, 28(F)
Kasaga, 101(F), 102(F)
Katafa, 82(T)
Katebale, 67(F)
Kawa kasa, 35(F)
Kedidromo, 65(F)
Keri keri sai, 72(F)
Ketedromo, 65(F)
Ketekete, 67(T)
Kikau, 74(F)
Kikaulevu, 76(F)
Kikauliki, 74(F)
Kiki, 78(F)
Kiro, 47(F), 60(F)
Kitou, 74(F)
Kitu, 15(F)
Kiu, 114(T, N), 120(T), 121(T), 123(T)
   foa'unga, 120(T)
   lega lega, 121(T)
   tahi, 121(N)
Ko, 26(F)
Koki, 32(F), 33(F, T)
Kokosi, 59(F)
Kolavalu, 24(F), 25(F)
Kota, 101(N)
Ku ku, 25(R)
Kukuru, 19(F)
Kula, 29(F)
   lailai, 78(F)
   oso, 65(F)
   wai, 30(F)
Kulukulu, 25(T, N)
Kuluvotu, 24(F), 25(F)
Kuma, 12(F)

Lafu, 85(T), 86(T), 87(T), 88(T),
   93(T)